D1882653

UNDERSTANDING AND SCOUTING WITH PHYSICALLY HANDICAPPED

UNDERSTANDING AND SCOUTING WITH PHYSICALLY HANDICAPPED

Editor
O. P. Goyal

ISHA BOOKS
DELHI-110 033

Understanding and Scouting with Physically Handicapped

Rs. 880

ISBN: 81-8205-146-0

© O. P. Goyal

All rights reserved. No part of this book may be reproduced in any manner without written permission.

Published in 2005 in India by
Isha Books, D-43, Prithviraj Road,
Adarsh Nagar, Delhi-110 033

Laser Typesetting at : Shree Vaishnavi Creations, Delhi
Printed at : Chawla Offset Press, Delhi

Contents

Preface

The term "disability" refers to a wide variety of conditions, including blindness, deafness, mental retardation, and mobility impairments. Some health professionals also consider the term to encompass learning disabilities, mental illnesses such as autism, and chronic or long-term illnesses such as epilepsy, diabetes, cancer, or AIDS.

People with disabilities face special problems. These problems often affect personal and community lives. Limited ability to perform ordinary daily activities is a major problem. Psychological problems may be experienced because the disability makes them feel different than most other people. Yet, some disabled people consider their disability a challenge to overcome.

Social relationships can often be difficult for disabled individuals. Those who don't have disabilities often feel uncomfortable in the presence of the disabled because they don't want to be reminded that disabilities exist. Learning to put others at ease is one of the most important skills that disabled individuals need to learn.

Lack of knowledge by most individuals builds many obstacles for people with disabilities. How much a disabled person can achieve is often not realized by the majority of the community. This can result in much exclusion of the disabled from many community activities.

Since the mid-1960s, a growing number of activists have sought to overcome these discrimination by enforcing legislation that protects the rights of people with disabilities and by changing negative public attitudes about the disabled. Many disability-rights advocates contend that the disabled are a minority group that suffers from discrimination. In their opinion, activists should concentrate on promoting acceptance of people with disabilities as valuable members of society. Other commentators argue that science should focus on eliminating disabilities entirely so that in the future no one will face the problems that having a disability can entail.

The social, legal, educational, and ethical issues faced by different segments of disabled persons are elaborately described in the present volume. It gives practical advice to legal, professional and academic people to mainstream the disabled form their tragic conditions. It also provides guidelines to individuals with disabilities to enable them to raise self-confidence, overcome challenges become the part of nation building. Besides disabled people, policy makers, academics, counsellors, social workers and teachers and trainers will find this work of utmost use.

Editor

1

Introduction

There are over 500 million persons with disabilities worldwide—or 10 per cent of the global population. Approximately two thirds live in developing countries. In certain developing countries nearly 20 per cent of the general population is in some way disabled; if the impact on their families is taken into account, 50 per cent of the population is affected.

The number of disabled persons continues to increase in tandem with growth of the world population. Factors causing the increase in their number include war and other forms of violence, inadequate medical care, and natural and other disasters. Not surprisingly, many of the disabled are poor. The overwhelming majority—perhaps 80 per cent—live in isolated rural areas. Almost that many live in areas where the services needed to help them are unavailable. Too often their lives are handicapped by physical and social barriers in society which hamper their full participation. Because of this, and in all parts of the world, they often face a life that is segregated and debased, and without help, many will live in isolation and insecurity.

"Disability is not a tragedy, it's an inconvenience." —A disabled woman and leader of a non-governmental organization The United Nations has dedicated itself to defending the basic human rights of all persons, including those with disabilities. Through its development work, it has shifted the focus, in ways that have often inspired national legislation and policy-making, from people's disabilities to their abilities.

The United Nations was founded on the principle of equality for all. The Preamble to the Charter affirms the dignity and worth of every human being and gives primary importance to the promotion of social justice. Persons with disabilities are, de facto, entitled to all the fundamental human rights upheld by the Charter and other human rights instruments. The General Assembly established the foundation for the promotion and protection of human rights in 1948, when it proclaimed the Universal Declaration of Human Rights.

Further anti-discrimination principles were established by such human rights instruments as the International Covenant on Civil and Political Rights and the International Covenant on Economic, Social and Cultural Rights, which came into force in 1966. Together they form the most comprehensive international code of binding legal provisions in the area of human rights. The two Covenants develop and supplement the provisions of the Universal Declaration, and the three instruments together make up what has come to be known as the International Bill of Human Rights.

Disability is perhaps the area in which the importance of recognizing the indivisibility and interdependence of human rights and fundamental freedoms, as both Covenants do, is most evident and sharp. This historical overview and accompanying chronology will trace the activities of the United Nations in relation to the disabled population. It will also discuss some of the activities undertaken by the specialized agencies of the United Nations such as the World Health Organization (WHO), which has helped to equalize opportunities for the disabled while providing technical assistance; the United Nations Children's Fund (UNICEF), which supports childhood disability programmes and technical support in collaboration with Rehabilitation International; and the International Labour Office (ILO), which works to improve access to labour markets and to increase economic integration by establishing international labour standards and implementing technical cooperation projects.

The United Nations' commitment to assisting the disabled has been evolving since it began addressing the needs of individuals injured in the Second World War. Injuries resulting from violent conflicts continue to receive the Organization's attention today in various organs and agencies of the system. For example, the Mine Clearance and Policy Unit of the Department of Humanitarian Affairs, United Nations Secretariat, works throughout the world to rid former war zones of deadly anti-personnel mines which are responsible for disabling hundreds of thousands of people.

The World Health Organization, in its International Classification of Impairments, Disabilities and Handicaps, makes a distinction between impairment, disability and handicap. These three concepts are defined by it as follows:

1. Impairment is "any loss or abnormality of psychological, physiological, or anatomical structure or function". Impairments are disturbances at the level of the organ which include defects in or loss of a limb, organ or other body structure, as well as defects in or loss of a mental function. Examples of impairments include blindness, deafness, loss of sight in an eye, paralysis of a limb, amputation of a limb;

mental retardation, partial sight, loss of speech, mutism.

2. Disability is a "restriction or lack (resulting from an impairment) of ability to perform an activity in the manner or within the range considered normal for a human being". It describes a functional limitation or activity restriction caused by an impairment. Disabilities are descriptions of disturbances in function at the level of the person. Examples of disabilities include difficulty seeing, speaking or hearing; difficulty moving or climbing stairs; difficulty grasping, reaching, bathing, eating, toileting.
3. A handicap is a "disadvantage for a given individual, resulting from an impairment or disability, that limits or prevents the fulfilment of a role that is normal (depending on age, sex and social and cultural factors) for that individual". The term is also a classification of "circumstances in which disabled people are likely to find themselves". Handicap describes the social and economic roles of impaired or disabled persons that place them at a disadvantage compared to other persons. These disadvantages are brought about through the interaction of the person with specific environments and cultures. Examples of handicaps include being bedridden or confined to home; being unable to use public transport; being socially isolated.

Handicaps are "concerned with the disadvantages experienced by the individual as a result of impairments and disabilities; thus, handicaps reflect interaction with and adaptation to the individuals' surroundings." Disabled people do not form a homogenous group. For example, the mentally retarded, the visually, hearing and speech impaired, those with restricted mobility or with so-called "medical disabilities" all encounter different barriers, of different kinds, which have to be overcome in different ways.

The following definitions are developed from the perspective in the World Programme of Action Concerning Disabled Persons:

1. Prevention is any measures aimed at preventing the onset of mental, physical and sensory impairments (primary prevention) or at preventing impairment, when it has occurred, from having negative physical, psychological and social consequences (secondary prevention);
2. Rehabilitation is a goal-oriented and time-limited process aimed at enabling an impaired person to reach the optimum mental, physical and/or social functional level, thus providing the individual with the tools to change her or his own life. It can involve measures intended to compensate for a loss of function or a functional limitation (for example, by technical aids) and other measures intended to facilitate social adjustment or readjustment;
3. Equalization of opportunities is the process through which the general system of society, such as the physical and cultural environment, housing and transportation, social and health services, educational and work opportunities, cultural and social life, including sports and recreational facilities, are made accessible to all.

Prevention and rehabilitation, then, relate to an individual's particular attributes (or lack thereof) and may entail special needs. Equalization relates to the process of building a suitable environment to reasonably accommodate those needs

2

Societal Responses to Disability

The production of disability therefore is nothing more or less than a set of activities specifically geared towards producing a good -the category disability -supported by a range of political actions which create the conditions to allow these productive activities to take place and underpinned by a discourse which gives legitimacy to the whole enterprise.

In order to understand societal responses to long-term disability, it is necessary to understand that the production of disability is in transition. In this process of transition, the move away from an individualised, medical view of disability does not imply that there is no role for medicine in the world to which we are moving. Clearly part of the experience of disability will remain an individual one. But in order to develop more appropriate societal responses to disability, it is important that we all understand -health care professionals and disabled people alike -that this is a partial and limited view.

In other words;- what is the nature of disability;what causes it and how is it experienced. These basic questions raise different sets of issues at different levels of abstraction. The ontological level requires issues to be addressed in terms of grand theory. The epistemological level requires issues to be addressed in terms of middle range theorising. The experiential level requires issues to be addressed in terms of developing an appropriate methodology for understanding the experience of disability from the perspective of disabled people themselves.

Table 1. The Hegemony of Disability

Level	*Question*	*Way of understanding*
Ontology	What is the nature of disability	Grand theory
Epistemology	What causes disability?	Middle range theories?
Experience	What does it feel like to be disabled?	Methodology

These levels do not exist independently of each other except in a conceptual sense. Rather, they interact with each other in producing what might be called the totality, or indeed, the hegemony of disability. The hegemony of disability, as it is produced by capitalist society - and it should be emphasised that other kinds of society have produced disability in different forms-stems from the ontological assumptions it makes about the pathological and problem oriented nature of disability.

These ontological assumptions link directly to epistemological concerns about the causes of disability in individuals with a view to eradication through prevention, cure or treatment. Hence the assumption is, in health terms, that disability is pathology and in welfare terms, that disability is a social problem. Treatment and cure are the appropriate societal responses to pathologies and problems.

In recent years, the hegemony of disability has been under a sustained and persistent attack in late capitalist society. At the ontological level this has lead, not to a denial of the problem oriented nature of disability, but of its assumptions of pathology. At the epistemological level middle range theorising has been turned on its head;disability is caused not by the functional, physical or psychological limitations of impaired individuals but by the failure of society to remove its disabling barriers and social restrictions.

At the experiential level disabled people are increasingly seeing their problems as stemming from social oppression and institutionalised discrimination. In other words, disability is something wrong with society. Thus the argument that the problems of disability are societal rather than individual problems and that these problems stem from oppression by society rather than the limitations of individuals is an essential part of developing an understanding of societal responses to long-term disability. Further, there is plenty of evidence to show that most policy and practice in this area has failed because it has been based upon individual rather than social models of disability; the individual model being a product of exclusion, the social model currently being produced by demands for inclusion.

However, in attempting to understand hegemony of disability, the ways in which the individualising of disability is interconnected at the levels of society, policy and practice and personal experience is crucial. These interconnections are crucial to the attempt to reformulate disability as an issue for society and develop a more appropriate social understanding of policy responses, professional practice and personal experience. The individualising of disability permeates all three levels and connects them in that disability is seen as a personal tragedy which occurs at random to individuals, that the problems of disability require individuals to adjust or come to terms with this tragedy and that research has used techniques designed to 'prove'the existence of these adjustment problems.

The alternative view suggests that disability occurs in structured ways dependent upon the material relations of production, the problem of adjustment is one for society, not individuals and that research should be concerned to identify the ways in which society disables people rather than the effects on individuals.

Table 2: Exclusionary and inclusionary visions

Way of understanding	*Dominant*	*Alternative*
Grand theory	Personal tragedy	Political economy
Middle range theories	Adjustment/	Social adjustment
Methodology	Disengagement	Emancipatory
	Positivist/Interpretive	

Grand theory: A Phenomenon of Disability

Grand theory, in sociological terms, is concerned with providing an all- embracing explanation of particular phenomena at the highest level of abstraction. Undoubtedly, in terms of the phenomenon of disability, the dominant grand theory has been personal tragedy theory. This suggests that disability is a tragic happening that occurs to unfortunate, isolated individuals on a random basis. It further influences compensatory policy responses and therapeutic interventions designed to help individuals come to terms with tragedy. At the level of individual experience, many disabled people come to see their lives as blighted by tragedy.

The problem is that personal tragedy theory does not provide a universalistic explanation of disability;in some societies disability is seen as the ascription of privilege, as a sign of being chosen by the gods. In others it is seen as bringing important social benefits such as bilingualism, as illustrated by the pervasive use of sign language throughout the community that was Martha's Vineyard. Further, even within some capitalist societies policies are moving away from compensation and towards entitlement.

Therapeutic interventions are also moving away from adjustment and towards empowerment. Finally, with the developing of a politics of personal identity, the experience of disability is being reinterpreted in positive rather than negative terms. Political economy, on the other hand, suggests that all phenomena (including social categories)are produced by the economic and social forces of capitalism itself.

The forms in which they are produced are ultimately dependent upon their relationship to the economy. Hence, both the categories of ageing and disability are produced in the particular forms they appear by these very economic and social forces. Further, they are produced as an economic problem because of changes in the nature of work and the needs of the labour market within capitalism;and that this is true of both ageing and disability separately.

"The political economy perspective points to the structural dependency of the aged arising from conditions in the labour market and the stratification and organisation of work and society". In other words, old people no longer play a key role in the process of production and no longer participate in the labour market. The same is true of disabled people and has been so, except in times of severe labour shortage, since the coming of the industrial revolution.

Hence the economy, through both the operation of the labour market and the social organisation of work, plays a key role in determining societal responses not just to ageing and disability but consequently also to ageing with a disability. Both old people and disabled people are forced into situations of dependency because they do not participate fully in the processes of production. However, it would be wrong to assume that old disabled people simply experience a double dose of dependency;to put the matter simply, to be old and disabled is not twice as bad as merely being old or merely disabled.

In order to explain this, it is necessary to return to the crucial question of what is meant by political economy and whether it is possible to have separate political economies of ageing and disability, or indeed race, gender, welfare or any other category. The following is a generally agreed definition of political economy, "The study of the interrelationships between the polity, economy and society, or more specifically, the reciprocal influences among government the economy, social classes, state and, status groups.

The central problem of the political economy perspective is the manner in which the economy and polity interact in a relationship of reciprocal causation affecting the distribution of social goods". There are two problems with such an agreed definition. To begin with, it is an explanation which can be incorporated into pluralist visions of society as a consensus emerging out of the interests of various groups and social forces as well as materialist theories of society which, in the last instance, see economic factors as determining. In addition, such political economies often themselves become oppressive in they divide up the experiences into an arbitrary set of socially constructed categories;old age, race, gender, disability etc.

Political economy, as it is used here, takes a particular theoretical view of society;one which sees the economy as the crucial, and ultimately determining factor, in structuring the lives of groups and individuals. Further, while the relationship between various groups and the economy may differ in qualitative ways, the underlying structural relationship remains.

All are rooted in the social-economic structures of society. All deprive certain groups of status, the right to control their own lives and destinies with the end result of powerlessness. All have resulted in economic and social discrimination. All rob (American)society of the energies and involvement of creative persons who are needed to make our society just and humane. All have brought on individual alienation, despair, hostility, and anomie".

As is usual in discussing the oppressions for which isms become shorthand, disablism does not merit inclusion. The reason for this is simple;even those writers who have specifically examined oppression have internalised the dominant, individualised world view of disability and have failed to conceptualise it as social oppression. Equally importantly, such theorising about oppression leaves the relationship between the various isms as non-problematic;with the exception of Abberley there have been no attempts to analyse the similarities and differences between the oppressions of disability, race and gender.

The 'politics'part of political economy comes in the ways in which ageing and disability are constructed as particular kinds of problems. Any society wishing to appear 'civilised'must make provision for those groups and individuals who cannot provide for their own needs through work or resources built up through previous work. Hence both ageing and disability are socially constructed as 'problems'.

Earlier it was suggested that producers of categories have an interest in shaping the ways they are produced, both disability and old age are constructed as social problems because of the needs of the welfare system and the professionals who operate it rather than the needs of old disabled people. Both are constructed as health problems because. of the needs of the health care system and because of the imperialism of the medical profession which has proclaimed a whole range of social phenomena from crime to homosexuality through addiction and onto naughtiness in children as problems requiring medical intervention.

Middle range theory -adjustment, disengagement or social adjustment? Middle range theories are usually concerned to link the abstract concepts of grand theory to the specific experiences of particular phenomena. In terms of ageing and disability;loss has been the dominant metaphor for developing these perspectives. They have been operationalised in the study of ageing in terms of middle range disengagement theories and in the study of disability in terms of middle range adjustment theories.

Until recently, the field of gerontology -the systematic study of ageing - has been dominated by theories which sought to explain how individuals react to the ageing process. Firstly, there are a range of individualist and psychological models which are primarily preoccupied with explaining 'normal'and/or 'successful'ageing -i. e. adaptation to old age. Here, ageing is viewed as part of an ordered life process moving from birth to death, with each stage (e. g. adolescence, early adulthood etc.) having it's own set of expectations and behaviours. From this perspective, successful adaptation to ageing is represented by an individual accepting the changes that he or she has experienced and, ultimately, accepting the inevitability of death.

At the same time, failure to undergo such change is often taken as evidence of pathological personality development. One of the most influential models of ageing has been disengagement theory. This theory suggests that the life course is marked by stages such as 'middle old age', 'young old age'and 'old old age'. Here, the main emphasis is on 'social roles'rather than personal psychology. From this perspective, ageing is characterised by various patterns of 'disengagement'whereby -'as people grow older their behaviour changes, the activities that characterize them in middle age become curtailed, and the extent of their social interaction decreases'.

These developmental approaches to ageing have a certain usefulness in that they focus on individual experiences over the totality of the life course. There are several reasons, however, why theories based on. disengagement and role change do not provide an adequate analytic framework for studying the experiences of ageing with disability. Firstly, the models of ageing implicit in these theories take little or no account of social factors which are external to individual psychological states or interpersonal behaviour such as the levels of pensions paid or the social attitudes to ageing. Secondly, ageing is usually conceptualised in terms of an inevitable and pathological process; consequently, older people are viewed as victims lacking control over their own lives. These theories do not, therefore, take account of individual differences in attitudes, expectations and resources. All of these factors may have a significant effect on how anyone individual may experience ageing-either positively or negatively.

More recent studies have also indicated that, where it does occur, any reduction in social involvement is much more closely associated with infirmity and poverty, than with age itself. In other words, if some older people are less socially active, it is due to these external social factors which vary independently of chronological age. Because the individualistic approaches to ageing do not take sufficient account of factors external to the individual, they make the basic error of assuming the observable association between such problems and old age are actually caused by ageing itself.

Just as studies on ageing have been dominated by middle range disengagement theories, so studies of disability have been dominated by middle range adjustment theories. The argument suggests that when something happens to an individual's body something happens to the mind as well. Thus, in order to become fully human again, in order to form a disabled identity, the disabled individual must undergo medical treatment and physical rehabilitation as well as the process of psychological adjustment or coming to terms with disability. Further, in order to adjust satisfactorily, the individual may need to grieve and mourn for lost ability and pass through a series of stages before adjustment is complete.

However, the conceptual framework provided by middle range adjustment theory has been severely criticised on theoretical grounds as well as on the grounds that it does not accord with the actual experience of disability and alternative frameworks such as social adjustment and social oppression have beer developed. But it is not just disabled people who have provided theoretical and experiential criticisms of this framework, researchers also have found it difficult to provide empirical evidence.

Initial work on the long-term effects of spinal cord injury suggested that the occurrence of a disability as a significant event in an individual's life is only a starting point for understanding the practical and personal consequences of living with disability. The work further suggested that the social environment, material resources and -most importantly -the meanings which individuals attach to situations and events were the most important factors to be considered in developing an adequate conceptual model which has been called social adjustment.

In a subsequent study on ageing, this basic approach has been built on to consider the longer term experiences of people who are ageing with a spinal cord injury. As previously, the concepts of 'significant life events' and 'career'are essential components in the conceptual model being developed. Before proceeding, therefore, it is necessary to explain what is meant by these terms and how they have been used in previous work. While much of the existing work which has utilised the concept of life events has focused on negative life events, there is no logical reason why it cannot be applied to positive aspects of people's life experience. The only essential criteria are that a life event should be disrupting or have the potential to disrupt, and, that this should have some significant meaning for the individual. This means that a whole range of life events can be considered including leaving school, working, marriage, having children, getting divorced, losing one's job as well, of course, as the range of life events often associated with ageing (e. g. retirement, the death of a spouse, etc.).

Since the understanding of the significance of ageing for older disabled people has been a central concern, the concept of life events provides a very useful conceptual tool. Thus, just as the occurrence of a spinal cord injury is not simply a single, isolated event, so the intervening impact of ageing cannot be considered as a self-contained life event, or even as a series of discrete life events.

Consequently, the concept of career is a further essential component of the model as it allows consideration of people's experiences throughout their lives including, but not restricted to, their experiences of disability and, subsequently, ageing with a disability. Equally importantly, and this relates back to appoint made in the previous section, using the concept of career does not require the experiences of ageing and those of disability as conceptually or experientially discrete and separate.

The concept of 'career'as an aid to the analysis of life experiences was developed by the American sociologists Strauss and Glaser and has subsequently been used in variety of contexts such as education, work experience and marriage, as well as in some studies of the experiences of disabled people. The main utility of the concept of a 'disability career'is that it focuses not only on the experience of disability, but also on the interaction between this and other aspects of an individuals total life experience.

Methodology of understanding Disability

The central methodological issue concerns the purpose of research and whether this is to interpret or understand particular phenomena. As far as disability research is concerned, most has gone for the interpretive approach but the problem is that it has been located within the medical model with its in-built positivistic assumptions which see disability as individual pathology, rather than the social model of disability, as articulated by disabled people themselves, which sees disability as social restriction or oppression. Consequently, most of this research is considered at best irrelevant, and at worst, oppressive.

The persistent lack of fit between able-bodied and disabled people's own articulations of their own experience has implications for both the provision of services and the ability of individuals to control their own lives. As Davis points out, research on disability has consistently failed to involve disabled people except as passive objects for interviews and observations designed by researchers with no experience or sensitivity to the day to day reality of disability -a situation which, whilst it may be of benefit to researchers, does nothing to serve the interests of disabled people. Thus many disabled people have become alienated from disability research;a not uncommon problem for research subjects, according to one commentator.

The term alienation in its original marxist sense referred to the process of labour whereby workers became estranged from the products they produced. In a powerful critique of most of what passes for social research, Rowan argues that alienation is the outcome of the process of this research. By this he meant ".... treating people as fragments. This is usually done by putting a person into the role of 'research subject' and only then permitting a very restricted range of behaviour to be counted. This is alienating because it is using the person for someone else's ends -the person's actions do not belong to that individual, but to the researcher and the research plan".

Further, in Rowan's terms, the researchers and the researched were alienated from each other in the way the research was carried out. Disabled people either filled in a postal questionnaire or were interviewed, not by the principal OPCS workers but by part-time interviewers. Further, "It is in the nature of the interview process that the interviewer presents as expert and the disabled person as an isolated individual inexperienced in research, and thus unable to reformulate the questions in a more appropriate way. It is hardly surprising that, by the end of the interview, the disabled person has come to believe that his or her problems are caused by their own health/ disability problems rather than by the organisation of society.

This alienation from the most extensive and most expensive disability research ever carried out in Britain is not simply and isolated example but symptomatic of a wider crisis that exists between disabled people and the research community. As disabled people have increasingly analyzed their segregation, inequality and poverty in terms of discrimination and oppression, research has been seen as part of the problem rather than as part of the solution. Disabled people have come to see research as a violation of their experience, as irrelevant to their needs and as failing to improve their material circumstances and quality of life.

This disillusion with existing research paradigms has raised the issue of developing an alternative, emancipatory approach in order to make disability research both more relevant to the lives of disabled people and more influential in improving their material circumstances. The two key fundamentals on which such an approach must be based are empowerment and reciprocity. These fundamentals can be built in by encouraging self-reflection and a deeper understanding of the research situation by the research subjects.

Peoples' Attitude Towards Physically Handicapped Individuals

Attitudes are complex structures with many components. Attitudes refer to the beliefs and feelings that are related to a person or event. They are an effective way to interpret the environment. Feelings that someone may have can guide their reactions when they are in situations where they must respond quickly. For example, a person who believes that handicapped individuals are incompetent or inferior may feel dislike for them. These feelings may then lead the person to act in a discriminatory manner. Attitudes are learned through social and environmental experiences rather than determined by one's genes. They can be altered or changed, however, this is often a difficult task because attitudes can be extremely resistant.

There are three dimensions used to assess attitudes:

— an affective component,

— a behavioral component, and

— a cognitive component.

The affective component refers to feelings or emotions that shape the attitude. The behavioral component refers to the intentions and the actual reactions of the person. Behaviors such as avoiding a person with a disability is an example of this component. The cognitive component consists of an individual's thoughts, ideas, and perceptions. Meyers' definition of attitude is defined as a favorable or unfavorable evaluative reaction toward something or someone, exhibited in one's beliefs, feelings, or intended behavior. This definition includes all three of the components that are characteristic of attitudes.

The World Health Organization (WHO) recognizes that the effects of physical impairments do not focus solely on the individual's motor strengths and needs. Instead, the cultural influence of the family and community environments and the physical impairments are inter-related and impact one another. This is termed continuum of disablement and it includes three levels: impairment, disability, and handicap. The International Classification of Impairments, Disease, and Handicaps defines each of these levels. Impairment is a loss or abnormality of structure or function.

Disability is defined as the restriction or inability to perform an activity in the manner considered normal for humans. Finally, handicap is the social and psychological results of the impairment. Handicap refers to the problems and labels that society uses when associated with disabilities.

Most physical disabilities are characterized under two different categories, orthopeadic and neurological disorders. Individuals with an orthopeadic disorder may be born with or acquire problems with bones, muscles, fascia, and joints. Disorders under this category can be a result of genetic, chromosomal, or environmental related problems. Some common orthopeadic disorders include Spina bifida, Scoliosis, Cystic Fibrosis and Cerebral Palsy.

Neurological disorders are problems related to the nervous system. They can also be inherited or acquired. Acquired disorders may result from trauma, disease, or as a part of the normal aging process. Traumatic disorders like spinal cord injuries are most often caused by motor vehicle accidents, falls, violence, and sports (diving and football). The age group most often affected is between 15-25 years and men are affected four times as often as women. Depending on the level of the injury, all limbs may be affected or only the lower trunk and legs may be affected.

Common disorders from disease include Multiple Sclerosis, Parkinson's disease, and muscular dystrophies. Multiple Sclerosis is a disease in which patches of demyelination occur in the nervous system. This will lead to disturbances in the conduction of messages along the nerves. The conditions usually develops between 15-45 years of age. Common symptoms include weakness, fatigue, and an alteration in sensations. If the disease is progressive, severe disability is the result.

Non-disabled individuals also tend to attribute success by handicapped persons to effort or luck rather than ability. They also perceive failures as a result of lack of ability rather than effort or luck. Those individuals who possess these negative attitudes tend to perceive people with handicaps as different, incompetent, and inferior to themselves.

There are factors that are associated with the attitudes of non-disabled individuals. Boys tend to have more negative attitudes than do girls. Attitudes also tend to vary with age. Attitudes of non-disabled children toward individuals with a handicap improve from early childhood through early adolescence. However, attitudes in late adolescence are less favorable, while attitudes of young adults are again more positive. Researchers have concluded that that stereotypes and attitudes vary according to the nature of the handicap. Attitudes tend to be more favorable toward those who are competent and appear normal than toward those who appear incompetent and abnormal.

Numerous studies have suggested that negative attitudes of peers have a tremendous impact on the life of an individual with a handicap. The person's self-concept, cognitive and social development, academic performance, and general psychological health may be largely affected. When an individual is not accepted by his or her peers, their educational environment and social opportunities in the school, community, work, and home may greatly suffer.

3

Human Rights of Persons with Disabilities

People with disabilities constitute a sizable global population, yet the often appalling human rights condition of this group has yet to be effectively addressed. Although the human rights system encompasses the principles of equality and non-discrimination, people with disabilities are commonly the subjects of de jure and de facto discrimination on a daily basis. Although at the domestic level some governments have adopted a social inclusion and rights-based approach to disability issues, many more rely on narrow and paternalistic charity and medical models of assistance.

All general international human rights instruments provide safeguards extending to persons with disabilities. These provisions may take the form of principles of equality and non-discrimination or more specific protections on a range of civil, political, economic, social or cultural rights.

The Universal Declaration of Human Rights (UDHR), adopted by the United Nations General Assembly in 1948, is the starting point for any consideration of the content of modern international human rights law. In its expression of general human rights principles in the area of civil, political, economic, social and cultural rights, the UDHR emphasizes its applicability to all people, underscoring that "all human beings are born free and equal in dignity and rights ...all are equal before the law, and [all]are entitled without any discrimination to equal protection of the law. "While the UDHR is a declaration and not an international treaty, it is now widely recognized as part of customary international law and therefore possesses legal force.

The adoption of the UDHR was followed by the drafting of two international treaties which, together with the UDHR, comprise the International Bill of Human Rights and the core of modern international human rights law. In 1966, the UN General Assembly opened for signature the International Covenant on Civil and Political Rights (ICCPR) and the International Covenant on Economic, Social and Cultural Rights (ICESCR). These treaties legally oblige States Parties to implement their provisions, subject to any qualifying reservations. They articulate binding international human rights standards that are applicable to people with disabilities.

While the International Bill of Rights provides protections applicable to all people, it should be noted that there is no explicit mention of discrimination on the grounds of disability in these instruments. In addition to expressions of human rights that apply equally to all human beings, in some instances international human rights instruments may specifically refer to people with disabilities in specific provisions. For example, Article 25 of the Universal Declaration of Human Rights provides for the right to an adequate standard of living.

In that provision, disability is explicitly referenced as one of several grounds for the "right to security "to preserve an adequate standard of living. Article 23 of the

Convention on the Rights of the Child is specifically devoted to the rights of mentally and physically disabled children. Notwithstanding these references, no international human rights convention (apart from one regional treaty) addresses the rights of people with disabilities in a comprehensive manner.

Early developments in international human rights law served to bolster the concept that human rights standards, and the violation of those rights by a state against its own nationals, are indeed a matter of international concern. It was soon discovered, however, that additional legal measures were required in order to address human rights abuses experienced throughout the world by individuals belonging to particular social, ethnic, religious and other groups.

Beginning in the mid-1960s, the United Nations began to recognize the vulnerability of certain populations to human rights abuses that were not addressed with any degree of specificity in existing international human rights law. Well- coordinated international campaigns led to the adoption of a number of specialized human rights instruments to address gaps in the law and establish permanent mechanisms for more effective monitoring of violations.

These include, among others, the UN Convention on the Elimination of All Forms of Racial Discrimination, the UN Convention on the Elimination of All Forms of Discrimination Against Women, the UN Convention on the Rights of the Child, the International Labour Organization Convention Concerning Indigenous and Tribal Peoples in Independent Countries, and the International Convention on the Protection of the Rights of All Migrant Workers. These treaties create legal protections that address in concrete terms the social, political and cultural circumstances that impact the human rights conditions of these populations.

The majority of these specialized instruments frequently provide for the establishment of permanent treaty-monitoring bodies composed of recognized experts in the field of human rights. Such bodies are mandated to scrutinize and promote State Party compliance with treaty provisions. Once the treaties have entered into force, they provide a forum for the consideration of human rights issues insofar as they pertain to the treaty.

In the same way that international human rights norms and standards have been developed in relation to a range of specific populations, efforts have also been made to draft disability- specific standards within the United Nations system. For example, during the 1970s, the Declaration on the Rights of Mentally Retarded Persons and the Declaration on the Rights of Disabled Persons were the first international human rights instruments to embody human rights principles relating specifically to people with disabilities. These were significant steps in terms of raising awareness about the human rights of people with disabilities.

They came under heavy criticism by the disability community, however, for their expression of outmoded medical and charity models of disability which serve to reinforce paternalistic attitudes about people with disabilities. Thus, for example, the 1971 Declaration on the Rights of Mentally Retarded Persons was criticized for qualifying the scope of rights for people with intellectual disabilities both in providing that "the mentally retarded person has, to the maximum degree of feasibility, the same rights as other human beings "and in terms of its goal for societies which is to promote "their integration as far as possible in normal life."

Although further progress was made in the development of international standards relating to disability, these efforts did not culminate in legally binding measures. These efforts included the United Nations Decade of Disabled Persons (1982-1993) , during which the World Programme of Action Concerning Disabled Persons and two new international human rights instruments pertaining to disability were adopted by the UN General Assembly.

In 1993, the UN Standard Rules on the Equalization of Opportunities for Persons with Disabilities were adopted as a blueprint for policy-making and provide a basis for technical and economic cooperation among states. The UN Standard Rules establish a monitoring mechanism through the appointment of a Special Rapporteur who reports to the Commission on Social Development. The Principles for the Protection of Persons with Mental Illnesses and the Improvement of Mental Health Care (MI Principles) were adopted in 1991, setting forth principles that can serve as a common standard for the evaluation of the implementation of human rights practices in national mental health systems. These documents do add content to existing human rights provisions found in the general international human rights instruments.

Nonetheless, they are not housed in a treaty, nor are they widely regarded as having attained the status of customary international law. Most significantly, the UN Standard Rules and the MI Principles do not establish permanent bodies to monitor compliance with their provisions. In addition, the UN Standard Rules leave important issues unaddressed. For example, they do not address important civil and political rights, such as the right to vote and be elected in free and fair elections held by secret ballot. In addition, the MI Principles have come under heavy criticism from psychiatric survivor groups who have argued with persuasion that some of the core principles serve to reinforce the status quo, thereby perpetuating human rights abuses against people with mental disabilities.

These and numerous other "softer "instruments are significant both insofar as they express support for people with disabilities, for their value as authoritative interpretations of broad treaty obligations of relevance for persons with disabilities, and for their potential contribution to the corpus of customary international law in the field of disability rights. It should be noted, however, that they may have severe limitations resulting from their framing of issues in outmoded and inappropriate ways. Many other articulations of standards and guidelines, such as those addressing accessibility in environmental or informational contexts, information, or trade provisions on the import of assistive devices, are also relevant in terms of providing a foundation for norm creation.

While the foregoing category of international human rights standards relating to disability represents progress, the current framework does indeed have shortcomings that have generated calls for further developments.

First, without specific attention and language devoted to the most common practices leading to the violation of human rights for people with disabilities in any single international human rights treaty, many governments. remain unaware of their legal obligations. Consequently, the international human rights framework is rarely used to protect people with disabilities.

Second, as a recent study by the Office of the High Commissioner for Human Rights demonstrates with persuasive force, the existing human rights treaty-monitoring bodies established by a variety of international human rights treaties only marginally address, if at all, the routine human rights violations to which people with disabilities are subjected. There is thus a notable lack of jurisprudence on the rights of people with disabilities as a matter of international human rights law.

International Courts and Tribunals and Their Relevance for Disability Norms and Standards

The jurisprudence of international courts and tribunals constitutes an additional repository of international norms and standards applicable to persons with disabilities as well as authoritative interpretations of existing human rights norms. Regional human rights tribunals, communications and general comments mechanisms of human rights treaty- monitoring bodies, and international administrative law tribunals of the United Nations, the World Bank and other intergovernmental organizations have the potential to advance the disability agenda through the interpretation and application of general principles of human rights law applicable to persons with disabilities as well as disability-specific standards.

Regional Human Rights Systems and Disability Norms and Standards

There are three regional human rights systems established to implement and enforce regional human rights instruments in Europe, the Americas and Africa. The African Charter of Human and Peoples ' Rights is the only one of the core regional human rights treaties that specifically references generalized protection for people with disabilities. Article 18(4) of the African Charter provides for the "right of the aged and disabled to special measures of protection. "It should be noted, however, that the language of this provision does not reflect current thinking about disability.

In general terms, the regional systems have not developed the competence to address the rights of people with disabilities in any consistent or ongoing basis. There are, however, some recent promising developments in this regard. In 1999, the first regional instrument specifically addressing the rights of people with disabilities was adopted by the Organization of American States. This instrument, the Inter-American Convention on the Elimination of All Forms of Discrimination against Persons with Disabilities , has the objective of preventing and eliminating all forms of discrimination against people with disabilities and promoting their full integration into society.

In addition, the Inter- American Commission, one of two bodies mandated to promote human rights within the Inter-American Human Rights system, has on occasion considered complaints specifically addressing the rights of people with disabilities.

Towards the Further Development of International Norms and Standards on the Human Rights of People with Disabilities

Efforts to further develop international norms and standards relating to disability have been ongoing within the United Nations as well as regional human rights systems during the past several decades. Most recently though, there have been numerous calls for an international convention on the human rights of persons with disabilities by actors within the global disability community. During March 2000, participants at the World NGO Summit on Disability convened in Beijing to discuss a possible treaty delineating the human rights of people with disabilities.

The Declaration, which was issued from that meeting, urged "all heads of state and government, public administrators, local authorities, members of the United Nations system, people with disabilities, civic organizations that participate in the development process, and socially responsible private sector organizations, to immediately initiate the process for an international convention. "

The momentum for a treaty was continued when, on November 28, 2001, the UN General Assembly adopted, by consensus, a resolution initiated by Mexico, which calls for the establishment of an Ad Hoc Committee mandated to elaborate "a comprehensive and integral international convention to protect and promote the rights and dignity of persons with disabilities, based on the holistic approach in the work done in the field of social development, human rights and non-discrimination. "This step builds on the efforts of other countries in recent years, most notably Ireland, to develop support within the United Nations for a treaty on the rights of people with disabilities.

The first meeting of the Ad Hoc Committee occurred July 29 -August 9, 2002, and during that time the Committee discussed how its work should be organized and how the treaty drafting process should progress, as well as how non-governmental organizations (NGOs) should be involved in the process. The meeting resulted in a commitment to meet again, as well as an agreement that NGO participation was a necessary part of the process and that further work should be done to enhance accessibility of the Committee meetings to facilitate the involvement of people with disabilities in the process.

Implementation of International Norms and Standards on Disability

At the international level, norms and standards on disability may be invoked as a basis for the critical analysis of periodic State reporting before treaty-monitoring bodies, as guidelines for fact-finding by inter-governmental and non-governmental bodies, as a frame of reference for international and regional human rights commissioners and special rapporteurs, and as persuasive authority or as a guide to the interpretation of human rights obligations of a general character in international legal procedures.

In a domestic context, international norms and standards may be used to further the cause of the disability agenda through a variety of strategies. Disability norms and standards may be directly incorporated into a domestic legal system through treaty mechanisms, customary international law, domestic legislation, and through domestic courts in reliance upon international norms and standards as authoritative guides to the interpretation of constitutional provisions, treaties or domestic law statutes.

Creating a Culture of Disability Rights

Effective monitoring and reporting mechanisms are critical if norms and standards are to be fully implemented. Yet realizing human rights and fundamental freedoms for all frequently depends less upon the crafting of new laws and more on the development of a culture in which diversity is accepted and accommodated. Thus, equalization of opportunity for people with disabilities implies not only drafting new laws and introducing new models of disability policy but also exploring ways to ensure that the social construction of disability leaves room for difference.

Such a perspective challenges the notion of hierarchy whereby persons without disabilities are placed above those with disabilities. Legal approaches to challenging ill-conceived hierarchical conceptions must include an examination of the processes through which decision-making regarding the rights and concerns of persons with disabilities takes place. Advocacy in this regard recognizes that the development of a society for all depends upon the utilization of all human resources, and that persons with disabilities are vital actors in fulfilling the different needs of society.

Creating a culture within which the rights of persons with disabilities are respected and where persons with disabilities are not passive recipients but critical participants in the process of building a disability rights culture is a core component of the new advocacy. Examples of strategies for advocacy include mainstreaming disability rights within human rights organizations, incorporating the disability perspective into all human rights trainings, constructing analytical tools to assess the impact of policy proposals at the national level (e. g. , disability impact assessments) , and ensuring the participation by disability rights organizations and persons with disabilities in all international conferences where the interests of persons with disabilities are affected.

Researchers and experts have played a significant role in identifying and defining human rights policy issues and in formulating proposals to address them. Research forms an important source of information and creates an impetus for policy development. Unfortunately, there is a long history of disabled persons being excluded from participation in the decision-making processes that directly affect them. Working to ensure the rights of persons with disabilities through service in international organizations, national governments, advocacy groups and non-governmental organizations and academic institutions not only invites but requires the full participation of persons with disabilities at the local, national, regional and international level.

The expertise of professional communities can inform the content of a disability rights strategy. Professionals such as lawyers, scholars, aid workers, and others have a reservoir of respect within many communities. The values of participation and inclusion can be furthered in drawing from the experience and expertise of a full range of persons working in, and affected by, laws and policies pertaining to disability. Disabled persons themselves are the key players in this process, both as experts and as advocates. Future regional and international standard-setting processes must do more to ensure that people with disabilities are included as full participants, both in the processes used to develop the standards and in the mechanisms and strategies used to implement them.

A New Human Rights Treaty in a Disability Framework

1. A disability convention should primarily contain rights that are enforceable, and it should incorporate measures to enable persons with disabilities to exercise their human rights and fundamental freedoms. In particular it should be grounded on the values of liberty, independence, dignity, self-determination, equality, social solidarity and recognizing that these values apply equally to diverse groups of persons with disabilities and shall result in
2. Standards below already existing human rights standards must not be accepted.
3. It should build on the existing positive achievements of the human rights treaty bodies

Ensuring Consistency with Existing Human Rights Standards

4. A disability convention should complement and strengthen the monitoring of disability rights by the treaty monitoring bodies under the six core Human Right Treaties.
5. The Standard Rules and the World Programme of Action and other instruments of relevance should be used as reference tools in seeking implementation measures.

Ensuring Sensitivity to Diverse Groups and Socio-Economic

6. The situation of all disability groups and the diverse conditions related to gender, race, colour, age, ethnic and other considerations must be taken into account when elaborating
7. When elaborating the convention, special attention should be paid to the conditions of persons with disabilities in developing countries and countries in transition..

Active Participation of Persons with Disabilities as an Essential Precondition

8. The drafting process must be based upon the fullest possible participation of people with disabilities through their representative organizations, including of parents of people with severe intellectual disabilities unable to represent themselves. States should engage in broad consultations with organizations of disabled people and should include representatives of organizations of people with disabilities in their own delegations to the treaty drafting meetings of the UN.

The UN should ensure the wide participation of representative national, regional and international organizations of people with disabilities in the process of drafting the convention like those united under the International Disability Alliance. Active efforts must be made to ensure the participation of organizations of people with disabilities coming from developing countries and of women with disabilities.

Providing a Strong Mechanism of Enforcement

9. The relevant treaty monitoring bodies, both at the international and national level, should be established and strengthened, with the purpose to monitor and

report on the implementation of the treaty, including dealing with individual and group complaints.

10. A mechanism for the participation of organizations of persons with disabilities in the monitoring and implementation of the treaty should be provided.

Worldwide View on Methodology in the Analysis of Disability Laws

Many different approaches are used to examine disability laws around the world. These include:

1) *Civil Rights-Based:* One approach closely associated with the examination of disability rights, vis-à-vis the ADA is the guarantee of e quality of opportunity by proscribing discrimination. This approach applies to legislation in Australia, Canada, Great Britain and New Zealand for example.
2) *Special Needs-Based:* Special needs-based aims at ensuring equality of results by emphasizing special needs over equal rights mandating quotas. Traditionally, this has been the continental European and Japanese model. Though efforts are underway even in continental Europe and Japan to base their laws on the approach in (a) above.
3) *Special Needs, Rehabilitation and Sanction-Based:* Another approach combines the ADA type of equality-based and special. needs-based models without quotas. Here special needs and rehabilitation are emphasized. Failure to comply by proprietors culminates in penal sanctions. This, for example, is the Zimbabwean model.
4) *Constitution-Based:* Constitution-based is found in many of the countries especially in Sub-Saharan Africa. These countries primarily guarantee disability rights as part of the constitutional norm on fundamental human rights of the individual prior to its regulation in statutory instruments.

5) *Religious &Customary Law-Based* :Another approach to the issue of disability is under indigenous customary laws and also Islamic law. This model invariably is present in traditional societies in Sub-Saharan Africa and in those countries of the world where Islamic law is prevalent. By and large,this method is uncodified.

Generally, the key is the equal treatment approach of the ADA in that it is viewed from a civil rights perspective. To this extent, it requires neutrality or "blind justice" in dealing with those protected by the legislation. The ADA approach is to prohibit employment discrimination per se. In contrast, however, the European and Japanese models emphasize the need to protect differences and analyze disability as a category that must be accorded special consideration, supported by the assistance of the state. The salient feature of the European and Japanese models is by and large the employment quota. As noted above, a movement is currently underway in Europe and Japan to move from quotas to ADA-type regulation.

The ADA interprets equality through the lenses of sameness and non-discrimination, that is, the ADA mandates that people with disabilities be treated in the same way as other citizens with reasonable accommodation of their differences. Under the ADA, therefore, emphasis is placed on the removal of barriers that jeopardize equality of opportunities. This outlook finds expression in large part through codified rights and claims to representation.

The British Disability Discrimination Act, 1995 (DDA) as examined an important turning point in the history of civil rights in Great Britain. Under the DDA, a person is identified as disabled if s/he "has" a physical or mental impairment, which "has" a substantial and long-term adverse effect on his/her ability to carry out normal day-to-day activities. There are five key elements to the DDA definition, namely (a) impairment;(b) substantial nature of the impairment;(c) long-term effects of the impairment (d) adverse effects of the impairment and (e) impact of the impairment on normal day-to-day activities.

The ADA includes three different ways to consider a person disabled and the classification of disability as "a physical or mental impairment that substantially limits one or more of the major life activities" is crucial to all three definitions of an individual with a disability. This. definition holds that work constitutes a major life activity. Significantly the definition of disability under the DDA is purely in the present tense. It does not incorporate an individual with a history of disability. "Is" is determined by the verb "has" in the critical clause "a person" has "a disability for the purpose of this Act if he" has "a physical or mental impairment."

The Five Elements of the Definition of Disability under British Law:

a) *Impairment*: Impairment may be either physical or mental. The DDA does not include alcoholism or drug addiction as disabilities. But the effect of these conditions may constitute impairment under the Act.
b) *Substantial*: The word "substantial" means an effect that is more than minor for the purpose of the Act.
c) *Long-term*: The effect of an impairment is long-term if (1) it has lasted at least 12 months (2) the period for which it lasts is likely to be at least 12 months or (3) is likely to last for the rest of the life of the person affected. Where impairment ceases to have a substantial effect, it will still qualify if it is likely to reoccur. The likelihood of recurrence is therefore a main factor.
d) *Adverse Effect*: When determining adverse effect, a tribunal considers what the individual either cannot

do or can do only with difficulty, not what the individual can actually do.

e) *Normal day-to-day activities:* Normal day-to-day activities constitute mobility, manual dexterity, physical coordination, continence, the ability to lift, carry or otherwise move everyday objects, speech, hearing or eye sight, memory or ability to concentrate, learn or understand and the ability to perceive the risk of physical danger.

Perspectives to Anti-Discrimination Legislation

Early European legislation on disability required employment quotas. Europeans were mandated to employ a certain percentage of disabled war veterans. Waddington and others have examined the quota system and anti-discrimination legislation. She also reviewed the reassessment of disability employment policy that is ongoing in some European countries, such as the United Kingdom.

Claire Feikert and Edith Palmer with respect to Germany take up a similar analysis while Karl Wennink has worked on the law's status in the Netherlands where a quota bill awaits final approval to be effective in 2003. The analysis by Waddington also incorporates three different legislative approaches countering on disability (employment) discrimination as follows:

a) Constitutional

b) Civil law

c) Criminal law

In some respects, the current European movement to adopt disability employment and anti- discrimination statutes, founded on civil rights (as in the United States) and in Sub-Saharan Africa, where disability is first and foremost a constitutional principle, and second where it is part of the fundamental human rights of the individual (civil rights) or where it is part of the State Principles and Fundamental Objectives of Government (non-justiciable), can be viewed as a return to the concept of duty, though in a variant form.

A full appreciation of the current wave of disability law in Europe necessarily involves. some understanding of the emergence and development of the quota system on the continent. The first quota systems originated in the post-First World War era and were tailored primarily to veterans:

"These quotas were based on the idea that society owed those who have been disabled while serving their country, and by the end of 1923, Germany, Austria, Italy, Poland and France had all adopted such systems. "However, some countries did not follow this path to impose mandatory requirements on employers to employ a certain number of disabled war veterans. Rather, they sought to encourage their voluntarily compliance. But the failure of voluntarism led most of the non- mandatory European countries to go back to the quota system in the post-Second World War era.

The second generation quota system was extended to include civilian populations. "A consequence of the extension was that, the concept of duty, which had existed when the systems were exclusively targeted at veterans was lost, and the new quotas became part of overall social welfare policy.. . "By 1996, ten of the fifteen members of the European Union still utilized quotas to employ the disabled. Even certain non-members of the Union have quotas for the employment of the disabled, for example, Poland. All quota systems require the employment of a certain percentage of disabled people. But even within this general framework of the quota system, variations exist. Consequently, one could not speak of a unified European quota system. Three main variations exist:

a) The Legislative-Based Quota System

Under the legislative based quota system, employers are typically not required to employ a certain percentage of disabled employees, but it is recommended that they do so. This system operates in the Netherlands, for example. Prior to 1986 in the Netherlands, a quota system, similar to that found in Great Britain in the post-Second World War era, was in force. This system imposed a legislative obligation without sanction. However, in 1986, the Handicapped Workers Employment Act (WGW) supplanted the Employment of the Disabled Act, 1947. The Law of 1986 introduced a new quota system and removed the registration requirement of disabled persons. Still, there was no significant improvement in the employment of the disabled.

Under the WGW, public and private employers were still required to facilitate the employment of disabled persons, and a quota target between three and five percent to be achieved over three years was set. But the quota was voluntary, and the WGW did not provide for any sanctions in case employers did not make the requisite quota. Rather, the government indicated that it intended to initiate a legislative obligation founded on a quota of between three and seven percent depending on the branch of the industry or public sector involved if it was discovered. that after three years employers were still not making the quota. This mandate was to be supported with a fine for every position not occupied by disabled persons in each year. Employers who exceeded their quota were similarly to receive compensation of a certain amount of money for every position filled by a disabled person in each year."

By 1989, there had been little improvement in the employment situation of the disabled people, and an official government report showed that only 2. 2%of workers with a contract of fifteen days or more were disabled. The government did not respond to this problem by introducing a compulsory quota as it had threatened to do, but rather concluded that such a quota across all sectors of industry was not'a practicable policy '. . . The Dutch experience suggests that a voluntary quota. . . which imposes no legal obligation upon employers and provided for no sanctions has little impact on the numbers of disabled people in open employment." The British pre-war experience was similar.

b) Legislative Model without Effective

Sanction Under this system employers are under legislative mandate to employ a quota of disabled people. The law does not provide any effective sanctions when the quota is not made. Britain typified this system of quotas subsequent to the Second World War with the Disabled Persons Employment Act, 1944. This act has been supplanted by the DDA."

In practice, the British quota was not successful in promoting employment of disabled people, and each year progressively fewer employers met their quota obligation. By 1993, only 18. 9%of employers achieved the 3%quota compared with 30. 4%in 1984.

c) Legislative Obligation Backed-Up by Sanction (Levy-Grant System)

The levy-grant system is the form of quotas, which, through modification of the quota system, attracted the most attention in the early 1980s and 1990s. It requires setting a quota, all covered employers who do not meet their obligation pay a fine or a levy that generally goes into a fund. The German legislation of 1974 set quotas of six percent for all public and private employers with sixteen or more employees. The quota could be adjusted as low as four percent or increased to ten percent.

"The German quota system undoubtedly has made a greater contribution to promoting the employment of disabled people than the two previously described systems. However, in recent years, the German quota has become progressively less effective. Since 1982, when the average percentage of severely disabled workers employed within firms had fallen to 4. 3%. . . the German quota has proved itself incapable of maintaining the targeted level of employment for severely disabled people during a period of economic recession. The economic difficulties, combined with the relatively low levy, seem to make payment a more attractive option than the unknown risks of hiring a severely disabled worker."

These three approaches of the quota system could be varied or adopted in toto in any given country. Another adaptation is the setting of the pertinent quota percentage. Among the quota systems that operate in the European Union, the percentage varies from two percent in Spain to fifteen percent in Italy, where the quota system is extended to cover people with disabilities, widows, orphans and refugees, according to the analysis provided by Giovanni Salvo. The minimum number of workers that must be employed also affects the obligation imposed on employers, and the means of calculating this number before an employer is subject to the quota. The number varied from sixteen employees in Germany to fifty in Spain. Additionally, targeting the public sector, the private sector, or both varies the quota.

"In most European Union Member states, both kinds of employers are covered, although in Ireland, the legislation only applies to the public sector, while in the United Kingdom, the provisions of the recently abolished DPEA did not apply to the public sector, the Crown, however accepted the same obligation. . . where quotas are based on the levy-grant system, the size of the levy can be altered."

Japanese disability law should also be mentioned in regards to the use of a quota system. The law defines a person with disability as "a person whose daily life or life in society is substantially limited over the long term due to a physical disability. . ." The Japanese government recognizes 6 million, or 5%of the general population, people as having some form of disability or another, whether it be physical, intellectual or psychiatric. This is a low percentage compared to other countries, for instance, 10%in Germany, 20%in the United States and over 30%in Sweden. The number is low primarily because Japanese law strictly limits the forms of disabilities that the law recognizes. For instance, AIDS/ HIV, alcohol, chemical dependency, epilepsy, rheumatism and other learning disabilities are not recognized as disabilities under Japanese law."

Furthermore, official surveys only include those people carrying a shougaisha techou or disability handbook, which lists the name, type and severity of the individual's disability. Carrying this card is not a requirement, but it is the only way to receive a host of welfare and tax benefits. Many disability activists see this card as reproducing the stigma associated with disabilities, but cannot afford to forfeit the benefits associated with it. Students attending special schools are encouraged to apply for a handbook, as are job seekers at their local public employment security office. Only handbook owners can officially claim to be disabled and thus count for a company's legal employment quota."

However, Japan has instituted a sophisticated system of rehabilitation and welfare benefits that service people with disabilities. Its vocational rehabilitation network is internationally well-known for its administration of the levy and grant system and its operation of the vocational training and placement services at its public employment security offices. The National Institute for Vocational Rehabilitation, constitutes a central institution for the nation-wide rehabilitation centers. It conducts surveys and research, trains rehabilitation counselors, collects and disseminates information on the employment and rehabilitation of people with disabilities. It also provides technical assistance to employers.

In Asia, Japan is considered a leader in vocational rehabilitation. It also provides support and research to establish similar systems in the region. The quota system imposed in Japan in 1960 became a legal requirement in 1976. However, employers not in compliance with the quota system were required to draw up a plan for such employment and would be" urged" to follow through or face a fine. These employer plans might require employers to adapt existing facilities, build new ones or provide additional supervision and training. The costs incurred were to be covered by grants, which in turn would be covered by the monthly levies gathered from noncompliant employers.

Today in Japan, the employment quota is 1. 8%for the private sector and 2. 1%for the public sector. Corporations that fall short of the employment quota are levied 50, 000 [yen] per employee per month. However, currently, only those corporations with 300 or more employees are actually levied. But awards are given to those entities that exceed their quota. For example, corporations with 300 or less employees are awarded 17, 000 [yen] per person per month, and companies with 300 or more employees are awarded 25, 000 [yen].

The actual employment rate for people with disabilities in Japan is still below the legal requirement of 1. 47%, which means that half (49. 8%) of all businesses do not reach the quota. The Ministry of Labor in Japan has indicated that when it comes to compliance with quotas, only small corporations truly comply.

Very large companies have developed a way to comply with the quota by establishing special "barrier free" subsidiary companies (tokurei kogaisha). These companies primarily hire people with disabilities who then count for the parent company's employment quota.

This de facto re-segregation into separate workplaces falls short of the U. N. -integrated mandate, but is promoted by the Japanese government as the best compromise and preferred means to boost the employment of people with disabilities. "In the same token, the educational system is also segregated against children with disabilities. The vast numbers of students with disabilities are educated in special schools (yougo gakkou (yougo gakkou). Placing disabled children into regular schools and/or classes constitutes an exception. Such schools do not receive any governmental subsidy for their special needs. Parents of disabled children waged a long struggle, but ultimately won the basic education rights for their disabled children in the 1970s. Compulsory education for disabled children was not enforced until 1979. For children without disabilities, compulsory education was mandated as far back as 1948.

Disability activists and policy makers in Europe have become increasingly active in promoting legislation to protect the rights of persons with disability through anti- discrimination measures. However, this has not been the case in Great Britain, where the Equal Opportunities Commission and th Commission for Racial Equality vigorously enforce sex and race discrimination. But it may be too early to judge whether European anti-discrimination measures will be any more effective than the long standing quota systems in promoting the rights and employment of disabled persons.

Anti-discrimination laws have always been part of the legislative environment in order to promote parity for women in Europe. Some other countries have also adopted this approach with respect to racial, religious and indigenous minorities. Only recently has this approach been utilized.

The United States was one of the first countries to adopt disability anti-discrimination legislation. The Civil Rights Act of 1964 prohibited discrimination on the basis of race, color, religion, sex and national origin. Thereafter, many people, including people with disabilities, started seeing disability as a category in need of anti-discriminatory protection. A campaign ensued which culminated in the Rehabilitation Act of 1973. Title V of this Act prohibits employment discrimination. Title V covers all federal government programs and activities supported by federal funds, including hospitals, schools and firms contracting with the federal government.

Subsequent to the Rehabilitation Act 1973, disability activists mounted a vigorous campaign to extend anti-discrimination requirements to employers in the private sector. These efforts culminated in the Americans With Disabilities Act of 1990. This statute not only exceeded the basic principle of anti-discrimination legislation concerning employers with fifteen or more employees, but also outlawed discrimination on the grounds of disability in housing, public accommodation, education, transportation, communications, recreation, institutions of people with disabilities, health services, voting and access to public services. The ADA is considered a comprehensive law that recognizes that disability discrimination pervades all areas of society and cannot be addressed on an ad-hoc basis.

Canada was the first country in the world to include a full equality clause in its Constitution that unequivocally incorporated "disability" in its wording, consistent with the Canadian Charter of Rights and Freedoms of 1982 as analyzed by Steve Clark. Despite similarities between the Canadian and American legal cultures, the Canadian anti-discrimination legislation has developed in a way that is distinct.

The first part of the Canadian regime reflects human rights instruments that adopt an individualized approach. The second part signifies laws that require proactive measures to fight against disadvantages and discrimination. The latter adopts a more categorical approach. Both types of instruments are not targeted exclusively at people with disabilities although the disabled are always specifically cited as a protected group. At the federal level, the most notable human rights instruments include the Charter and the Canadian Human Rights Act of 1985, also discussed in the report by Steve Clark. For example, section 15 of the Charter secures and guarantees the "right to equal protection and equal benefit of the law without discrimination." This section also covers discrimination founded on "mental or physical disability." However, the concept of disability is not defined further. The Charter permits, but does not mandate, positive action in favor of disadvantaged groups. It is limited in coverage to the extent that it applies only to federal and provincial legislative activities.

On the other hand, the Human Rights Act prohibits instances of discrimination, including disability. It also proscribes certain discriminatory practices. The Act extends to all of the federal government, crown corporations and businesses and industries that are within the jurisdiction of the federal government. In the same way as the Charter, the Canadian Human Act allows positive action to eliminate or reduce disadvantages.

Even though the legislative program for persons with disabilities in Australia is not as comprehensive as the ADA, basic rights for the disabled are codified on several levels. Under federal law, the Federal (Commonwealth) Government only has constitutional authority to legislate on a restricted number of subjects. The federal government is constitutionally responsible for external affairs, an area of responsibility that enables legislation mandating state compliance with treaty obligations.

Federal legislation in Australia mandates state compliance with the International Convention on the Elimination of All Forms of Racial Discrimination, the International Convention on Civil and Political Rights and, most importantly, the International Labor Organization's Discrimination (Employment and Occupation) Convention. With this background, Donald De Glopper has examined the Disability Discrimination Act of1993:

". . . the Disability Discrimination Act, one of the most comprehensive rights-based pieces of anti-discrimination that the world has yet seen, and a major reform in the law prohibiting discrimination against people with disabilities. Since 1993, the Disability Discrimination Act has been in operation throughout Australia. . . . [it covers]people with all kinds of impairments. By choosing to deal with disability in legislation separate from other instruments dealing with discrimination, the Act is sending out a clear message to disabled people that their situation should not necessarily be lumped into one whole, and that discrimination on the grounds of disability raises a whole set of discrete issues that are different from those associated, for example, race or gender. The Federal Human Rights Equal Opportunity Commission has responsibility for its operation, via the newly appointed Disability Commission. . . The burden of proof that discrimination has occurred rests, however with the disabled person."

In addition, state laws, though less important since the Disability Discrimination Act, also protect disability rights. State legislation is ultimately the most critical when it comes to the concept of affirmative action. Laws secure the civil rights of the physically disabled in four of the seven Australian states. These include New South Wales, Victoria, South Australia and Western Australia. Other than South Australia, this protection incorporates discrimination on grounds of intellectual impairment. In Victoria and Western Australia, mental disorder is also a covered disability

The Intellectual Disabled Persons Services Act, 1986 (IDPSA) and the Disability Services Act, 1991 (DSA) both enacted by the state of Victoria. The IDPSA sets standards for providing services, admission and treatment of the mentally disabled in residential institutions. The IDPSA also instituted a code of conduct or established principles founded upon the concepts of equity, integration, participation and civil rights. On the other hand, the DSA regulates the funding of disability services for both physically and mentally disabled people, premised on a set of prescribed principles set forth in the Act.

For example, the DSA states that persons with disabilities possess rights that must be respected so as to insure their human dignity at all times. No distinction is made between people with disabilities and others when it comes to human rights. The law aims to insure that persons with disability are able to realize their potential for physical, social, emotional and intellectual development on a level playing field. In practical terms this means unrestricted access to services to support a reasonable quality of life. The law intends to guarantee persons with disabilities the liberty to enjoy services and resources without limitations on their rights and opportunities. They are also empowered to pursue grievances in relation to services where their rights are abridged.

In the recent past, European disability activists and policy makers have paid increasing attention to disability discrimination and the effective use of anti-discriminatory legislation. France has been noted as one of the first countries in Europe to extend legal protection to victims of disability discrimination. Germany followed when it amended its Constitution to include an equal protection clause, which explicitly cites the disabled as a protected group.

The British enacted the DDA in 1995, addressing disability discrimination, and the Irish followed suit with similar legislation. These four countries have adopted different approaches in crafting disability laws, following either a constitutional model as in constitutional model as in constitutional model Germany;civil law as in Britain and Ireland and the criminal law as in France .

Disability laws in Sub-Saharan Africa also reflect constitutional and criminal law bases. In Germany, it was through the constitutional amendment as noted above. In the United Kingdom, there is little tradition in the United Kingdom of a rights-based approach to the problems faced by people with mental and/or physical disabilities action. This approach arose from activists to private members' bills, as ably examined by Feikert below. Various pieces of legislation provide for special assistance to disabled in given situations such as rights to special financial benefits, to housing adaptations, special parking facilities, access to special services and so forth. The mentally disabled, subject to the restrictions contained in the Mental Health Act, including detention, are still given special rights and protections by law.

"The concept of an overarching protection from discrimination on grounds of disability, either in specific settings (as in the United States) or generally (as in Canada) has to date found little favor in the United Kingdom."

In the Irish Republic, the government published proposals for employment discrimination legislation under the Employment Equality Bill. Together with the Equal Status Bill, this legislation covers discrimination and the provision of goods, services and facilities. Both bills include disability discrimination in their provisions. Consequently, the Irish Commission on the Status of People with Disabilities was established in December 1993 with the purpose of presenting the Irish government with proposals that would give disabled people the same opportunities to participate as others in the life of the Republic.

In France, the French Parliament in 1990 adopted Law No. 90-602 concerning the protection of persons against discrimination on grounds of their state of health or handicap. This law amended the Labor and Penal Codes as noted by Nicole Atwill below. By amending the Penal Code, Parliament made it a criminal offense for providers of goods and services to refuse an individual or association on the grounds of state of health or handicap; it also makes it illegal for an employer to decline to hire or to dismiss an individual on these grounds. The Penal Code also covers discrimination based on origin, sex, custom, marital status, ethnicity, nationality and religion.

The European Community has also taken a keen interest in promoting the employment of disabled people since the 1970s. This interest has taken the form of financial support from the European Social Fund and a number of actions and programs concerning the disabled. This includes a Recommendation in 1986 on the Employment of Disabled People. Until recently, however, disability discrimination was not addressed at all at the community level, and the European Community has even been criticized for its discriminatory treatment of its employees."

Instead in the 1980s, both the Commission and the European Parliament tended to focus on the quota system as a means of promoting the employment of people with disabilities. The Commission recommended that all Member States adopt some form of quota. . . and commissioned a report on this subject, while the European Parliament pushed the Commission and Member States to take further action in this area. The 1990s has seen a shift in focus, with first the European Parliament and now the Commission addressing the issue of disability discrimination."

In Sub-Saharan Africa, a multiplicity of laws and legal systems are operative. The diversity of jurisprudential models makes it impossible to analyze all countries in a generic way. Even though the subject matter may be identical or similar, the systems of law and their cultural contexts are unique.

The National Constitution of Argentina, as noted by G. I. Rodrigues-Ferrand, incorporates protection for the basic human rights of people with disabilities first in Article 23. This constitutional provision is a grandfather clause enabling the Congress of Argentina to legislate on matters that promote affirmative action, ensure equal opportunity and treatment of people with disabilities and their full enjoyment and exercise of the rights recognized by the constitution. These rights of people with disabilities are by their very nature secured, protected and enforced under international human rights instruments that deal with the rights of people with disabilities to which Argentina is a party.

A number of legislative instruments have been promulgated in Argentina to deal with the basic rights of disabled persons. These include Law, No. 24657/96 as described by Rodriguez-Ferrand which established The Consejo Federal de Discapacidad. It comprises superior institutions, Consejo Federal de Discapacidad. It comprises superior institutions, Consejo Federal de Discapacidad agencies and organs of the government that deal with the protection of people with disabilities in the provinces and Municipality of the City of Buenos Aires. This body coordinates national policy on prevention, rehabilitation and equal opportunity aspects of the rights of people with disabilities at a provincial level. It also disseminates information on the subject.

The other significant piece of legislation is Decree No. 10247/94. Under this Decree, directives are issued to various and relevant government bodies and agencies to execute policies pertaining to the disabled as set forth in Law No. 22431 highlighted below. Another relevant statute is Decree No. 1101/87, which established the Commission Nacional Asesora para la Integracion de Personas Discapacitadas as an executive body, which relates to the three branches of the Argentinean government.

This body constitutes a regulatory agency for the Sistema Unico de Prestaciones Basicas para Personas con Discapacidad and provides Prestaciones Basicas para Personas con Discapacidad and provides Prestaciones Basicas para Personas con Discapacidad prevention and rehabilitation treatments, education, therapeutic programs, and special transportation needs and devices for disabled people.

Law No. 22341/81, as amended by Laws Nos. 24314/94;24901/97, and Regulatory Decree No. 498/83, reflect a "comprehensive" protective system of rights of people with disabilities. This law deals with measures against employment discrimination for people with disabilities, specific educational allowances to families with disabled children, security and protection of rights concerning public services and transportation. Amended Law No. 24314/94 ensures public facility accessibility to provide independence, self-sufficiency and safety in transport-related areas. Amendment 24314/94 specifically prohibits physical barriers to mobility for people with disabilities.

Law No. 24204 deals with telecommunications. It requires that telephone companies provide public telephones that are duly equipped to service those physically disabled with hearing and speech impairment. Other supporting legislative regimes are also available in this area to deal with matters of telecommunications. A series of other statutory enactments deal with sanctions on anti-discrimination measures.

Canada does not have a single statutory enactment that controls the basic human rights of people with disabilities in similar manner to the ADA. Emphasis in Canada appears to be on "access to justice and enforcement rather than on enactment of new legislation. . ." The Canadian "Bill of Rights" as part of the Constitution of Canada was adopted in 1983 with a clause on equal protection before the law. The Charter specifically proscribes discrimination based on mental and physical disability. However, as noted above, the Charter is not applicable to the private sector, is only applicable to government and is only enforceable through court action. This has given rise to an evolving body of case law enforcing these provisions concerning disabilities.

First, the Human Rights Act of Canada constitutes the primary focus of anti-discrimination measures. It is equally applicable to government and the private sector. Provinces of Canada also have their own human rights legislation. Variances are prevalent in form and language between the different provincial legislation. Human rights commissions as quasi- judicial tribunals enforce the human rights laws through binding orders that are enforceable with process and procedure for judicial review invested in the provincial courts. At the federal level, decisions of the Canadian Human Rights Tribunal are reviewed by the Federal Court of Canada.

Second, The Employment Equity Act is a federal statute enforced by the Canadian Human Rights Commission. The province of Quebec also has a similar employment equity law. Both the federal and provincial legislation are designed to increase the employment of women, aboriginals, visible minorities and persons with disabilities. Two of the ADA topical headings are found in Canada's statutory scheme of. protection for persons with disabilities: employment and public services/ transportation.

In the area of employment, the subject areas within each major topic above as identified also comport. Under ADA, these seven categories are covered entities that are prohibited from discrimination, actions considered discriminatory including retaliation and/or coercion, enforcement/penalties and/or sanctions, exemptions and/or defenses to actions of discrimination, administering authority, certification for meeting or exceeding statutory requirements if any and agencies responsible for coordination.

Canadian legislation is classified in the same manner as the ADA. However, this Canadian classification is tailored to its own unique national circumstances so that the Canadian employment major topical heading also includes employment equity. As to the particular detail in each and every subject area, these are by definition particular to Canada, and the requester/reader must examine the individual Canadian report by its author to grasp exactly how Canada has dealt with these areas.

The public services and transportation subject matter category comports with the ADA. Under this heading, Canadian legislation has dealt with two aspects that are ADA subject areas. These reflect covered entities and actions considered discriminatory. Canadian laws may have dealt with the other ADA type classifications within the seven areas identified above, but, under Canadian laws, these are not similarly formulated or identified. Second, Canadian laws only comport with the two ADA type areas of employment and public services/ transportation, and they do not comport with the other major subject areas of ADA as well. To this extent, therefore, Canada, as Argentina, is also comparable in a limited and specific sense.

The Constitution of Mexico secures and protects the rights of people with disabilities, declaring "the social security law is of public interest and shall insure against disability." Indirect guarantee of these rights is also evident in the other portions of the Constitution that includes an equal protection before the law clause. These rights as secured and guaranteed under the Constitution cannot be abridged.

Statutory measures that protect the rights of disabled persons in Mexico are not contained in one single statutory instrument such as the ADA. They are found in various statutory enactments such as The General Law of Health. This law regulates a citizen's right to health as secured by the Federal Constitution. The Health Law also governs prevention of discrimination against persons with disabilities as well as cure and rehabilitation. Protection is with respect to mental and physical disabilities.

A federal agency is responsible for the administration and enforcement of the Act. The other piece of legislation applicable to people with disabilities is The Law on the National System of Social Assistance. This instrument constitutes an enhancing and reinforcing measure of those protections found in the Health Law. The responsible authority under the Law on the National System of Social Assistance is the National Social System for the Integral Development of the Family. This body enjoys a broad mandate to cover a wide spectrum of social, economic, educational and welfare programs that address the needs of the disabled.

The 31 Mexican states including the Federal District of Mexico City have statutory measures that, in one form or other, deal with some aspects of rights of people with disabilities as covered by Gutierez in the Mexico report.

There appears to be no constitutional provisions that govern matters of the persons with disabilities in the Czech Republic. The rights of people with disabilities enjoy statutory protection notwithstanding the apparent absence of constitutional safeguards: "The rights of persons with disabilities are protected by a combination of special and general legislation. The judicial mechanism available to. protect the rights of persons with disabilities is a legal remedy through the courts.

The non-judicial mechanism is an administrative remedy through the offices of public administration. The Czech Republic enacted legal provisions concerning persons with disabilities along the lines of the Americans with Disabilities Act of 1990. These provisions deal with the employment of disabled persons, user-friendly public transportation for people with disabilities, accessibility of public accommodation to people with disabilities, and also provisions for the improvement of services for the hearing and speech-impaired." A committee at the governmental level reports to the Office of Prime Minister. The committee constitutes representatives of concerned Ministries and organizations of persons with disabilities. This has led to the improvement of coordination and other interactive measures to better serve the needs of disabled persons.

There seems to be no constitutional provisions in France that guarantee the rights of people with disabilities. This is because the French approach to new anti-discrimination measures as noted above was approached from the standpoint of criminal law. There are a number of statutes that regulate disability rights in France as follows:

(i) Law 75-534 of June 30, 1975. This law constitutes the primary law on disability. It is a consolidating legislation that harmonizes prior disability laws on the subject. It covers all aspects of the rights of people with disabilities from personal to organizations and agencies that deal with matters of people with disabilities.

(ii) Law 89-486 of July 10, 1989. This law deals with education-related

(iii) Law 90-602 of July 12, 1990 as amended by Law 2001-1066. This Law protects individuals against discrimination due to their state of health or disability.

(iv) Law 91-663 of July 13, 1991. This law incorporates several measures to improve accessibility of disabled persons to housing, work places and public buildings. The policy-making institution of government is the Conseil National Consultatif des personnes handicacapeds. The enforcement and/or administering agency the commission technique d'orientation et de reclassement professionnel also known as d'orientation et de reclassement professionnel also known as d'orientation et de reclassement professionnel COTOREP.

From the point of view of the four major classifications encountered under ADA, French law is in comport. With respect to the seven categories within the four topical headings, French law does not identify these subjects in a similar manner. Concerning employment French law provides as follows:

With respect to public service/transportation, French law covers education of disabled children. But the subject of transportation is not covered under public service. Thus, in addition to the various pertinent legislative measures examined above, Law 82-1153 of December 30, 1982 reinforces disability measures with respect to urban transportation. As regards public accommodation and services by private entities, French disability law regulates these matters in the following manner:

i) Access to housing, public buildings, public and private roads
ii) Access to culture and sports
iii) Discrimination from the point of view of sanctions contained in the general criminal law.

Concerning telecommunications, this is also dealt with to highlight accessibility and non-discrimination of people with disabilities in matters of telecommunications and applicable technologies. Therefore, French law exhibits major components of its disability law that are identical and comparable to the ADA classification of four and seven subject areas identified above. Variance in force and scope between the ADA and French law, therefore, stems from local exigencies in French law tailored to French society.

The Germany constitutional amendment of 1994 specifically prohibits discrimination based on the disability of the person. This clause appears affirmatively enshrined and has led to substantial case law, enforcing the basic human rights of people with disabilities. A number of statutory enactments are in force in Germany in one form or another that touch on the protection of the rights of people with disabilities. These include:

— The Act Combating Unemployment among the Severely Disabled. This law expands employer obligations to hire people with disabilities and improve their working conditions.

— Title 9 of the Social Code, which codifies prior scattered provisions on rehabilitation, and employment of people with disabilities. It has also instituted new administrative structures for the efficacious implementation of this law.

— The Disability Equalization Act constitutes the primary legislation on the rights people with disabilities in Germany and may be comparable to the ADA in subject matter coverage.

— The Anti-Discrimination Act is in drafting stages. Once in force, this law will implement the equal treatment directive of racial and ethnic minorities, required by the European Union.

However, the German legislation intends to go beyond the Union's requirements to strengthen local mechanisms that deal with anti- discrimination. The local German law will formulate a civil rights- based law that would enable filing of civil suits against discrimination, not only protecting the rights of people with disabilities, but also other disadvantaged groups as well. The reach of the proposed legislation will extend to private contractual matters and also employment and housing.

The Germany law is in comport with ADA's four and seven category classifications with natural variances in the German legislation to suit local conditions and circumstances. Consider the broad four ADA categories, the German statute is also similarly outlined in terms of. employment;public services/transportation;public accommodation and services by private entities and telecommunications. The German statute is in accord with the ADA in subject classification. Consequently, in accord with the ADA in subject classification. Consequently, in accord Palmer observes:

> "The German Disability Equalization Act is similar to the Americans with Disabilities Act. . . however, there are some differences between the two acts. The German Act is not as detailed and comprehensive as the American Act. Some of the areas covered in the Americans with Disabilities Act are covered in provisions of Title 9 of the Social Code. This is particularly true of employment law. In addition, much of the assistance for the disabled continues to be provided by social service providers, even though, the newly enacted laws stress the qualitative rights aspects of the entitlements of the disabled. On the whole, much of German legislative frame work for the disabled creates the impression of mixing formerly prevailing welfare philosophy with the new thinking of anti-discrimination measures."

It follows therefore, that, while there are similarities in the American and German positions on disability, variances are also necessary to reflect the distinct societal, developmental and prevailing conditions in each country. In Germany, for example, prior law on disability emphasized a "welfare philosophy" according to Palmer. This history necessarily influenced legislation on the subject, even though the current movement is towards anti-discrimination, consistent with the American legislative position under the ADA. Accordingly, Germany has dealt with the major topical headings of (1) employment to cover the following areas: employment to cover the following areas:

Employment

— Hiring requirements
— Definition of disability
— Compliance through payment of levies
— Enforcement/sanctions/penalties under German law described as prohibition of discrimination and affirmative requirements
— Legal remedies
— Administrative Authority, under German law, described as Agencies and Institutions Involved.

ii) Public Services/Transportation: This area under German law incorporates:

— General mandates imposed on public entities
— Specific requirements
— Schools and Universities

iii) Transportation: Transportation is also separately examined. It includes:

— Enforcement
— Agencies involved.

iv) Public Accommodation and Services to Private Entities:

This area is prescribed under German law thus:

— Requirements in the hotel and restaurant industries
— Transportation as pertains to this sector
— Barrier-free-environment
— Housing
— Enforcement within this specific area of public accommodation and services by private entities.

Palmer has observed with respect to the barrier environment: "An obligation to create barrier-free-environments is imposed on industry in general by the

Equalization Act's definition of "barrier-free," which indicates that the concept applies not only to public accommodation, but also to industrial producers of daily use. However, the statutory concept of "barrier-free" is somewhat elusive, in that it has to be established for each industry or type of service by agreements between the associations of the disabled and the representatives of industry.

Free from barriers are buildings and other installations, means of transport, technical articles of daily use, information processing systems, acoustical and visual sources of information and communication devices, as well as other spheres of daily life, to the extent that they are accessible or usable for disabled human beings in the generally intended manner, without special difficulty and in principle without the help of others. . ."

Italy has constitutional provisions that secure and protect the rights of people with disabilities. A variety of statutory instruments have been in force in Italy over the years to protect the rights of people with disabilities. These include The Organic Law of 1992 or Law No. 104 of February 5, 1992 as amended. This is considered the Charter of the rights of disabled people. Another Charter of the rights of disabled people. Another Charter significant legislative instrument is Law No. 68 of 1999 and the right to work for people with disabilities.

There appears to be no constitutional provisions in the Netherlands that deal with the rights of people with disabilities. A number of statutory enactments are currently in force. Some significant statutory measures have been proposed and are almost law that will comprehensively regulate the rights of people with disabilities in Holland. First, The Equal Treatment of People with Handicap or Chronic Illness Bill "is similar to the Americans with Disabilities Act, but Chronic Illness Bill" is similar to the Americans with Disabilities Act, but Chronic Illness Bill not nearly as extensive. "Once approved, the Bill would become law in 2003. The Law on (Re) Integration of Persons that Have a Disability to Perform Labor, 1998 (The Law) replaced the Law on Labor for Disabled Employees of 1986 as amended. Also pertinent is the Building Decree, 1992, which contains national uniform rules with respect to buildings.

The Law of 1998 is for the reintegration of persons with disabilities into the labor force. It extends existing legal instruments and removes institutional barriers that obstruct this reintegration of people with disabilities into the labor force. In terms of the ADA's four major topical classifications, Dutch law has also adopted the following categories:

i) *Employment*. This area is covered by the Law of 1998 and also the proposed Bill.

ii) *Public Services/Transportation*. Wennink has observed under this category as follows:

> "Public services will be added in the future to the Bill. However, it should be noted that people with disabilities have access to a large number of national insurance schemes. . . People with disabilities can benefit from a large number of programs, services and activities. Vocational education is one of the areas in which the Bill explicitly forbids discrimination. It is prohibited to discriminate against people with disabilities."

iii) *Public Accommodation and Services by Private Entities*. In the Netherlands, the Building Decree, 1992 noted above provides that "all buildings not meant for housing must be made accessible for people with wheelchairs."

iv) *Telecommunications.* The Bill requires accessibility of all telecommunications to employees with disabilities. Furthermore, the Minister responsible for telecommunications on November 8, 2001 installed an ICT Platform on Care for People With Disabilities.

Consequently, Internet cafes for people with disabilities were opened in the campaign "Drempels Weg or Thresholds Removed." This initiative "Drempels Weg or Thresholds Removed." This initiative "Drempels Weg or Thresholds Removed started to make available to people with disabilities web sites of governments, corporations and other institutions. The campaign was also intended to encourage people with disabilities to get fully engaged in participating and utilizing web sites as means of communications. Thus far, 62 of the most important web sites in the Netherlands have agreed to make their sites accessible to the disabled.

"The Republic of Poland does not have a comprehensive law similar to the ADA. The rights of disabled people are regulated by almost 60 various laws and regulations." The primary statutory instrument appears to be The Resolution of the Sejn of the Republic of Poland, better known as the Charter of the Rights of Disabled People. This law deals with all aspects of the rights of disabled persons. The four broad categories and the seven sub-divisions as identified under ADA are not applicable to Poland.

The Constitution of the Russian Federation, 1993 requires that "each person shall be guaranteed social security in old age, in the event of sickness, disability, or loss of a family's primary provider for the raising of children and in other cases specified by law. . . The Constitution also defines the system of state-supported economic, social and legal measures that secures the conditions necessary to compensate disability- related restrictions."

The primary law on the basic human rights of disabled people in the Russian Federation is Federal Law No. 181 of November 24, 1995 on Social Protection of People with Disabilities. This law enunciated and formulated the official state policy concerning the social protection of people with disabilities. The law also extends this protection to equal opportunities for people with disabilities to implement their economic and political rights.

Under this legislation, the four ADA broad categories examined above are also present in the Russian Federation that cover the following areas:

i) Employment
ii) Public Services/Transportation
iii) Public Accommodation (without services by Private Entities)
iv) Telecommunications

Concerning the area of *Employment*, Roudik observes that: "In order to secure the employment of people with disabilities, the law requires a particular number of positions to be reserved for people with disabilities. Local authorities establish employment quotas for people with disabilities in all enterprises with more than 30 employees, regardless of the form of ownership. This quota shall be no less than 3% of the entire number of employees. The law states that special working places which accommodate the needs of the disabled be created."

With respect to *Public Services/Transportation*, the law in the Russian Federation requires that the institution of conditions that enable people with disabilities to have unrestricted access to objects of social infrastructure constitutes a duty of the federal, state and local executive authorities. Accordingly, the law requires that transportation, government buildings, sport establishments and places of recreation and entertainment must be accessible to all people with disabilities including those that require the use of wheel chairs.

The Russian Federation Law with respect to *Public Accommodation* grants people with disabilities and their families with children a right of priority to receive municipal residences. These must be equipped according to standards that ensure safeguard of the needs of people with disabilities.

Telecommunications is another area of the Russian Federation Law, which comports with the ADA. According to this law, in order to secure the basic human rights of people with disabilities, federal and state authorities are under a mandate to provide information restriction free.

Enforcement/Administering Authority is similar to other countries examined above and below where a central executive agency is responsible for the administration and enforcement of the statute. Under the Law in the Russian Federation, the agency with such responsibility, The Ministry of Social Protection of Population (which is similar to the Social Security. Administration in the United States) with branches and other field offices throughout the provinces is responsible for the implementation and enforcement of all laws protecting the basic human rights of people with disabilities.

There seems to be no "constitutional" measures that govern protection of the basic human rights of people with disabilities in the United Kingdom. This is consistent with the British tradition of an "unwritten single Constitutional Instrument" in the manner found under United States law and/or other countries with a tradition for a written constitution.

The primary legislation on the basic human rights of people with disabilities in the United Kingdom is the

Disability Discrimination Act, 1995, better known as the DDA. The four ADA broad categories are also present under the DDA that, in addition, to the four has added education, while public transportation also does not include Public Services. Thus, employment, public transportation, public accommodation and services by private entities and telecommunications are part of the scope of coverage of the DDA. The DDA, as other countries noted above and below, including the Russian Federation, has included in the five broad categories Enforcement and Monitoring of the DDA. This enforcement is general and covers all aspects of the statute.

First, from the United Kingdom report by Feikert, it is evident that even the seven subcategories found under the ADA are also present in the DDA, albeit in manner variant from that found under the ADA. As noted in the case of the Russian Federation, and by large in the countries of Sub- Saharan Africa, enforcement here is a broad category to govern the entire enforcement here is a broad category to govern the entire enforcement statute. Second, the inclusion of education in the five categories under DDA is also similar to other countries in Asia, Europe, Latin America and Africa, as observed in the case of France, Italy, the Netherlands, Poland and the Russian Federation as well as in Argentina, Mexico and Canada. In these countries the basic human rights of disabled students are emphasized as a distinct social group on its own that requires special. attention.

There are no constitutional provisions that secure and guarantee the basic human rights of people with disabilities in Egypt. Law No. 39 of 1975 constitutes the Law on Rehabilitation of Disabled Persons. It governs matters of people with disabilities. The four and seven categories of subject matter classification as found under the ADA are not applicable to Egypt.

According Gholam Vafai, "There is no reference to. .. people with disabilities and their basic human rights per se in the Constitution. . . of Iran. . . 1979 as amended in. .. 1989." The primary law regulating the rights of the disabled in Iran came into force in November of 1959. This instrument approved Recommendation No. 99 concerning Vocational Rehabilitation of the Disabled as adopted by the General Conference of the International Labor Organization (ILO) following its meeting on June 1, 1955. The Iranian law defines the term "disability" as "an individual whose prospects of securing and retaining sustainable employment are substantially reduced as a result of physical and mental impairment. . ."

This law deals with the scope of vocational rehabilitation, administrative. organization, enforcement of civil rights for people with disabilities and employment. The categories of ADA are not applicable to the Iranian law.

However, Ruth Levush has stated: "In interpreting the law, Israeli courts have been guided by the 1999 Law, other provisions in various laws, as well as by the general principles of the legal system, particularly those enumerated in the Basic Law: Human Dignity and Freedom. . ." The primary law protecting the rights of people with disabilities in Israel is The Persons with Disabilities Law 5758 of 1998, effective January 1999. Under this statute, the four broad ADA categories have also been adopted to cover the following:

i) Employment/Special Accommodation under Employment,
ii) Public Services/Transportation,
iii) Public Accommodations and Services by Private Entities,
iv) Telecommunications, and
v) Enforcement/Implementation that covers all aspects

of the statute, not only the four ADA-type classifications.

Within these four broad categories, the seven areas under ADA, as examined above, are also available in a variant form. For example, these are classified as definition, illegal discrimination, enforcement and/or implementation, administering agency, special accommodations, proper representation for people with disabilities in the work force, judicial interpretation, special programs and complaints. These are within the purview of the seven categories even if they are not classified in exactly the same or similar manner under Israeli law. Judicial review by Israeli courts under the Law of 1998, effective 1999 is another important source of disability law. The administering agency is the Equal Rights Commission for Persons with Disabilities.

The law has imposed certain requirements in the employment of persons with disabilities. These requirements vary according to the size of the business entity" and the burden imposed on the employer by compliance. "Also significant under the heading of employment is employment is employment the proscription of discrimination in admission, tests and conditions of services, promotion, professional advancement, severance and severance pay, benefits and retirement compensation in matters of employment. Concerning special accommodations, Levush states: ."

An employer is required to provide accommodations for the employment of persons with disabilities. These include the work place and equipment accommodations, job requirements, hours of work, employment admission tests, training and work procedures. Accommodations are required, however, only as long as the adjustments shall not impose on the employer a too-heavy burden. To be considered too heavy, the burden must be unreasonably heavy in the circumstances in consideration among others, of the cost of the adjustment and its nature, the size of the business, the scope of activities, size and composition of labor force and the existence of exterior or national financing resources or carrying out the adjustment. "

Thus, in dealing with the broad category of employment under Israeli employment under Israeli employment law, the following must also be examined:

— Illegal discrimination,
— Special Accommodation,
— Judicial Interpretation,
— Enforcement/Implementation,
— Special Programs, and
— Complaints.

The Law of 1998, which became effective in 1999, has declared that those with disabilities are entitled to public transportation services. These must be accessible and suitable for their use. Such public transportation must maintain a reasonable frequency in their schedules. Persons with disabilities also must have unrestricted access to stations and ports where such public transportation keeps its routes. Therefore, public transportation covers such carriers as buses, trains, aircraft ships and other means of public transportation for the use of the public. Authority is reposed in the responsible Ministers of Transportation and Treasury to promulgate regulations that implement the various requirements for accessibility. Infringement of these requirements may culminate in fine on the public transportation carrier.

The Law of 1998, effective 1999 mandates that employers must provide special accommodations to persons with disabilities, including places of work and also equipment accommodations. But these are provided based on the test of "reasonable in the circumstances."

According to Levush, "Although the law does not specifically require suitable telecommunications services to persons with disabilities, such a requirement exists based on the general requirement on providers of public services to provide such persons with the appropriate level of service subject to necessary adjustments."

Sub-Saharan Africa constitutes numerous reports by the author of this comparative analysis that cover both constitutional regimes and statutory measures pertaining to people with disabilities in the 31 Sub-Saharan African countries. The study covers 31 Sub-Saharan African countries in English and French-speaking Africa as regards constitutional provisions that either directly or indirectly address the basic human rights of disabled persons. Other constitutions have general provisions that are deemed applicable to persons with disabilities. Concerning national legislation, certain examples are available from English-Speaking Africa that also either directly or indirectly governs the basic human rights of people with disabilities.

The Zimbabwean Disability Act, 1992 or any other law in Sub-Saharan Africa does not contain similar ADA type classifications examined above. But the Zimbabwean law deals with protection of the basic human rights of disabled persons in terms of the following classification:

i) Enforcement, Penalties, Sanctions
ii) Administering Authority
iii) Rule-Making Powers
iv) Scope of Legislation

However, the Zimbabwean legislation has topical headings of employment and access to public premises, services and amenities that may be gleamed using ADA-type guidance.

The Constitution of the Peoples Republic of China protects the lawful rights and interests of people with disabilities. The governing law regulating the rights of disabled people in the PRC is The Protection of Disabled Persons Law divided into 54 articles and 9 Chapters. These regulate rehabilitation, education, employment, cultural life, welfare, environment, legal disability and other ancillary provisions. The four and seven ADA classification of subject is not in explicit accord with the approach taken in the PRC, but these are discernible. The Chinese law is classified in the following manner:

According to Hsia &Zeldin a disabled person in the PRC is defined as "one who suffers abnormalities, the loss of a certain organ or function (psychologically, physiologically, or in anatomical structure), or the loss wholly or in part of the ability to engage in activities in a normal way. Disabled persons are those with visual, hearing, speech, or physical disabilities;mental retardation;mental disorders;multiple disabilities; and/or other disabilities. Criteria for classification of disabilities are established by the State Council. . ."

Hsia &Zeldin also indicate that the law in the PRC contains a general provision that proscribes all discrimination against disabled persons, rather than targeting as done by the ADA with respect to discrimination against public and private entities. Even though the general law of disability prohibits all acts of discrimination, it does not contain a list of actions that are deemed discriminatory as contrasted with the various enumerations of the ADA in this regard.

Similarly, the Law in the PRC does not contain provisions that permit public and/or private entities to take certain actions or measures against disabled persons. For example, the PRC Law does not contain a provision. refusing a food handling position to an individual who has a disease that is transmittable through food handling if reasonable accommodation has been provided.

On the contrary, the Law requires that people with disabilities enjoy full and equal rights with other citizens and that their rights and their personal dignity be secured and protected by law. Therefore, discriminating against people with disabilities, and insulting or abridging the rights of people with disabilities in all manners is prohibited by article 3 of the Law. Article 7, on the other hand, enjoins all Chinese citizens to interact with people with disabilities based on compassionate humanitarian grounds that show understanding, respect, care for and providing assistance to people with disabilities. Society in general must support the work of persons with disabilities.

"Other general provisions deal with, among others, providing special services to people with disabilities, incorporating projects for their benefit into plans for social and economic development at all levels of government, and giving special attention to those wounded or disabled in the service of the State. . . The China Disabled Persons' Federation and its local branches are charged with representing the common interests of persons with disabilities and protecting their lawful rights. . . The Law also obliges disabled persons to abide by the law and to "display an optimistic and enterprising spirit" and "have a sense of self respect, self confidence, self exertion and self reliance."

The State guarantees the right to work for all disabled persons;however, a quota system also exists under Chinese Law. The people's governments at the provincial level determine these quotas. Welfare institutions and others dealing with disabled persons and disabled persons that are self- employed enjoy tax reductions or exemptions. According to article 34 of this law, "no discrimination shall be practiced against disabled persons in employment, engagement, status regularization, promotion, determining technical or professional titles, payment for labor, welfare, labor insurance or in other aspects".

Consequently, no enterprise or institution can deny employment to a disabled person assigned to such an enterprise by the State. Public service agencies are under mandate to provide preferential treatment and auxiliary services to disabled people. Whenever they board public transportation systems, they must be accommodated and be given convenient and special treatment. They are permitted to bring on board, free of charge, any equipment necessary for their mobility. The law also contains other numerous provisions that secure and protect the basic human rights of disabled people in the country. .

The Constitution of India in articles 245 to 246 enshrines provisions for the welfare of people with disabilities. "The Constitution gave the Central Government authority to legislate on the subject at the national level to give effect to India's obligations to the international community. . ."

"The rights of persons with disability are protected by a combination of special and general legislation. "However, the primary legislation is The Persons With Disability (Equal Opportunities Protection of Rights and Full Participation) Act, 1995. Under this Law, the following classification has been adopted:

i) Definition
ii) Coordinating Committee
iii) Prevention and Detection
iv) Education
v) Employment that incorporates the following:
v) Employment that incorporates the following:
   — Affirmative Action
   — Prohibited Actions;Non-discrimination
   — Research and Manpower Development

vi) Competent Authority
vii) Social Security
viii) Penalties
ix) Rule-Making Powers Regulations.

The four and seven categorization of ADA is not utilized in the Indian legislation, though these are discernible from the discussion provided by Nehra.

"Fundamental human rights are secured under the Constitution. . . Article 14 of the Constitution provides for the equality of the people. Although, it does not specifically prohibit discrimination based on disability, it is commonly understood such discrimination is prohibited. . ." In addition, the Japanese Constitution in article 98 (2) requires that treaties and customary international law have both domestic legal force in Japan and therefore prevail over Diet statutes.

According to Umeda, Japan does not have an ADA type legislation that protects the basic human rights of people with disabilities. Numerous laws are available in Japan that are deemed pertinent to rights protecting people with disabilities. A particular law is available that mandates an employment-based quota system. Another law promotes the welfare. of disabled people and another, which requires compliance to disabled rights with respect to public transportation and buildings. By and large these instruments do not grant rights to people with disabilities, but rather mandate certain actions of the government and the private sector.

These statutory instruments include the Basic Law of Disabled People of 1970 as amended in 1999;the Physically Disabled Welfare Law, 1949 as amended in 2002; the Intellectually Disabled Welfare Law, 1960 as amended in 2002 and the Law Concerning Mental Health and Psychotic's Welfare, 1950 as amended in 2002.

Others include the Law Concerning Promotion of Employment of Disabled People, 1960 as amended by

Law, No. 35 of 2002; The School Education Law of 1947 as amended in 2000; The Law Concerning Promotion of Easy Transportation for Elderly and Disabled via Public Transportation, No. 68 of 2000;The Law Concerning Promotion of Building, Specified Buildings Easy to Use by Elderly and Disabled Law, No. 44 of 1994 as amended by Law, No. 68 of 2002 and the Law Concerning Promotion of Business which Facilitate the Use of Telecommunications and Public Broadcasts by Disabled of 1993 as amended in 1999.

The Basic Law of Disabled People contains policies that address promotion, independence and participation of disabled persons in the Japanese society. Under this law, the government is under mandate to institute the Basic Plan Concerning Policies for Disabled People to implement requisite stipulated policies.

Welfare law denotes the Physically Disabled Welfare Law and the Intellectually Disabled Welfare Law. These set forth welfare measures and other requirements for people with disabilities among state, prefectures and municipal government entities. The municipal government provides various services that cater to the needs of people with disabilities. Prefectures are under mandate to establish clinics. They also have qualified welfare officers. The national government operates specified facilities and reimburses a portion of the welfare costs spent by the local government.

The Law concerning Mental Health and Psychotic's Welfare also contains welfare measures. This law also permits mandatory hospitalization and other restrictions of hospital psychotic's activities according to standards prescribed by the Minister of Health, Labor and Welfare. The various statutory enactments regulate the specific subject areas they cover. The classification is as follows:

i) Constitutional authority

ii) Basic law on the disabled
iii) Mandatory employment.
iv) Education
v) Barrier-free transportation
vi) Barrier-free public buildings
vii) Telecommunications

The four and seven ADA category classification of ADA is inapplicable to Japan. The philosophies and evolution of the law on disability as seen in Heyer's piece is variant between the United States and Japan.

There appears to be no constitutional provisions governing the rights of people with disabilities in Pakistan. The Disabled Persons (Employment and Rehabilitation) Ordinance of 1981 constitutes the primary law on matters of disability. The other instrument is the Voluntary Social Welfare Agencies (Registration and Control) Ordinance of 1961. The Law of 1981 classifies the subject as follows:

The Federal Government has constituted a National Council, and each province in Pakistan has constituted a Provincial Council that carries the objectives of the Disabled Persons (Employment and Rehabilitation) Act. The National Council formulates policy on employment, rehabilitation and the general welfare of people with disabilities. The Provincial Council executes the policies established by the National Council. The Pakistan Society for the Rehabilitation of the Disabled is legally recognized under the Voluntary Social Welfare Agencies (Registration and Control) Ordinance, No. 46, 1961 for its operations to rehabilitate the people with disabilities.

ii) *Public Services/Transportation*. The National Council establishes guidelines that govern free community housing, accessibility to buildings including schools, hospitals, rehabilitation centers and all forms of public transportation (land, sea, air, etc). These must be accessible to people with disabilities. The national authority and local governments regulate control and enforcement of accessibility measures.

iii) *Accommodation and Services by Private Entities*. There is no specially designed community housing for people with disabilities in Pakistan. However, private entities are amenable to respect and protect the rights of disabled persons.

iv) *Telecommunications*. "Sign language for deaf people is recognized as the main means. of communication between deaf persons and others. There are no government measures for encouraging media and other forms of public information to make their services accessible to persons with disabilities. There is no legal provision to assist them to obtain audiometer supplements. . . to improve their lives." The classification of subject matter comports with ADA with respect to the four categories. The seven point classification, however, is not applicable.

There are no constitutional provisions on disability in Taiwan. The law governing the basic human rights of people with disabilities in Taiwan is The Law on the Protection of the Physically and Mentally Handicapped of 1980. The following classification is utilized under this Law:

i) Definition of Disabled
ii) General Provisions on Reporting Requirements;
iii) Employment
  — Covered entities
  — Actions considered discriminatory
  — Enforcement
  — Exemptions or Defenses to sanctions for discrimination
  — Administering Authority
— Certification for Meeting or Exceeding Statutory Requirements

iv) Public Service/Transportation
- Covered entities
- Enforcement
- Exemptions or Defenses to sanctions for discrimination
- Administering Authority
- Certification for Meeting or Exceeding statutory requirements
- Agencies Responsible for Coordination.

v) Public Accommodation and Services by Private Entities

vi) Telecommunications.

There appears to be no constitutional provisions dealing with the rights of the disabled in Australia. The law governing disability rights is the Commonwealth (Federal) Disability Discrimination Act, 1992, better known as the DDA. De Glopper has stated:

> "The framework for disability rights in Australia is provided by the Disability Discrimination Act 1992 and a body of case law. The Act is enforced by the Commonwealth Human Rights and Equal Opportunity Commission, which promotes education on disability issues and responds to complaints of discrimination with an approach stressing conciliation, although appeal to the Federal Court is possible. Both the terms of the Act and governing practice take a cost-benefit approach to disability issues, with statements of rights qualified by such terms as "impose an unjustifiable hardship on" employers or educators.

"Under the DDA, the following classification as been adopted:

i) Regulations under the DDA

ii) Human Rights and Equal Opportunity Commission (HREOC)

iii) Commonwealth Government Initiatives and Programs
iv) Disability Standards
v) Employment
vi) Public Services/Transportation and Public Accommodation and Services by Private Entities
vii) Telecommunications
viii) Case Law

Australia's classification of the subject though slightly variant is consistent with the categories found under ADA especially in the four major categories. The role of case law here is also similar to ADA as it is under Canadian, German, French, Czech, British and Israeli legislation.

4

Educating Children with Disabilities

Defectology is usually associated with the education of children with disabilities in special schools, separated from other children. These schools clearly do not encourage any social integration, particularly when they take the form of large-scale residential institutions of the type that exist in some parts of the region. However, the education of children with disabilities and others who experience difficulties in school (often referred to as "having special needs") remains a subject of fierce debate in other industrialized countries.

As a result of the 1990 World Conference on Education for All: Meeting Basic Learning Needs, the challenge of exclusion from education has been put on the political agenda in many countries. This has helped to focus attention on a much broader range of children who may be excluded from or marginalized within education systems because of their apparent difficulties. Such children may include:

— Those who are already enrolled in education but for a variety of reasons do not achieve adequately.

— Those who are not enrolled in schools but who could participate if schools were more flexible in their responses.

— The relatively small group of children with more severe impairments who may have a need for some form of additional support.

Given this broad range of children, all of whom may be seen as having special needs, it is essential to consider policies and practices in relation to overall educational arrangements within any given context. This points immediately to a major difficulty facing anybody wishing to summarize international trends in this field. That is to say, when suggesting "patterns", one must take care to engage with the ways in which children come to be defined as special within particular places. Put bluntly, a child categorized as having special needs in one country might not so categorized in another. This means that attention needs to be given to the forms of education provided for all children within a given context, including a consideration of which children are given the opportunity to participate in schools and which children are excluded. Bearing these concerns in mind, one may suggest certain overall trends that seem to be evident in many countries.

The field of special education has developed relatively recently and unevenly in different parts of the world. Its development has involved a series of stages during which education systems have explored different ways of responding to children with disabilities and others who experience difficulties in learning. As a result, special education has sometimes been provided as a supplement to general education provision, whereas in other cases it may be totally separate.

For a number of reasons, attempting to define the numbers of children who receive special forms of education presents considerable difficulties. In particular, care has to be taken in considering any data that are presented since terminology and categorization systems vary considerably from country to country. Furthermore, in some countries it is very difficult, even impossible, to obtain reliable and recent data. To illustrate these difficulties, figures reported in the same year with regard to children with disabilities in so-called "developing countries" range from 31 million , through 117 million to 160 million . What is beyond doubt is that around the world many children do not receive any form of conventional schooling, including large numbers who have disabilities.

Considerable concern also exists about the poor quality of teaching offered to children in many schools, particularly in developing countries , whilst in the developed world, although sufficient school places are usually available, the problem still exists of finding forms of schooling that will enable all children to experience success in their learning. Sadly, for too many children their attendance at school is a largely unsatisfying experience, leaving them despondent about their own capabilities and disillusioned about the value of education to their lives. Indeed, it has been argued that in some countries such circumstances are the major cause of children becoming categorized as having special needs and, as a result, being marginalized in or even excluded from general education. These realities exist despite the fact that it is now more than 50 years since the nations of the world, speaking through the Universal Declaration of Human Rights, asserted that "everyone has a right to education".

A helpful source of data with respect to patterns of special education provision internationally arises out of a survey of 63 countries carried out recently , although once again great care needs to be taken in interpreting the findings because of the way in which data were collected. Overall the evidence from many of the countries in the sample implies that integration is a key policy idea, although only a small number spelled out their guiding principles explicitly. The report suggests that there is a case for "guarded optimism" in that, since UNESCO's previous survey in 1986, special educational provision has become much more firmly located within regular education at both the school and administrative levels. However, the pattern of provision varies from country to country.

In 96 percent of countries the national ministry of education holds sole or shared responsibility for the administration and organization of services for children with disabilities. Other ministries sharing responsibility are mostly ministries of health and of social welfare. State funding is the predominant source of finance, whilst other funding comes from voluntary bodies, nongovernmental organizations and parents. Most countries acknowledge the importance of parents in matters relating to special educational provision, and some give them a central role in the processes of assessment and decisionmaking. There was also evidence of a substantial increase in in-service training of staff related to special needs.

Having said that, the report also warns against complacency in that many countries face fiscal and personnel constraints such that even maintaining the existing level of investment may not be easy. Furthermore, pressures created by more general school reforms in many countries could, it is argued, reduce the priority given to provision for children seen as having special needs. An analysis of the history of special education provision in many Western countries suggests certain patterns .

Initial provision frequently took the form of separate special schools set up by religious or philanthropic organizations. This was then, eventually, adopted and extended as part of national education arrangements, often leading to a separate, parallel school system for those pupils seen as being in need of special attention. There is also some evidence of similar trends in developing countries.

In recent years, however, the appropriateness of having such a separate system has been challenged both from a human rights perspective and, indeed, from the point of view of effectiveness. This has led to an increased emphasis in many countries, both developed and developing, on the notion of integration . As an idea, this can take many forms and in itself remains a topic of considerable debate. Such an emphasis, involving attempts to increase the flexibility of response within neighbourhood schools, seems sensible for economically poorer countries given the extent of the need and the limitations of resources. It is also important to recognize that in many developing countries substantial "casual" integration of children with disabilities in local schools already occurs, particularly in rural districts.

The existence of well-established separate provision in special schools and classes creates complex policy dilemmas, leading many countries to operate what Pijl and Meijer refer to as "two tracks". In other words, these countries have parallel but separate segregation and integration policies, something that may well become a trend in Central and Eastern Europe. A rather obvious problem here, of course, is the costing implications of maintaining such parallel arrangements.

In some countries integration still largely represents an aspiration. In Germany, for example, while some pilot initiatives based on the idea of integration are under way, students who are declared eligible for special education must be placed in a special school. In the Netherlands it is reported that almost 4 percent of all pupils aged 4 to 18 attend full-time special schools, although the exact proportion varies with age. So, for example, 7.4 percent of 11-year-olds are in special schools. Recent national policies are attempting to change this emphasis. Similar developments in other counties, such as Austria, England and New Zealand, have led to major discussions about the future roles of special education facilities and support services within a system driven by a greater emphasis on integration.

Some countries (for example, Australia, Canada, Denmark, Italy, Norway, Portugal and Spain) have shown considerable progress in implementing the integration principle universally. A problem reported from a number of industrialized countries is that, despite national policies emphasizing integration, paradoxically there is evidence of a significant increase in the proportions of pupils being categorized in order that their schools can earn additional resources.

Policies in Australia, England, Scandinavia and the United States, Fulcher suggests that the increased bureaucracy that is often associated with special education legislation and the inevitable struggles for additional resources have the effect of escalating the proportion of children who are labelled as disabled. As an illustration, she describes how in Victoria, Australia, during the 1980s, some pupils in regular schools came to be described as "integration children". She notes that over 3,000 children were in this category, which had not existed prior to 1984, and that often schools would argue that these pupils could not be taught unless extra resources were made available. It is because of situations such as this, of course, that data gauging changes over time in the numbers of children with special needs said to be integrated must be treated with caution.

Dissatisfaction with progress towards integration has caused demands for more radical changes in many countries. One of the concerns of those who adopt this view is the way in which pupils come to be designated as having special needs. They see this as a social process that needs to be continually challenged. More specifically, they argue that the continued use of what is sometimes referred to as a "medical model" of assessment within which educational difficulties are explained solely in terms of child deficits, prevents progress in the field, not least in that this distracts attention from questions about why schools fail to teach so many children successfully.

Such arguments lead to proposals for a reconceptualization of the special needs task. This suggests that progress will be much more likely when it is recognized that difficulties experienced by pupils come about as a result of the ways in which schools are currently organized and the forms of teaching that are provided. In other words, as Skrtic puts it, pupils with special needs are "artifacts of the traditional curriculum". Consequently, it is argued, the path forward must be to reform schools and improve pedagogy in ways that will lead them to respond positively to pupil diversity, seeing individual differences not as problems to be fixed, but as opportunities for enriching learning. Within such a conceptualization, a consideration of difficulties experienced by pupils and, indeed, teachers can supply an agenda for reforms and insights as to how these reforms might be brought about.

However, it has been argued that this kind of approach is probably only possible in contexts where there exists a respect for individuality and a culture of collaboration that fosters and supports problemsolving.

All of this has helped to encourage the emergence of another orientation in many countries, that of "inclusive" education. This adds yet further complications and disputes to those that already exist. Driven in part at least by ideological considerations, the idea of inclusive education challenges much of existing thinking in the special needs field, whilst at the same time offering a critique of the practices of general education. Put simply, many of those who are supporting the idea are raising the question:

Why is it that schools throughout the world fail to teach so many pupils successfully? Thus, instead of an emphasis on the idea of integration, with its assumption that additional arrangements will be made to accommodate exceptional children within a system that remains largely unchanged, they are arguing for inclusive education, where the aim is to restructure schools and classrooms in order to respond to the needs of all children. This new, inclusive orientation is a strong feature of "The Salamanca Statement on Principles, Policy and Practice in Special Needs Education", agreed by representatives of 92 governments and 25 international organizations in June 1994.

Specifically the Statement argues that regular schools with an inclusive orientation are: "the most effective means of combating discriminatory attitudes, creating welcoming communities, building an inclusive society and achieving education for all; moreover they provide an effective education to the majority of children and improve the efficiency and ultimately the cost-effectiveness of the entire education system."

Implicit in this orientation is a fundamental shift with respect to the way in which educational difficulties are addressed. This shift in thinking is based on the belief that methodological and organizational changes made in response to pupils experiencing barriers to their learning are, under certain conditions, likely to benefit all children, thus linking together the pursuit of equity and excellence. It involves a continuous process of school improvement aimed at using available resources, particularly human resources, to support the participation and learning of all pupils within a local community. In this way those pupils seen as having special needs come to be regarded as the stimulus that can encourage developments towards a much richer overall educational environment.

Moves towards inclusion are also endorsed by the UN Convention on the Rights of the Child. Specifically the adoption of the Convention by the UN General Assembly and its subsequent ratification by 187 countries impose a requirement for radical changes to traditional approaches to provision made for children with disabilities. The Convention contains a number of articles which require governments to undertake a systematic analysis of their laws, policies and practices in order to assess the extent to which they currently comply with the obligations they impose in respect to such children.

In other words, the Convention allows no discrimination in relation to access to education on grounds of disability. Advancing towards the implementation of this new orientation is far from easy, however, and evidence of progress is limited in most countries. Moreover, there is not full acceptance of the inclusive philosophy . There are, for example, those who argue that small specialist units located in the standard school environment can provide the specialist knowledge, equipment and support for which the mainstream classroom and teacher can never be a full substitute. In this view, such units may be the only way to provide feasible and effective access to education for certain groups of children.

Consider educational provision for children with disabilities and those who experience difficulties in learning in the countries of Central and Eastern Europe and compare this with international trends, these trends are in themselves riddled with uncertainties, disputes and contradictions. However, what can be said is that throughout the world attempts are being made to develop more effective educational responses for such children and that, encouraged by the lead given by the Salamanca Statement, the overall trend is towards making these responses, as far as possible, within the context of general educational provision. This is leading to a reconsideration of the future roles and purposes of specialists and facilities in the special needs field.

In scrutinizing data about countries within the region, one must be very sensitive to the profound differences that exist among them. For example, historians and others have pointed out the limitations of the concept of "Eastern Europe" in any analysis of the region. Traditionally the use of the term was limited to eight or nine countries, that is, Poland, Czechoslovakia, Hungary, Romania, Albania, Yugoslavia, Bulgaria and, at times, East Germany. These countries shared certain geopolitical similarities when they became nation-states in that they were all at one time or another part of the former Russian, German, Austro-Hungarian or Turkish empires. Further commonalities also exist in that these countries have shared a communist system of one form or another from just after the Second World War to the late 1980s or early 90s. However, these similar experiences do not seem to have created the notion of a region that is a single entity.

The situation becomes further complicated when countries of the former Soviet Union are included in the umbrella term "Eastern Europe". The diversity within the former Soviet Union requires its own space. Here, differences are found in respect to ethnicity, religion and other cultural dimensions. Effectively, these countries remained under direct Soviet rule until the early 1990s. Countries that are today seen as being Eastern and Central European were also under the Soviet political sphere of influence.

These historical and political events have played important roles in educational developments in this region and are often deep rooted. For example, Hungary inherited its school system from the Austro-Hungarian Empire and was seen as being "German-like" . In Germany special schools were established from the 1880s after the Education Act of 1872 . There was a tradition of strict segregation which affected the social status of children in special provisions. The Hungarian special education system initially based its practice on this German model and even called itself "remedial education", a term derived from the German "Heilpädagogik".

Definitions are highly problematic in the field of special needs education. Primarily, there is the problem of the country- and culture-specific nature of the definitions used. Consequently, terms have to be defined within the context of each individual country. There is also the need to look at the sociopolitical context within which disability is defined. For instance, in one Russian city, Saratov, there has been a marked increase in the number of children categorized as having disabilities. In 1989 there were said to be 2,745, but by 1994 the number had increased to 6,780. This increase was attributed to the change in the definitions of disability in Russia. The Ministry of Health Care Act in 1991 broadened the definition of disability to include all "inherent and generic illnesses leading to a partial disturbance of life activity and social disadaptation".

In addition, perceptions differ even within countries, and this can cause havoc when one seeks to present statistics on disability. So, for example, it has been reported that in Hungary each institution has its own criteria of classification. The category "mental disability" may have been defined using separate medical, educational and social classifications. Since the definitions used may therefore be different, it is not possible to assume a coherent figure when incidence-prevalence data are quoted at the national level.

Issues of perceptions are even more sensitive when "outsiders" carry out surveys using predetermined categories that do not fit the realities within a specific situation. Indeed, many in the field argue that for this reason the idea of a "standard methodology" using global categories is neither possible, nor desirable . It follows logically that the figures cannot be fully relied upon if problems exist at the fundamental levels of definitions and perceptions. However, there is an even more basic problem in that recent statistics of any kind may not be available for some countries. For example, in Slovenia it is reported that there are no recent figures available for the number of people, of all age groups, that have various special needs . Meanwhile, in Bosnia-Herzegovina there are problems because of destruction caused by war .

Even where available, statistics are often inconclusive because they are susceptible to omissions. In some cases, for example, certain categories of children are not included in surveys that are carried out. Furthermore, since schools provide a vital statistical base, children who are not within the educational system at all are likely to be excluded from most figures. For example, it is estimated that a large percentage of Romany children do not attend school in some countries in the region. In Hungary it has been reported that only 5 percent of the

Romany population attend mainstream primary education.

On the other hand the figures in Hungary also suggest that Romany children make up between 30 and 40 percent of the special school population. Clearly, these figures are not able to tell us the full story, though they point to some interesting questions that could be investigated and suggest certain deductions that might be made. So far the focus has been largely on quantitative data. However, qualitative data are not without difficulties. The problems of perception that plague statistics are just as evident here.

On the other hand, recent moves in the field of special education away from the so-called "medical model" towards an orientation that places much greater emphasis on the role of context in explaining difficulties in learning have increased the use of qualitative forms of enquiry. This does not deny the place of statistics in the field of special education, but rather points towards what is perhaps their most useful function, that is, supporting and working alongside more in-depth, qualitative forms of enquiry.

Special Education in Transition

The educational systems of Central and Eastern Europe have gone through their fair share of upheavals. So, too, has the special educational subsystem. In particular, consideration is given to the overall context of the general education system, dominant approaches in special needs education, recent developments in the field, excluded groups, and the process of change. Education systems are often vulnerable to changes that take place at the sociopolitical and economic levels. Certainly this can be illustrated by the strong influence that Soviet policy had on the educational systems of Eastern European countries. For example, the educational systems in

Romania, Hungary, Bulgaria and Poland saw pre-1989 reforms which appeared to adopt Soviet educational plans, curriculum and textbooks indiscriminately.

In Hungary, the level of control that politics had in the education sphere is well illustrated. The school system was highly centralized and the curriculum seen as state law. It was presented and given official interpretation in state textbooks. Teachers who did not follow the method and interpretation presented were in danger of being accused of failing to observe state law. To ensure that the teaching was in line with policy, supervisors were sent into schools to assess teachers, although it is difficult to say how strict this was implemented in individual schools. Nevertheless, it serves to illustrate the control that the political system had in schools.

The economic transformation that Eastern Europe is currently undergoing has also had a huge bearing on the education sector. In particular, the transition to a market economy seems to have aggravated the existing socioeconomic difficulties. As a result, the meaning of "basic free education" has undergone significant changes. Across the region, services that were once free or provided for minimal fees are now offered at market prices. In the light of budget constraints, schools are increasingly encouraged to raise their own funds and introduce fees for "extra" services.

Local foundations linked to individual schools in Poland and Hungary, for example, run commercial businesses and transfer their profits to the schools. Fees have been introduced, both at primary and secondary levels, for extracurricular activities, elective courses, tutoring and participation in hobby clubs. Meanwhile, availability of textbooks and school supplies has become an acute problem. As a result, children from poorer households increasingly face difficulties in access to schooling.

The impact of the competitive market economy has often meant that the education system itself moves towards a market-based approach where attainment becomes totally performance related. In such a context there is a growing danger that educational reform will add to, rather than lessen social divisions and inequalities. On the other hand, some have argued that the freer economic situation can benefit systems by, for example, opening the doors for private and church schools which are seen to provide more opportunities to children who have severe learning difficulties.

Broadly speaking, educational systems in Central and Eastern Europe have been described as being highly academic, rigid and conservative in their uniformity . In the Czech Republic, for example, the curriculum has been undergoing change, and so far the concern has been with making each aspect of the curriculum more demanding in the belief that this will raise standards in education. Similarly, in Bosnia-Herzegovina the curriculum is dense and overloaded, making it difficult for teachers to respond to pupil diversity. More encouraging in this respect, however, are the recent reforms that have led to the introduction of a national core curriculum in Hungary.

Emphasizing flexibility, this new curriculum is seen as a framework which provides the basis for working out more detailed plans at the school level. Particular attention is given to the importance of strengthening minority identities, and principles are laid out as to how the "special needs of challenged pupils" are to be addressed. Separate institutional provision for children who are perceived as special was largely consistent with other aspects of educational policy in the communist period. The strict streaming of secondary school pupils was associated with their separation into academic, technical and vocational schools. In this sense, the physical separation of different types of pupils was rather taken for granted in education systems in general. And, of course, the lack of flexibility in school curricula and the rigidity in the methods of teaching did not favour the participation of children who might experience difficulties in learning.

Dominant approaches

The influence that Soviet educational philosophy had on Eastern and Central Europe has been widely recognized. In the field of special education, the Soviet impact was particularly felt through the theory of defectology originally developed by Vygotsky, a scholar best known internationally for his work in developmental psychology and linguistics. At the Scientific Research Institute of Defectology, in Moscow, he developed "an area of scientific scholarship devoted to problems of diagnosing, educating and rehabilitating children with physical and mental handicap [known as 'defects']".

Vygotsky utilized disciplines such as psychology, philosophy, sociology and political thought to find effective ways to assess children with disabilities and to determine how progress could be made in the learning process of these children. In addition, he directed his theory towards the analysis of the broader social and cultural implications of disability . Some believe that his theory addresses the problems that are faced today in attempting to educate children seen as having difficulties in mainstream school settings.

Indeed, Vygotsky argued that children with disabilities should not be socially cut off from mainstream society and that they would be better served if they learned in interactive environments . Thus, a closer analysis of the original theory of defectology shows that the environmental factors which affect the child are seen as being of the utmost importance. For this reason, Knox and Daniels present "defectology" as being closer to what they describe as the "social paradigm". Within the social paradigm normal functioning is seen as relative to cultural values and beliefs.

In addition, the characteristics of students are believed to be both socially constructed and culturally mediated identities . According to some interpretations of Vygotsky's work, the two words "socially constructed" are the key to defectology, in that "one of the best learning situations for a child is believed to be in an environment of shared activity". This interpretation of defectology is, of course, quite contrary to the medical paradigm. It does seem, however, that within the region the term defectology has come to be seen more generally as a means of defining and, indeed, justifying various forms of separate special educational provision.

Having said that, it has to be kept in mind that the concept of defectology may well mean different things in different countries. This last point is an important one in highlighting the fact that present trends and practices in special education are often interpreted and applied in the context of a particular area, taking into account unique environmental conditions. It is worth noting, for example, that a number of countries in Eastern and Central Europe did participate in the conference that led to the preparation of the Salamanca Statement, though that does not necessarily mean that the interpretation and application of the principles found in the statement will be identical among and within countries.

It seems reasonable to conclude that in many countries within the region the ideas that have become associated with defectology have encouraged ways of working that are largely consistent with what has been referred to as a "medical paradigm"; that is, "...people are labelled as diseased and separated on the basis of their diagnosis into separate programmes where they are made functional for their place in society as a handicapped person... it concentrates on the individual, at the expence of context". Certainly there is very strong evidence that the scientific nature of the theory of defectology has meant that it has been an influential legacy in the field of special education in many parts of Eastern and Central Europe.

In addition to the strong inclination that special needs education has had towards institutional provision, this scientific-medical emphasis has also encouraged the development of practices that have proved difficult to change. The influence of the medical model in determining which label a child is given has been very strong. In Russia, for example, children said to have mental disabilities are defined in terms of their IQ scores, despite the fact that some of those who have put forward Vygotsky's theory argue that, if a child is not seen holistically, then an erroneous diagnosis will be made. Meanwhile, assessment is usually seen as leading to a diagnosis, thus implying that treatment of the perceived disease is a necessity.

The concept of diagnosis is undoubtedly medical in orientation and suggests a narrow, within-child interpretation of educational difficulties. This kind of methodology can have negative consequences for a child and, indeed, for the development of educational provision within a community. In the Czech Republic, for example, a large number of children were considered to be ineducable following a process of formal assessment that they received at the age of 6. Often these children were not even accepted by special schools .

In some countries, however, processes of assessment are changing progressively, including developments that encourage the involvement of multidisciplinary teams. Parents are also becoming more involved in some areas, however weak their voices may seem by the standards of some Western countries. In Hungary, the 1985 Education Act set up a state committee that determined what kind of a school a child should go to . The committee carried out medical, psychological and pedagogical tests and evaluated the reports of teachers.

With the parents consent, a proposal for placement was suggested. The committee's decision was binding on the parents, and, although the parents could appeal, it was reported that this rarely occurred. Similar to most countries in Western Europe and North America, the dominant approach to the care and education of children with disabilities has involved provision through various kinds of institutions. This is often associated with a strong belief that children with special needs are best catered for in specialist contexts where there is an emphasis on rehabilitation . This is clearly consistent with the ideas of defectology that have placed the issue of disability within the medical field and, as a result, away from other possible forms of assessment and intervention. This legacy has been so strong in a country like Hungary that legislation pertaining to disability has continued to emphasize medical concepts.

The objective of special education in Hungary has been to prepare children for independent life and general socialization and, in addition, to reduce the disability. This is perhaps best illustrated by the idea of conductive education. This is an internationally known method for correcting physical disabilities that was developed by Andras Peto in Budapest. Since it is so highly specialized a field it is seen as quite separate from other approaches and may not necessarily reflect the general picture of special educational provision in that country.

In most of the countries an institutional-based approach has been used extensively to guide the development of special educational provision. In the Russian Federation, for example, special schools are known as "specialized correcting educational establishments", the aim of which is to provide education, correct development problems, give medical treatment, and create appropriate conditions for social adaptation. In 1990-1 there were 1,817 of these establishments. There has been an annual increase of institutions such as these, and by 1995-6 there were 1,871, all of this despite the rhetoric of integration. In fairness, however, it also has to be noted that the overall numbers of children in these schools had actually fallen over this period from 312,100 to 270,900.

Different types of institutions concerned with special education exist across the region, and for this reason it is impossible to make generalizations about their nature and condition and about the children who can be found in them. In Romania, for example, there are orphanages, homes for disabled children whose parents cannot give them adequate care, and others for children from dysfunctional families and children seen as having emotional or behavioural difficulties. All these children are considered to have special needs. Some schools also specialize in children with particular disabilities; thus, in the 1996/7 school year there were 124 schools for children with mental disabilities, 12 for children with hearing impairments, and three for children with visual impairments . In Lithuania, on the other hand, until recently some children with serious disabilities had no teaching provided for them at all, so they would not have been included in statistics on children in special schools or special classes.

Although the proportions of children placed in institutional establishments within the region are relatively high by international standards, in a country like Hungary it has been argued by some that there are still categories of pupils for whom special schools do not exist, for instance, children with behavioural difficulties, those with various forms of learning difficulties (such as dyslexia, attention deficit), and socially disadvantaged children. It is also suggested that those with relatively mild difficulties are often integrated into mainstream schools. However, it would be ill advised to assume that the nonexistence of special schools is evidence of moves towards more inclusive arrangements.

Special schools are usually maintained by the state and are more expensive to run than mainstream schools. Therefore, their reduction in number may have more to do with financial policy decisions. Certainly moves towards the integration of children with disabilities can be found in various countries, including the Czech Republic, Hungary, Slovakia, Poland, Slovenia, Romania, Latvia and Lithuania. Children with disabilities in the Czech Republic have been progressively integrated into regular schools since 1990, both in ordinary and special classes. However, despite a drop of some 15 percent in the number of children in separate special schools at the primary and lower secondary levels, the overall share of enrolments in special schools at there levels grew because of the falling number of children in the age group. Indeed, the share rose from 4 percent in 1989 to 4.4 percent in 1996, the highest figure in any country for which data from the region are available. In addition, the number of children in upper secondary schools rose by 10 percent, to more than 17,000.

This information can be interpreted in at least two ways. On the one hand, there are positive signs of moves towards integration, but, on the other, it appears that there are relatively large numbers of children categorized as having special needs, the reasons for which remain unclear. It is reported, for example, that Romany children in the Czech Republic are a noticeable presence in special schools, where, it has been suggested, they may be placed because they are not able to communicate sufficiently well in the language of instruction of regular schools.

Slovenia is another country where there have been significant moves to integrate children with special needs into mainstream schools, including into regular classrooms. Available data suggest that the number of children in special schools has fallen by one-quarter and that their share of total basic school enrolment in 1996 was 1.5 percent. However, provision is reported to be uneven across the country. Poland has also seen changes towards greater integration. However, of the 119,000 children classified as receiving special needs education at the basic level in Poland in 1996, 80,000 were still in separate schools (that is, 1.6 percent of total basic level enrolments) and only 5,800 in mainstream classes.

Bulgaria is a good example of the problems facing a country wishing to switch away from separate special schools. The number of children in special schools has fallen by 20 percent since 1989, but the share of enrolments overall in basic education (1.2 percent in 1996) has changed little, reflecting both the smaller size of the age cohort and a decline in all enrolments at the basic level. As of mid-1997 all children categorized as having special needs received their education in separate special schools. A 1995 law provides for the integration of children with disabilities in regular schools, but its implementation has been postponed because of a lack of financial resources, illustrating well the problem of the set-up costs of integration. There was a marked economic downturn in Bulgaria in 1996-7, and the shelving of the new legislation is a concrete example of the implications for vulnerable children of set-backs in the economy.

In contrast with Bulgaria, the process of integration seems to have progressed steadily in Lithuania following the 1991 Law on Education. The number of children in separate special schools at the basic level has fallen substantially as a result of stricter criteria for categorization, and there has been an increase in the number of children with special needs attending mainstream schools. Another positive development has been the recent move to ensure access to education for those with the severest disabilities, for whom there was previously no provision. In the majority of instances these children live with their parents, rather than in institutions, and attend newly established development centres.

Some commentators in Lithuania have argued that the process of integration has been implemented too quickly without sufficient preparation of appropriate facilities or retraining of teachers. Moreover, the situation in rural areas gives cause for particular concern. Some children with disabilities receive only limited teaching in their own homes; others are sent to mainstream schools, but without any planned attempt to integrate them, and as a result many are said to stop attending.

The figures in Moldova for children in separate special schools show a huge drop, from 11,400 in 1989 to 5,800 in 1996, that is, 1 percent of all enrolments. Part of this decline may reflect the exclusion of enrolments for the latter year among children in the region of Transdniester, but this cannot account for most of the change. There is no indication that the shifts in enrolment are due to increased integration into mainstream schools, and the data suggest a collapse in special provision.

Similarly, Moldova has suffered enormously during the transition period, with output in 1996 down by twothirds on its 1989 level, and no rise estimated for 1997.

Conditions in special schools have apparently deteriorated very badly due to the severe shortage of funds. There has been enormous neglect of buildings (including heating and water systems) and other equipment, and malnutrition and disease among children in special schools have apparently risen. Difficulties of interpretation are also presented when scrutinizing data from Russia. These show that the number of children in either special schools, or in special classes attached to regular schools have gone up appreciably in recent years. For example, the figure for 1995 represents 2.3 percent of total basic level enrolments, up from 2 percent in 1990.

Enrolments in special schools have gone down, and those in special classes have gone up during the same period. These data suggest positive trends, but without knowledge of what is driving the changes it is difficult to say anything conclusive. For example, the most marked addition in the numbers of children with special needs in regular schools has been in "classes to support psychic development", a category distinct from "classes for the mentally disabled". Meanwhile another report suggests that only one-third of children with cerebral palsy in Russia are enrolled in either special schools, or special classes, implying that one group of children at least is excluded from the data and, more importantly, from access to education.

It is also possible that the rising number of children in special classes in Russia might merely reflect the operation of an incentive to classify more children as having special needs. It is worth noting that the number of children officially recognized as disabled through receipt of an invalidity pension has risen enormously, from 155,000 in 1990 to 454,000 in 1995 (that is, 1.3 percent of all children), but it is known that this increase was due to a liberalization in the criteria used for awarding benefits.

Within the countries that make up former Yugoslavia the situation continues to be very uncertain, despite considerable international efforts to support development. For example, it is reported that recently the Ministry of Education in FYR Macedonia has set up a commission charged with developing new regulations for the education of children with disabilities and emphasizing the need to develop responses in ordinary schools. However, the implementation of new policies is likely to meet difficulties because of what are described as "deeply rooted systems of diagnosis, categorization and institutionalization" and economic constraints.

In Bosnia-Herzegovina the administration of education is carried out separately by two entities, the Federation of Bosnia and Herzegovina, where responsibility is delegated to the ten cantons, and the Republica Srpska. Both have severe economic difficulties and confusion about leadership responsibilities following recent conflicts, and these make improvement efforts difficult. In the Federation there are severe shortages of qualified teachers in some areas. There are also enormous difficulties because of the damage to build-ings, including the many special schools that were destroyed, and shortages of materials.

The current policy is to integrate children with disabilities into mainstream schools as far as possible, although some special schools in Sarajevo remain open, albeit with reduced numbers in attendance. It is reported, however, that many pupils with special educational needs are not receiving any formal education. Meanwhile teachers are faced with many new challenges in attempting to respond to children who suffered the trauma of war, those who have lost parents and, increasingly, those returning from exile in other countries, many of whom are not familiar with the language used in local schools.

In such a context it is becoming increasingly evident that all classrooms need to provide responses that are responsive to pupil differences. In this sense, somewhat paradoxically, the situation may eventually encourage moves towards more inclusive forms of education. The Republic Srpska has been described as a "humanitarian disaster area", with unemployment estimated in 1996 at 90 percent, and most of the population suffering from the deepest forms of material and social deprivation.

Furthermore, a confluence of factors has meant that few international efforts have been possible to alleviate this suffering. Some special schools exist, however, and neither pre-war, nor present-day policy seeks to integrate children with disabilities into the regular school system. On the other hand, it is reported that there are plans to develop pilot projects to include "mentally retarded children" in regular preschools. A consideration of the limited information and figures that are available suggests a possible, though somewhat uncertain, conclusion that the most dominant approach in special education has to date been an institutional approach.

Available statistical data for the region also suggest a variety of changes in overall access to education for children seen as having special needs. In some countries there is evidence of moves to provide for such children within the mainstream, whilst in others there appears to have been little or no change, or even a worsening of previous arrangements. It is also clear that the proportion of children categorized as having special needs varies significantly from country to country, as it does in other parts if the world. These and other uncertainties surrounding much of the available data underline the need for more detailed investigations.

In particular, children of Romany backgrounds, those with profound and multiple learning difficulties, and children who are socially disadvantaged have been identified as groups that are sometimes excluded from any type of educational provision. Exclusion from educational provision manifests itself in various ways, including the absence of these groups from legislation and assumptions by those who ought to facilitate their education that they are ineducable or, sometimes, undesirable. In the case of the Czech Republic it has been suggested that, even where there are laws in place, opportunities are not fully optimized because of the attitudinal, knowledge and skill gaps that exist amongst those who should implement the legislation.

In Central Europe, Romany people make up 2.5 to 4 percent of the entire population. The educational status of Romany children is usually low, as reflected in the 75-85 percent dropout rate in the Czech Republic and the 27.3 percent illiteracy rate in Romania. Romany children also make up a large portion of the pupils in special schools in certain countries, for example 30-40 percent in Hungary. The reason that is sometimes given for this is that mainstream schools do not seem to be able to meet the needs of these children, and, as a result, they end up in educationally inappropriate special schools in a way that appears to violate their rights to education.

The situation is similar in the Czech Republic, where between 25 and 100 percent of pupils in schools for children with moderate learning difficulties are from Romany backgrounds. In addition, mainstream schools are deemed to have too many socio-cultural and racial tensions and conflicts for Romany children. The fact that most of these children are then sent to special schools means that at a later stage their ability to compete in the job market is diminished. In the Czech Republic legislation has been the first step towards including Romany children into mainstream schools and society.

In 1991, the "Federal Government Policy Document on the Rom Ethnic Minority" provided broad aims covering equal rights and respect for all aspects of Rom culture and heritage. Unfortunately, the legislation seems to have had many loopholes. For example, since the legislation, the Ministry of Education's responsibilities have been devolved to schools and head teachers, and, as a result, participation is very much dependent upon the will of these people to accommodate such children.

Children with profound and multiple learning difficulties are also frequently excluded from special education within the region because they are con- 25 The Education of Children with Special Needs: Barriers and Opportunities in Central and Eastern Europe sidered to be ineducable. The number of such children that are currently in institutional care is probably not reflective of the actual population since there is evidence that a significant proportion stay at home. In Russia, statistics for children with these more severe disabilities are not available within the education sector since they are the responsibility of the health department.

Meanwhile, it is reported that in Lithuania such children who are placed in residential provision do not have any form of curriculum, and those in residential schools in Bosnia-Herzegovina are said to be living in very poor conditions. Concern has also been expressed about the conditions found in some residential institutions in FYR Macedonia and Romania.

The economic and social transition in the region has had mixed implications for the education of children seen as having special needs. On the one hand, more open attitudes to new teaching methods and concerns to build a more humane society have led to moves towards the integration of children with disabilities in some countries. On the other hand, a greater emphasis on academic competition and on selectivity into elite schools, coupled with a tradition of rigid curricula and pedagogy, creates an atmosphere that is not favourable towards children who experience difficulties of any kind.

Clearly this has not helped the integration of children with disabilities, still less any moves towards a more "inclusive" approach. Reduced national incomes has also hindered moves towards integration, given the set-up costs of training teachers and support staff, and of adapting buildings. And where children have remained firmly in separate special schools, economic downturn has threatened the quality of teaching and care provided.

There is also evidence of emerging pressures for yet further reform. For example, within the Czech Republic, a document entitled "The National Plan of Measures to Reduce the Negative Impact of Disability" has been produced by the government as a result of pressure groups composed of people with disabilities, their families and those who work with them. It will take time, however, for such developments to bring about the fundamental changes of attitude that will be necessary in order to provide more equitable education systems. As Peters suggests, "...obstacles to education result not from inherent incapacities, but from the physical and attitudinal barriers socially and politically constructed within the environment."

Since 1993 the Ministry of Education in Romania, with support from UNICEF, has carried out a series of initiatives in order to explore ways of encouraging the development of more inclusive practices. These have included a project based on the UNESCO teacher education resource pack "Special Needs in the Classroom". These materials, which have been distributed in over 50 countries, are intended to prepare and support teachers in regular schools to facilitate the participation and learning of children who might otherwise be excluded, particularly those with disabilities.

The Romanian initiative has included a programme of awareness-raising involving teachers, inspectors and teacher trainers from around the country. More recently, intensive action research has been undertaken in a small number of schools. This has demonstrated the relevance of the overall approach and, at the same time, drawn attention to how it can be used in the context of Romanian schools. In addition, these experiences are leading to the development of further training materials arising from local efforts and the identification of personnel who will be available to lead dissemination efforts. A strategy for wider dissemination is currently being formulated.

Meanwhile, efforts are under way to encourage special schools to develop closer working links with the mainstream and to reintegrate pupils with relatively mild disabilities. In this way, space can be made for those with severe difficulties, many of whom currently receive no form of schooling. Other teacher education initiatives, such as the Tempus programmes, which fund collaborative partnerships between Western universities and East European teachers and their trainers, have taken steps towards developing the understanding of leaders in this field about how to manage and support the process of change. For example, in Bulgaria between 1994 and 1997 there was a Tempus programme entitled "Action on Reflective Practice" that was situated at the Department of Special Education at Sofia University and at the Higher

Institute of Pedagogics at Blagoevgrad. The programme was intended to impact on the work of teacher trainers in special needs and the practice of all school teachers. Various problems were identified as a result of the programme, including a preoccupation with cost-effectiveness and the difficulties involved in changing "change agents".

Changing the attitudes of those who are part of the process is crucial to any kind of innovation within the field. The reported preoccupation with costeffectiveness is symptomatic of the difficulties to be faced. Attitudinal change takes time and is often difficult to evaluate. In the Czech Republic, it has been pointed out that teacher training had to be focused in specific areas if change is to be expected, for example, in responding to learning difficulties and in exploring teacher attitudes to children with learning difficulties. Lessons can be learned from other areas in the education field that can be useful in understanding the process of change in Eastern and Central Europe.

As a result of work in the area of reforms in school-leaving and university entrance examinations in the region, West has identified some important issues and barriers to change. Some of these seem to be equally relevant to the field of special needs education. Reform vis-à-vis teacher attitudes is one such issue. Another relates to the legacy of the highly centralized socialist system of policy planning and implementation. This legacy is seen to have negatively affected the ability of those at the grassroots to innovate and to participate in initiating and planning development programmes, leading them to shy away from making decisions. It seems that such bottom-up initiatives were not encouraged in highly centralized systems.

A widely used term such as disability is likely to mean different things to different people. The translation of a term such as disability into other languages necessarily puts it into different linguistic and cultural contexts. A typical dictionary definition focuses on "want of power" linked with notions of weakness, incapacity, and disqualification. It is easy to stray from the purely descriptive to a pejorative usage, the avoidance of which, in part, explains the coining of alternative terms such as "differently abled."

The United Nations, in providing recommendations for the conduct of national censuses defines a person with disability as:

> A person who is limited in the kind or amount of activities that he or she can do because of ongoing difficulties due to a long-term physical condition, mental condition or health problem (United Nations, 1998).

The World Bank Disability Group's Web site http://wbln0018.worldbank.org provides a section on Defining Disability:

> Defining what is meant by disability is sometimes a complex process, as disability is more than a description of a specific health issue; rather it is affected by people's cultures, social institutions, and physical environments.

International Classification of Functioning, Disability and Health

ICF presents a framework which encompasses the complex multifaceted interaction between health conditions and personal and environmental factors that determine the extent of disablement in any given situation. The International Classification of Functioning (ICF) model views disability as "...the umbrella term for any or all of an impairment of body structure or function, a limitation of activities, or a restriction in participation".

ICF essentially follows a top-down model. A group of experts, assisted by representative disability organizations, have produced a highly complex classificatory scheme with components of Body Functions and Structures, Activities and Participation, and Environmental Factors, each of which is comprised of various domains. This is used to provide a coding. Notwithstanding its complexity if ICF were to be fully implemented, the tripartite categorization of impairment (loss or malfunction at the level of organ or body part), activity limitation (work, school, self-care, or social interaction, and generally activities of daily living), and handicap (defined contextually in connection with survival roles), underlies much of the efforts to obtain national and international data sets in the disability field. Note, however, that there is much inconsistency in the use of these terms. In particular, the usefulness of making a distinction between disability and handicap is queried in that essentially external causes underlie both.

Zinkin and McConachie recommend the definitions agreed by disabled people's organizations:

> In essence, "impairment" is an individual limitation, whereas "disability" is restriction imposed by the current organization of society. "Impairment" is defined by WHO as "any loss or abnormality of psychological, physiological, or anatomical structure or function." Making descriptions at the level of the impairment allows focus on the individual child and her/his needs as an individual. When the emphasis is on children with impairments as a social group (original emphasis) we have used the term "disabled children," defining disability as the disadvantage or restriction of activity caused by contemporary social organization which takes

> little or no account of people who have ... impairments and thus excludes them from participation in the mainstream of social activities .

Jonsson and Wiman, in another World Bank publication on Education, Poverty and Disability in Developing Countries, point out that:

> The relevant terminology used in the education sector has changed dramatically during the last decades. The narrow disability based classifications and the resulting labelling of children are being replaced by wider definitions such as "disadvantaged children," "children in especially difficult circumstances" or "children with special educational needs." These broader terms include the whole range, from profound disabilities to minor difficulties in performing necessary functions.

The Organization for Economic Cooperation and Development (OECD) reported in a monograph and summarized in issues of the publication Education at a Glance , separates out three cross-national categories currently referred to as disabilities, learning and behaviour difficulties, and social disadvantages. These categories are derived from categories used in the collection of national educational statistics on children for whom additional resources are provided to enable them to access the regular school curriculum.

This type of resources definition is clearly wider than a more traditional medically based approach and is attractive as a means of operationalizing the broad educationally relevant definition advocated by Jonsson and Wiman. However, it is based on data from the industrialized countries that constitute OECD, with the initial development of the instrument used in these studies incorporating pilot work in developing countries.

The Central Registry for Rehabilitation in Hong Kong aims "To facilitate provision of services and to assist in their reaching out to people with a disability". In similar fashion, The National Intellectual Disability Database in Ireland is concerned "To provide information for decisionmaking in relation to the planning, funding, and management of services".

Types of Disability Data Sets

There are three main types of system for the collection of population level data on disability exist in the forms of national censuses, household surveys, and administrative registries.

National Censuses

Because of the great cost and substantial data demands of comprehensive national coverage in a census where the attempt is made to enumerate every person in a national population, the detail and depth of any questions about disability are severely limited. Nevertheless, there is a strong case for all national censuses to include a section on disability, and for this to cover childhood disability in order to help ensure that childhood disability becomes visible on the national policy agenda. The infrequency of national censuses limits their value as a tool for planning services and programs.

Following are the advantages of using a Census to collect data on disability:

1. *To provide small areas data*. The census is the only data collection activity nationwide that can provide detailed data at the level of the smallest geographic area. Data collected though surveys can hardly be used to estimate disability prevalence even at the smallest level of geographical detail due to the limited sample size and the related sample errors.

Data for program development and analysis at local level can only be collected through a census or a registration system, which is available only in a very limited number of countries.

2. *To provide data to compare persons with disabilities and persons without disabilities*: Every census collects data on living arrangements, employment, and education and if these characteristics are tabulated for persons with and without disabilities, different levels of participation related for example to education and work and employment can be easily measured.
3. *To allow for time-series analysis*: It is common in many countries that a census is undertaken on a regular basis, every five or ten years. If data on disability are collected in several censuses, time-series analysis can be performed in relation to disability prevalence rates and participation data.
4. *To use as a sample-frame for a follow-up survey*: Several countries, e.g., Canada, France, and New Zealand, have used the census to establish a sample frame for follow-up specialized surveys. In countries where a specialized disability survey is planned, persons identified through the screening module included in the census can provide a frame to more effectively design a sample frame for a more detailed survey on disability.

An additional advantage of using a census is that it has the ability to examine the impact of different types of disability. The number of respondents is large enough to allow for this type of cross-comparison.

Following are the disadvantages of using a Census to collect data on disability:

1. *Measuring the continuum*: Disability is not a phenomenon that can be easily described with a

binary classification yes/no. It is rather an experience that needs to be measured in a continuum to consider several issues such as intensity, duration, and environment. It is important that the instruments used be able to capture as much as possible the different points on this continuum. In this context the design of the question(s) used as a screener to identify the target population with disability should be carefully studied to be sure they do not exclude part of that population. To measure the complexity of this continuum, multiple questions to set context, clarify terminology, and define multiple domains are required. This aspect is particularly difficult in a census where the number of questions asked is restricted.

2. *Need for extensive training of enumerators*: The main focus of a census is the total counting of the population and their social and demographic characteristics. The collection of data on disability requires extensive training of enumerators on how to ask the questions, which may not be possible in a census.
3. *Special Population Groups*: The use of a short question in a census tends to underestimate special population groups such as, children, elderly, persons with cognitive and psychological impairments. Specialized surveys where longer instruments can be used are more suitable to measure disability in these sub-population groups.
4. *Use of proxy*: Censuses have an extensive use of proxy respondents.

Such testing as has been done in Australia; Canada and the United States has not been encouraging. The Australian study, for example, led to a decision not to include any disability questions in the 2001 census as they did not reach criterion requirements for reliability and validity. Although such studies provide valuable pointers toward improving validity and reliability, they are all in industrialized countries. Me and Mbogoni have analyzed the data available in DISTAT-2. They find that "person-level" questions (i.e., requesting information about individual household members) is associated with higher reporting of disability than "household-level" questions (i.e., is there anyone in this household who ...).

Hess, et al., comparing the two types of question in a United States study, although replicating the finding, also reported that household-level questions produced more reliable data than the person-level approach, and in a shorter interview time. However, Mathiowetz and Lair find that household-level reports of functional limitations are higher than self-reports. Overall this is an area wherein the research base is weak and many of the factors likely to affect the reporting of disability are poorly understood,, particularly when the focus is on childhood disability in developing countries.

Household Surveys

Household surveys involve the systematic sampling of households with the sample so constructed that it is possible to arrive at an estimate of the feature of interest. Such a survey could focus solely on disability issues, but it is more likely that these would be embedded within a more wide-ranging study, typically of general health issues. Examples include the National Health Interview Survey (NHIS) for the United States; an annual survey of health and health care. Questions on activity limitations and the presence of acute or chronic health conditions permit some assessment of disability. A 1996 survey of the West Bank in Palestine is a similarly structured one-off example.

Surveys of this type depend for their reliability and validity on the construction and implementation of well-designed, statistically representative, sampling frames, and high rates of response. They are resource intensive when the large scale samples needed to obtain accurate population estimates are employed, and the detail of disability related questions is likely to be severely limited.

Following are the advantages of questionnaire based surveys:

1. They provide a relatively simple and straightforward approach to the study of attitudes, values, beliefs and motives.
2. They may be adapted to collect generalizable information from almost any human population.
3. High amounts of data standardization.

Postal and other self-administered surveys

4 Often this is the only, or the easiest, way of retrieving information about the past history of a large set of people.

5. They can be extremely efficient at providing large amounts of data, at relatively low cost, in a short period of time.
6. They allow anonymity, which can encourage frankness when sensitive areas are involved.

Interview surveys

7 The interviewer can clarify questions.

8 The presence of the interviewer encourages participation and involvement (and the interviewer can judge the extent to which the exercise is treated seriously).

Following are the disadvantages:

General to all surveys using respondents

1 Data are affected by the characteristics of the respondents (e.g., their memory; knowledge; experience; motivation; and personality).

2 Respondents won't necessarily report their beliefs, attitudes, etc. accurately (e.g., there is likely to be a social desirability response bias - people responding in a way that shows them in a good light).

Postal and other self-administered surveys

3 Typically have a low response rate. As you don't usually know the characteristics of nonrespondents, you don't know whether the sample is representative.

4 Ambiguities in, and misunderstandings of, the survey questions may not be detected.

5 Respondents may not treat the exercise seriously, and you may not be able to detect this.

Interview surveys

6 Data may be affected by characteristics of the interviewers (e.g., their motivation; personality; skills; and experience). There may be interviewer bias, where the interviewer, probably unwittingly, influences the responses (e.g., through verbal or nonverbal cues indicating "correct" answers).

7 Data may be affected by interactions of interviewer/ respondent characteristics (e.g., whether they are of the same or different class or ethnic background).

8 Respondents may feel their answers are not anonymous and be less forthcoming or open.

Surveys incorporating disability related questions can be on an annual or other regular basis, permitting the assessment of change or trend. An alternative is to have a regular general survey wherein more extensive disability related questions are included from time to time. The Health Survey for England is an example of this approach. There are disability-specific household surveys, though these are typically on a one-off basis or at relatively infrequent intervals.

General health surveys in which disability questions form a minor part will be likely to present similar validity and reliability problems to those noted above in relation to censuses. Disability-specific household surveys can, in principle, avoid such problems, although question wording will require careful consideration and adequate pretesting. Durkin, who has devised such an instrument, has carried out studies on validity, reliability, and sensitivity of survey questions in three developing countries in relation to child disability.

Service Registries

This is an administrative record of the numbers of persons in receipt of a service or benefit. The most common forms are adult health and employment programs, and children's educational and social services. A large scale example is the Mexican Registration of Children with a Disability. Children of all education levels, from preschool upwards, are identified by type and number of disabilities together with basic demographic and socioeconomic indicators.

This type of record has the advantage that it is commonly collected routinely for administrative purposes. With current emphases on accountability, there is a strong argument for countries having good data on the recipients of services and benefits. It is, however, highly problematic for population level demographics, or for making cross-country comparisons (the number of children registered will be a complex function of the types of programs, the eligibility rules, and how positively the programs are perceived by the population). Even in industrialized countries, only a fraction of persons with a disability are typically in receipt of a service or benefit. Fujiura estimates, for example, that in the United States, only 11 percent of persons classified as "mentally retarded" are served by the long-term residential care system.

This is, of course, not to assert that such persons should be in a residential care system, only that the numbers in the system do not provide a reliable population indicator. In developing countries it would be anticipated that discrepancies would be large. For example, in Mauritius, the 1990 census identified nearly 28,000 persons with a disability. Half of them were in receipt of disability pensions but only 400 received services from rehabilitation programs .

The countries doing the most for children with disabilities inevitably appear to have the highest rates of disability. This may affect the willingness of government administrators to classify children as disabled. Service records are, nevertheless, useful and important in providing information on who gains access to services and programs.

Other Approaches

Other methods of data collection have been employed. For example:

Key informant surveys, which involve asking key people in the community, such as community leaders, teachers, and midwives, to identify all disabled persons in their community. This approach is attractive as low cost and feasible in developing countries. However, the method has been shown to be inaccurate when tried in various countries with serious underestimation of less physically obvious conditions. Cohort studies include organized longitudinal studies which follow a birth cohort, typically of several thousand children. They are heavily resource intensive and effectively ruled out because of this in developing countries.

Qualitative Studies on the Lives of Children in Developing Countries

Qualitative studies enable the experiences and feelings of people to be explored, permitting an understanding of their lives not accessible by means of quantitative surveys or other data collection techniques resulting in numerical information only. A wide variety of methods can be used, including the use of relatively unstructured interviews, focus groups or other group interviews, participant observation, and so on. Such studies are particularly important for marginalized groups such as children with disabilities in developing countries. In studying disabled childhood there is a tendency to rely on the views of parents, teachers, and other professionals, hence denying the voice of the child.

Shakespeare, et al., describe an ongoing qualitative study of life as a disabled child through the children's own experiences and perspectives. They focus on disabled children between 11 and 16 and include children with a wide range of physical, mental, and sensory impairments and who are from a range of backgrounds, in both inclusive and segregated settings. They aim to examine the role of structural factors, social settings, cultural contexts, and policy implementation by shedding light on all aspects of the lives of disabled children, their relationships with family, peer group and adults, their experiences at home, at school, and in leisure. Although their study is based in England and Scotland, the central features of their approach are applicable in all contexts, including developing countries.

The organization Save the Children has made outstanding efforts in this area and has practical manuals on carrying out such projects, for example Learning to Listen and Children and Participation. A booklet, Children's Statements, based on interviews with children involved in various Save the Children projects throughout the world, shows the profound sense of exclusion experienced by children who are disabled.

The United Nations Convention on the Rights of the Child (CRC) places great emphasis on the participation of children and the disabled in decisionmaking . Regional meetings have been proposed "...to which disabled children and young people, and local disability organizations would be invited to present their experiences of respect or lack of respect for their rights, what they would like to see changed and their suggestions for further action" .

Data Sets and Classificatory Frameworks

World Bank and other international organizations are collecting regarding children with disabilities and their education. The main international organizations involved, apart from the World Bank, are the United Nations, UNICEF, UNESCO, OECD, the European Community.

The World Bank

The World Bank is not a primary data collection agency for most areas other than living standards and debt. As a major user of socioeconomic data, however, the World Bank places particular emphasis on data documentation to inform users of data in economic analysis and policymaking.

The World Bank also supports projects which serve persons with disabilities, and projects in this area are currently growing in number. For example, in the education area, several projects have components that benefit persons with disabilities. They include:

— India Basic Education and District Primary Education Projects, which assists primary school teachers in the project districts in identifying and assessing children with disabilities and developing inclusive programs for their education.

— India Technician Education Project, which establishes two polytechnic institutions that are designed for students with disabilities.

— Nepal Second Basic and Primary Education Project, which supports inclusive education of children with nonsevere disabilities in primary schools.

— Yemen Vocational Training Project, which finances subprojects for vocational training and rehabilitation of persons with physical disabilities.

— Brazil Project on Education.

There are several papers on poverty and disability and a particularly useful one on "Education, Poverty and Disability in Developing Countries". Persuasive arguments are put forward in favour of an inclusive, mainstream education for children with disabilities, as against segregated residential provision, claiming that:

> Historically, the education of disabled persons, even those with mild disabilities (e.g., epilepsy) has been through institutions. These residential institutions were often run by charitable institutions and based on a medical model where the "patients" or "inmates" had to be diagnosed and, theoretically, cured. The model was then exported to developing countries by charitable NGOs and later by official development assistance.

The claim is made that few, if any, children who are disabled require segregated residential provision for educational or any other reasons.

The United Nations Statistics Division

The Statistics Division of the United Nations, which forms part of its Department of Economic and Social Affairs, produces extensive statistical databases. In the field of disability its central resource is the International Disability Statistics Data Base, DISTAT, the most up to date version of which is DISTAT-2, which is not yet fully available. Currently "...the only information we have on children with disabilities from DISTAT-2 are prevalence rates by age groups for those aged 0-14.

DISTAT (i.e., the original version of the database) included information on the socioeconomic characteristics of persons with disabilities, together with data on the educational attainment and school attendance of children. It is important to note that the database is a collection of census, survey, and administrative registration systems information as provided by countries, supplemented by information provided from correspondence with national statistical services.

The questions used to collect information in individual countries are available on the database. Because of the methodology used in compiling the database, it carries the important warning "...due to differences in the concepts and methods used in collecting data on disability, prevalence rates should not be compared across countries."

Although there is little or no indication that this basic methodology will change, the Statistics Division is clearly committed to providing advice and support in the development of statistical systems for assessing disability in developing countries. This appears to have been stimulated by urging from the World Program of Action Concerning Disabled Persons that the Statistics Division:

Together with other units of the United Nations Secretariat, the specialized agencies and regional commissions, ... cooperate with developing countries in evolving a realistic and practical system of data collection based either on total enumeration or on representative samples, as may be appropriate, in regard to various disabilities, and in particular, ... prepare technical manuals/documents on how to use household surveys for the collection of such statistics .

The resulting Guidelines and Principles for the Development of Disability Statistics, although oriented to statisticians, is intended to be useful to managers of disability programs "as they are essential partners in developing objectives for a data collection activity and the use of the resulting data". Use of the ICIDH/ICF framework is advocated.

It covers a wide range of issues that are central to planning and organization in collecting data on disability. There also are useful suggestions on sampling issues, and on the dissemination and use of disability data. It is intended to be applicable to both industrialized and developing world contexts.

Other activities of the United Nations Statistics Division (UNSD), summarized in Mbogoni have included participation in the DISTAB project, organizing meetings in the field of disability statistics, and carrying out regional training workshops on disability statistics, using the Guidelines and Principles for the Development of Disability Statistics document as the main training tool. DISTAB (a United States National Centre for Health Statistics initiative) seeks to examine the usability of ICIDH-2 (which became ICF) for coding disability and census data. Exercises have been undertaken to back-code existing survey data to ICIDH-2 codes. Attempts have been made to identify problems, and recommendations made to WHO on how to revise the classification. The group also has made recommendations on what countries need to make disability data more comparable, particularly in the area of questionnaire design.

The World Health Organization (WHO)

International Statistical Classification of Functioning, Disability, and Health (ICF) is a newly developed member of the WHO family of international classifications and seeks to describe how people live with their health condition. It is a classification of health and health-related domains that describe body functions and structures, activities, and participation. The domains are classified from body, individual, and societal perspectives, together with a list of environmental factors.

The precursor WHO classification, International Classification of Impairments, Disabilities, and Handicaps (ICIDH), was heavily criticized in relation to disability mainly because its conceptual basis was exclusively medical, leading to a medicalization of disability. The lack of involvement by persons with disability or their organizations also attracted criticism. ICF made attempts to counter this, with efforts to closely involve the organizations of people with disabilities and to remove "handicapism" language. ICF also recognizes that disability is a social construct.

There are three components of the classification:

— Body Functions and Body Structures,

— Activities and Participation, and

— Environmental Factors.

The United Nations Educational, Scientific, and Cultural Organization (UNESCO)

UNESCO has taken the lead role in worldwide organizations on matters concerning the education of children with disabilities and of special needs education more widely. The term "children with special needs," although variously defined, is commonly taken to include those with a range of difficulties and sometimes disadvantages, as well as those with disabilities.

The organization has, for example, published reviews of the situation in special needs education. The information in these reviews was collected by means of a questionnaire completed in the division or unit in the Ministry responsible for special education. In the 1995 exercise, 90 member states were contacted with 63 responses. Information was obtained on aspects such as:

— Number of countries using different forms of provision (e.g., boarding special schools);
— How pupils are recorded for official purpose (e.g., registered in disability groups);
— Presence or absence of policy of integration;
— Presence or absence of links between special and ordinary schools;
— Number of pupils in special schools as a percentage of school age population; and
— Preschool provision for children with special educational needs (e.g., available for less than 10 percent of children).

UNESCO has adopted a mission statement committing itself to the concept of "inclusive education" deriving from the Salamanca Statement and Framework for Action 1994. A typical project under this heading is "Steps towards inclusive education in Thailand and Lao PDR," which promotes access and quality education for children with disabilities.

UNESCO also has been involved, together with EUROSTAT and OECD, in a special study on data collection between 1996 and 1999, focusing on the revision of the International Standard Classification of Education (ISCED). As the title indicates, this is a classificatory system and has an analogous role in education to that of the ICF framework in the field of health. A central feature of the revised ISCED classification is that the prime criterion for assignment of an educational program to an ISCED level is the content of the program. Descriptions are given of the content expected for each level.

The very different nature of educational systems in different countries, including different organization of the cycles of education (e.g., some but not all countries distinguish between lower and upper secondary education) complicate this exercise and make international comparisons difficult. The UOE (UNESCO, OECD, EUROSTAT) data collection exercise discussed below focuses on industrialized countries with OECD membership and makes use of the ISCED framework.

In the field of special educational needs the assignment of some programs to ISCED levels has proved contentious. For example, a program for older students with severe or profound learning difficulties may in content terms appear closest to primary basic education. However, it also could focus on life and self-help skills which share some of the aspirations of programs for students coming to the end of their school education.

The Organization for Economic Cooperation and Development (OECD)

OECD takes the lead role in the UOE data collection exercise referred to in the preceding section. This is used, among others, to produce the yearly Education at a Glance handbook. It is a substantial and influential book currently running to approximately 400 pages. A wide range of indicators covers the context in which education systems work, the financial and human resources that OECD countries invest in education, access, participation, progression, and completion, the learning environment, outcomes, and student achievement.

Although coverage is mainly of the industrialized OECD countries, recent editions have included some indicators for nonmember countries participating in the UNESCO/OECD World Education Indicators program funded by the World Bank. Coverage of children with disabilities was, until recent editions, limited to information about students educated in segregated special schools. OECD countries made additional resources of various kinds available to students who had particular difficulties for a variety of reasons in accessing the regular curriculum, whether or not this came within a national definition of special educational needs.

A further complication is that although a large proportion of countries had national categories of needs, the actual categories employed varied widely, ranging from 2 to 19. Hence, in addition to adopting a resource based definition, three cross-national categories have been developed corresponding to disabilities, learning or behaviour difficulties, and social disadvantages). Through an iterative consensual process, national categories have been allocated to the three cross-national categories. Table 7 gives an example. Countries also provided definitions for the national categories, as the names of similar categories in different countries were commonly found to be different.

The indicators developed include the percentage of students receiving additional resources in primary and lower secondary education in different countries, both overall and within the cross-national categories; the location of their education in special schools, special classes, or regular classes; and the gender distribution in the different locations. A monograph giving further details and analyses of individual categories in relation to particular disabilities is available and a further monograph is in preparation.

The general message obtained is of very wide country to country variability. In some countries virtually all children of whatever disability or difficulty are educated in integrated settings (e.g., Italy and the New Brunswick province of Canada). In others almost all students with disabilities are in special schools (e.g., Switzerland and the Czech Republic). However, there is a high degree of consistency in gender distributions, with a 60/40 male/female split for different categories and cross-national categories. It is not possible to state with any degree of confidence whether this represents an inequitable distribution. Further data collection is planned that should help elucidate this finding.

Through collaboration with UNESCO, initial pilot work was carried out in Sri Lanka and Zambia. The data collection instrument was further tested in Chile, Costa Rica, the Philippines, Uganda, and Zambia, with encouraging results. The instrument is currently forming the basis for further related data collection exercises in the countries of South America. OECD also is responsible for PISA, the Program for International Student Assessment, a new regular survey of 15-year-olds assessing their preparedness for adult life. At present PISA does not appear to have fully taken on board what is needed to include students with disabilities.

OECD, through its Centre for Research and Innovation in Education (CERI), has carried out studies on integrating students with special needs into mainstream schools. These studies have incorporated other exercises in comparative statistical data collections. PARIS21 (Partnership in Statistics for development in the 21st Century) is based at OECD. It was launched in 1999 "...to act as a catalyst for promoting a culture of evidence based policymaking and monitoring in all countries, and especially in developing countries". It does not, to date, appear to have any disability focus.

The European Union

The European Union through its statistical arm EUROSTAT and EURYDICE (the information network on education in Europe, which is part of SOCRATES, the communities' program on education) provides extensive data on the education systems in Europe.

There is a now somewhat dated compilation of provision for students with disabilities largely based on national surveys and reports with different methodologies. The conclusion is that "information on the number of handicapped pupils in ordinary education is fairly rare, the only reliable data being for France". A handbook on *Disability and Social Participation in Europe* was published in 2001. It is based on data from the European Community Household Panel (ECHP), which is a longitudinal multisubject survey. The ECHP contains several questions on health, including a general question on restrictions on everyday activities caused by a health problem.

The United Nations Children's Fund (UNICEF)

UNICEF is involved in helping countries assess progress for children at the end of the decade in relation to World Summit for Children goals. Goal 6 is:

> Universal access to basic education, and achievement of primary education by at least 80 per cent of primary school-age children, through formal schooling or nonformal education of comparable learning standard, with emphasis on reducing the current disparity between boys and girls.

Relevant indicators are the proportion of children entering first grade of primary school who eventually reach grade 5; the proportion of children of primary school age enrolled in primary school; and the proportion of children of primary school age attending primary school. Unfortunately no data on disability are presented.

The data collection instrument known as MISC2 (Multiple Indicator Cluster Survey, second wave for end-of-decade assessment) did, however, include an optional module on child disability. This is based on the "Ten Questions" approach. By accessing the national reports of individual countries it can be seen that some countries did make use of this module, although this information has not been included in the standard reports.

The INNOCENTI Research Centre based in Florence is the main research arm of UNICEF. It publishes databases, for example, the TransMONEE database of socioeconomic indicators for Central and Eastern Europe. There is information about education (e.g., enrollment in different phases, pupil-teacher ratios, and public expenditure), but nothing on children and disability. Similarly, A Comparison of Survey Instruments for Collecting Data on Child Labor suggests ways of improving data collection in relation to education and health, but does not cover disability.

Children with Disabilities and the Education for All (EFA) and Millennium Development Goals (MDG) Global Initiatives

Education for All (EFA)

UNESCO has taken a lead role in the Education for All (EFA) global initiative. In 1990, the international community put education on the global agenda during the World Conference on Education for All which took place in Jomtien, Thailand. Ten years later, a World Education Forum at Dakar, Senegal, examined the results over the decade, producing the EFA 2000 Assessment which took stock of the status of education in some 180 countries and evaluated the progress achieved during the 1990s. This assessment pinpointed widespread shortcomings in many countries in achieving the goal of universal primary education. UNESCO was mandated to take the lead role in orchestrating global efforts to achieve EFA by 2015. The "DAKAR" objectives were:

1. Expand and improve comprehensive early childhood care and education, especially the most vulnerable and disadvantaged children.
2. Ensure that by 2015 all children, particularly girls, children in different circumstances, and those belonging to ethnic minorities, have access to, and are able to complete education that is free, compulsory and of good quality.
3. Ensure that the learning needs of all young people and adults are met through equitable access to appropriate learning and life-skills programs.
4. Achieve a 50 per cent improvement in levels of adult literacy by 2015, especially women, and equitable access to basic and continuing education for all adults.
5. Eliminating gender disparities in primary and secondary education by 2005, and achieving gender equality in education by 2015, with a focus on ensuring girls' full and equal access to, and achievement in, basic education of good quality.
6. Improving all aspects of the quality of education and ensuring excellence of all so that recognized and measurable learning outcomes are achieved by all, especially literacy, numeracy and essential life skills.

With the exception of objectives 4 (which is solely concerned with adults) and 3 (where the intention appears to be to target those aged 15 and above), the objectives have clear relevance to children with disabilities. This is explicit in objective 1, but in the other objectives it is indisputable that "all" includes children with disabilities. There is, for example, considerable concern about drop-outs and repeaters. It appears likely that children with disabilities are over-represented in these groups, and one might expect relevant data and analyses.

Given this, it is surprising that the EFA 2000 assessment appears to be silent on the education of children with disabilities. In particular, none of the 18 indicators used to assess the extent to which the objectives are being met include any mention of disability. Worryingly, a declaration in the DAKAR final report stating explicitly that additional indicators, including ones for people with disabilities, should be developed does not appear to have been taken on board at a later meeting on proposals for the future development on EFA indicators (UNESCO Institute for Statistics, 2001: Table 2). Neither in their proposals for short term, nor for medium term improvements in the existing indicators, is there any indication that attention is to be given to children with disabilities. It is therefore unsurprising that the most recent monitoring report on progress toward EFA (UNESCO, 2002) is similarly silent.

However, there are other UNESCO related activities that appear to be attempting to stimulate attention to disability issues. One of the 12 thematic studies for the World Education Forum conference on the EFA 2000 assessment covering "Education for All and Children Who Are Excluded" considers under the heading of "Protecting the Most Vulnerable" the position of children with disabilities. However, this is primarily a discussion of the philosophy of inclusive education with case study illustrations, rather than an attempt to provide linkage to indicators.

UNESCO clearly recognizes the need to link EDA and disabilities and has established what they term a "flagship" program the purpose of which is to focus extra attention on disability issues as key to achieving the overall goals of EFA . The main aim of this program appears to be to bring organizations from the disability community into the EFA dialogue. The Flagship has as one of its main strategies the gathering of data on children with disabilities in order to help this group of children be fully included in EFA.

The current work program of the United Nations Institute for Statistics includes the EFA Observatory. This is the international monitoring body that examines progress toward the objectives of Education for All. They have data on school entrance and duration, but none on disability in relation to their monitoring of EFA. Note however that the Institute's Web site covering the 2002 EFA Global Monitoring Report in a table listing EFA Flagship Programs includes one on "EFA and the Rights of Persons with Disabilities Towards Inclusion". This project, under the joint auspices of organizations, including those representing people with different disabilities, seeks amongst other activities to "Support research to produce the data needed top inform governments and international financial institutions." However, this program still appears to be at the planning stage. There also is an appreciation at the Institute that data on disability would be "good to collect".

Millennium Development Goals (MDG)

The Millennium Development Goals have grown out of agreements and resolutions of world conferences organized by the United Nations in the last decade of the 20th century. They have been commonly accepted as a framework for measuring development progress. The World Bank has taken a lead role in relation to MDG and the statistics associated with the achievement of these goals. They are:

1. Eradicate extreme poverty and hunger.
2. Achieve universal primary education.

3. Promote gender equality and empower women.
4. Reduce child mortality.
5. Improve maternal health.
6. Combat HIV/AIDS, malaria, and other diseases.
7. Ensure environmental sustainability.
8. Develop a global partnership for development.

The goals are operationalized with specific targets. The target for goal 2, for example, is to "...ensure that by 2015, children everywhere, boys and girls alike, will be able to complete a full course of primary schooling." The second goal has clear relevance to children with disabilities. It is indisputable that "universal" includes children with disabilities. Each goal has a number of indicators. For goal 2 these are:

— Net enrollment ratio in primary education;
— Proportion of pupils starting grade 1 who reach grade 5; and
— Literacy rate of 15- to 24-year-olds.
— Extensive data tables are provided for over 200 countries .

However, they do not appear to include anything relating to disability. The assessment is therefore straightforward. At present children with disabilities are not explicitly incorporated into the Education for All (EFA) and Millennium Development Goals (MDG) global initiatives. They should be. This could be achieved by developing indicators for EFA objectives 1, 2, 5, and 6, and MDG goal 2 which give explicit mention of children with disabilities.

Transportation of Person with Disabilities

Until the late 19 Century, most transportation in the entire world was on foot. Animal- drawn conveyances were used by wealthier people and for transporting smaller amounts of cargo. Waterways -rivers and lakes and oceans -provided opportunities to travel more quickly and with greater comfort and also to carry larger amounts of goods. For most people, travel was limited to some tens of kilometers of their residence. Life expectancies were shorter, and the survival rate among people with disabilities was especially low.

Currently, trains, cars, buses and aircraft have revolutionized life for many people. Especially in urban areas, people today commute daily the same distance their ancestors experienced in a lifetime. Yet it is important to remember the extremely unequal distribution of resources on the earth today. While the 20%most well-off of the world's population dispose of 85%of the world's GNP, the poorest 20%have about 1. 5%of GNP. The remaining 60%of the population dispose of 13. 5%of the world's GDP. The poorest 20%are confined to mainly using their feet for transportation, and their mobility is limited. The 60%consume mainly cheaper means of transportation -crowded buses and trains, but also bicycles and smaller motorbikes.

Thus, in most countries, the movement of people with disabilities depends on which class they belong to. Generally speaking, accessible transportation is only available for the richest 20%who drive or are driven in private cars or who can afford specialized door-to- door transportation. The poorer segment of the population, where most disabled people are found, generally lack mobility.

People with disabilities who seek inclusive transportation include persons with a mobility impairment (such as those who use wheelchairs, crutches, canes, and walkers) or who have a hidden disability such as arthritis. Other passengers with disabilities may have sensory impairments (such as those who are blind or partially sighted;or persons who are deaf, deafened, or hard-of-hearing), or a cognitive impairment.

It is difficult to quantify the precise number of disabled persons who are currently denied transport due to inaccessible transportation. The United Nations estimates that some 6-10% of people in developing countries are disabled at some level. The European Conference of Ministers of Transport estimates that around 20-30%of people traveling have a mobility impairment for one reason or another, taking into consideration temporary health conditions, pregnant women, parents with young children, and people carrying luggage or shopping bags. The population that would benefit from accessibility improvements is therefore much larger than the actual number of those with mobility, sensory, or cognitive impairments.

The inception report of a major study sponsored by the British Department for International Development (DFID) notes that "it is likely that in most developing countries the number of people with sensory disabilities (including blind, low vision, deaf, hard-of-hearing, and speech) amount to about 40 to 50%of all disabled people, while people with various physical disabilities are in the 20 to 50%range, and people with cognitive disabilities in the 7 to 15%range. "These figures are important because different features of universal inclusive design (and different specialized features as well) especially serve different segments of those with disabilities. Within this context, particular problems that afflict some countries or regions may result in sharp increases in the number of disabled persons.

These problems include nutrition, health problems such as AIDS, a bad public health environment, and injuries due to war and violence. For example, the New York Times reports that 40, 000 Cambodians have lost limbs to land mines, or one of every 250 people. This may cause Cambodia to have the highest ratio of amputees per capita in the world. The article goes on to note the grievous transport problems faced by this population.

Inaccessible Transportation

Impact of inaccessible transportation A lack of transportation contributes to a vicious cycle of disability, poverty, and lack of access to opportunities. The DFID study cited above found that the consequences of this vicious cycle were observed in all the countries studied: India, Mozambique, Malawi, and South Africa, as well as Latin American countries.

There is another, even more hidden, evil that flows from the tendency for public transportation to be designed and operated in an inaccessible manner in developing regions. Because accessible operating practices and safe operating practices are essentially the same, inaccessible transport actually causes a significant amount of disability. Many accidents and fatalities can be attributed to transport vehicle operation and design.

In Australia, for example, where safety standards are presumably superior to those of less wealthy regions, 28%of all disabilities of those ages 18-44 are nevertheless reported as caused by accidents or injuries, and 37%of these accidents are classified as road accidents, implying that 10%of disability in this age bracket is due to road accidents. Studies from Africa and Asia indicate that a disproportionate number of road accidents are caused by transit vehicles and especially by lack of proper operation by bus drivers. A study from Campinas, Brazil, reports that buses were involved in nearly one third of the traffic accidents affecting blind pedestrians and those with reduced vision.

The different design features and operating practices necessary for access to the entire trip chain also tend to reduce accidents and, in the process, mitigate the demonstrable safety concerns that may keep many seniors and women, as well as those with even the most modest disabilities, from using public transportation. Examples of problems of inaccessible design include a lack of vertical stanchions or failure to use non-skid flooring to help passengers avoid falls during sudden changes in vehicle speed or direction.

Many additional accidents caused by inaccessible design or operating practices may not even be categorized as traffic accidents. Further, seniors are far more likely to suffer increased injury or death from accidents than are younger passengers. Women may also be more at risk than are men. The lack of a "culture of safety "among drivers and fare takers may go hand-in-hand with a lack of respect for vulnerable passengers, which can aggravate the fears of many women, children, and disabled persons who might otherwise use public transport.

Promotion of Accessible Transportation

As used here, "promotion "refers to a spectrum of advocacy and support activities which, taken together, have placed accessible transportation on the agenda of agencies and NGOs around the world. These activities take place at international, regional, national, and local levels.

The United Nations

The UN's Standard Rules on the Equalization of Opportunities for Persons with Disabilities, adopted in 1994, provide an international framework within which advocates and legislators can address disability issues. More recently, an important Mexican initiative has resulted in a process to create a United Nations Convention on Disability Rights to promote and protect the rights and dignity of persons with disabilities. The United Nations General Assembly approved this process in December 2001.

As part of this process, the General Assembly also created a special committee, which has produced a comprehensive draft document that includes a provision that public transport vehicles and services permit access and mobility by passengers with disabilities. The process of producing this policy framework for member nations was moved ahead by the Quito Declaration, passed in April 2003 at a regional meeting of delegates from the Americas, held in Ecuador. The declaration acknowledges that 80%of the world's disabled persons live in developing regions and calls upon each country to guarantee access by disabled persons to a better quality of life, taking into account the development level of each country. The special committee will again meet at United Nations headquarters in New York, June 16-27.

International NGOs

The disabled community is well-organized at an international level, with conferences by international NGOs such as Disabled Peoples' International and allied NGOs such as Rehabilitation International. Other internationally-oriented disability NGOs, typically operated by and for persons with disabilities, include the Institute on Independent Living (Stockholm, Sweden), World Institute on Disability (Oakland, California, USA), and Mobility International (Eugene, Oregon, USA) . These and other agencies promote international exchanges of persons with disabilities, thus further encouraging the spread of advocacy around the world.

TRANSED

The triennial "TRANSED "series of conferences on Mobility and Transport for Elderly and Disabled People also provides an international venue for transit researchers and other professionals who in turn promote accessible transport in their home countries and, on occasion, introduce these concepts in less wealthy countries due to their international vision. Recent conferences were held in Australia and Poland, with the next conference scheduled for May 2004 in Japan.

Access Exchange International (AEI)

Access Exchange International (AEI) is an NGO based in San Francisco, California, which promotes accessible transportation around the world. AEI workshops have been held in eight Latin American countries and also in South Africa, Russia, Japan, China, Australia, Thailand, Malaysia, the UK, France, Croatia, and Poland.

For a number of years, AEI has worked with transport staff of the World Bank, facilitating and acting as a resource for workshops for bank staff held in 2001 and in January 2003. More recently, the International Centre for Accessible Transportation (ICAT) has been formed in Montreal, Canada, with close links to AEI and practitioners in the USA's Transportation Research Board.

DFID: At a global level, the largest single current effort in the field of accessible transportation is a project funded by the UK's Department for International Development (DFID), working with the UK's TRL Ltd., CSIR Transportek in South Africa, Access Exchange International, India's Central Institute of Road Transport, and agencies in Malawi and Mozambique. Titled Enhanced Accessibility for People with Disabilities Living in Urban Areas, the project is based on inputs from Africa, Asia, and Latin America. This international effort is focused on developing and testing a set of guidelines appropriate for different levels of development for use by stakeholders around the world. The project is further strengthened by concrete demonstration projects, which are planned or already created in India, South Africa, Malawi, and Mozambique. The project aims at a tool kit of guidelines to be published by March of 2004. The guidelines will be available to assist major financial institutions, such as the World Bank, to better incorporate criteria for accessible transportation into their own projects.

The World Bank

World Bank staff joined staff of the Inter-American Development Bank in a Funders Roundtable organized by AEI in Washington in early 2002. The Bank has hired an Advisor on Disability and Development, assisted by a core of five part-time and full-time staff. A recent Urban Transport Policy Review conducted by the World. Bank has acknowledged, for the first time, issues of inclusion of disabled passengers in its transport policies. In addition, AEI was asked by the Bank to contribute content and case studies to its Sourcebook for Poverty Reduction Strategies, and the Bank commissioned a working paper by a Finnish agency titled Transport, Poverty and Disability in Developing Countries .

UITP

The International Association of Public Transport (UITP), with 2000 members in 80 countries, adopted an official position in 2001 supporting access to transportation by disabled persons.

Regional advocacy

Promotion at national and municipal levels

In terms of local successes, national and municipal NGOs or coalitions, typically headed up or composed of advocates with disabilities, are beginning to have significant success in Latin American and Asia, inspired to some degree by the successes in western Europe and

North America of similar NGOs. Little has happened around the world without such advocacy.

Government ministries and transportation agencies do need to make sure that advocacy NGOs represent the full spectrum of disabled persons with mobility, sensory, and cognitive concerns who are now seeking inclusive transport. Millions of persons with disabilities in each category are currently completely denied their mobility due to lack of accessible design and operation of transport systems. The needs of those with "hidden "disabilities need to be fully recognized.

For example, the use of additional vertical stanchions in transport vehicles may especially help semi-ambulatory passengers with arthritis or similar concerns, but adequate use of this type of design element is often ignored because advocacy has not traditionally formed around such "unseen "disabilities. Yet these "more modest "mobility concerns may make it just as impossible to use public transport by a very large group of persons who especially benefit from design elements such as low first steps on transport vehicles or from operational practices such as the avoidance of sudden stops and starts.

Another concern is that advocates may not be able to fully represent the needs of the lowest-. income segments of the disability community. This is due to the inability of low-income persons with disabilities to get to meetings due to their lack of access to a private car or to public transportation. Such persons tend to be automatically excluded from participation.

Planning Accessible Transportation

In many countries, promotion and advocacy merge into a planning process. Some especially important issues include:

— The need for planners to fully involve persons with different disabilities in the planning process in order to make service design and operation user-friendly.

— The need to include different government agencies in the overall process, so that the entire "trip chain "of accessible transport will be accessible from trip origin to transit stop, on board the vehicle, and then from the vehicle to and within the final destination. Where ministries exist, planning and transport ministries need to work cooperatively with public works departments, traffic police, and health and social service agencies as well as more traditional advocacy groups such as disability NGOs.

— Especially in developing countries, planners should consult with their colleagues in other less-wealthy countries to benefit from their experience. The resources section of the AEI web site at www. globalride-sf. org lists resources in the field of advocacy, planning, and implementation of accessible transport.

— The DFID-sponsored project guidelines, referenced above, may prove of especial assistance to planners who need to take into consideration the development level of their countries.

— Finally, one must note that there are some modest differences between Europe and America in the way accessible transportation has been planned and implemented. The European approach has historically been to evolve technical advice and sub-national guidelines, test them out in practice, and then move to incorporate these standards in binding legislation in what might be seen as a "bottom up "approach, which has resulted in standards that are well matched to peoples' abilities. To a modest degree, the American experience has been seen as more of a "top down "approach. Neither the European approach (with its history of development of technical advice which is then put into practice) nor the North

American approach (with its greater reliance on legislative mandates) is wholly relevant to less developed countries. A major reason for this is a lack of targeted demonstration projects to assist transport planners in developing countries to quantify the tradeoffs between various approaches to inclusive design.

Inclusive Design Features

It is important that advocates, planners, and policy makers have a general understanding of the range of accessible features, which make a transportation system accessible to passengers with disabilities, bearing in mind that most of these features are (1) low cost, and (2) make transportation easier to use by all other passengers as well. all other passengers as well all other.

Examples of inclusive design

Here are some examples of how design elements and operating procedures that benefit disabled persons also tend to benefit everyone else.

— When separate street lanes with dividers are created for pedestrians, bicyclists, and motorized vehicles, each mode is safer to use. This benefits everyone, but especially assists pedestrians with disabilities.

— When a van or taxi operator brings the vehicle to a complete stop and waits while a passenger with a cane climbs on board and finds a seat, the driver has made it possible for that person to ride. But all other passengers also benefit from safe courteous treatment by their drivers.

— When a bus driver announces the most important stops to the passengers, a blind person may especially benefit, but everyone is given important information.

— Painting handrails a bright yellow on a bus or train especially benefits a passenger who is partially sighted, but it also benefits every passenger who wants to quickly find a way to hold on while entering.

— When a wheelchair user rolls onto a bus at floor level, he or she is able to ride even when unable to climb steps. But every passenger gets on faster by not having to climb steps .

— Well-located signs may be especially helpful in directing a deaf person to a bus or train in a transit terminal, but these signs may be equally important to tourists or anyone else who is not yet familiar with that terminal.

In other words, all passengers tend to benefit from inclusive design. Sometimes the benefit comes from an operating procedure : bringing a bus to a safe stop at a bus stop, or calling out important stops. Sometimes the benefit comes from an inclusive design feature : painting hand grips in a bright contrasting color, providing level boarding to buses, or installing good signs with large print at convenient locations.

Design issues for different transit modes

Pedestrian infrastructure includes streets, sidewalks, paths, and access to and within transit terminals, stations, and stops. Indeed, while door-to-door modes of transport can exist with relatively less emphasis on access to infrastructure, all fixed route systems depend heavily on access to transit terminals, stations, and stops. There is no such thing as an "accessible rail car "or an "accessible bus "viewed in isolation from an environment that permits an accessible trip chain, of which access within the vehicle is only one link in this chain.

It may be helpful to list major transportation modes with specific comments about some selected features that enhance the accessibility of each mode

1) *Pedestrian ways, including streets, sidewalks, and paths*
Pedestrian pathways and buildings serving the public should incorporate inclusive design (level pathways of adequate width, curb ramps serving wheelchair users and all other pedestrians, ramps to public buildings, accessible bathrooms, etc.), noting that new construction can be made accessible at relatively little cost compared with retrofitting old construction. Village roads, tracks, and paths should be kept free of obstacles and maintained in as accessible a state as possible.

2) *Stops, stations, and terminals*
Transit terminals should have well-located signs with high-contrast large print to assist deaf and visually impaired passengers or with icons to assist passengers who cannot read;a low ticket counter for use by wheelchair users and short persons;tactile guideways (where needed) to and within transit terminals and stops, and tactile warning strips at curbs and platform edges to assist blind persons.

Unpaved bus stops could be made more accessible with a short (e. g., 2 meter) yellow curb piece, thus helping blind persons to position themselves behind the curb piece, persons with reduced vision to see the stop marker, and persons with reduced mobility to step up on the curb as a way to reduce the distance to the first step of the bus (usually the most difficult step to reach) .

Subway and elevated rail lines provide a special case, requiring station access for those with mobility concerns using either elevators (preferred) or stair lifts. Elevators serve many additional patrons beside wheelchair users, including passengers carrying children or packages -their initial cost is higher, although their lifetime cost per trip may well be lower than for specialized stair lifts serving primarily those using wheelchairs.

3) *All vehicles*

Vehicle design should include large print destination signs to assist those with visual impairments; prioritized seats for disabled and elderly passengers;adequate hand grips and plentiful vertical stanchions at doors and inside vehicles, painted in a bright contrasting color;non-skid materials for step and floor surfaces;and, where feasible, a retractable first step at a bus entrance (or a movable stool) to assist semi-ambulatory passengers.

4) *Access by passengers using wheelchairs* is provided by different methods:

a) *High-floor buses with platform access.* Access can be gained by use of ramped "wayside "platforms serving all passengers at all stops in "Bus Rapid Transit "systems, using bridges operated from the bus or the platform to span the distance between platform and vehicle floor. Such systems can efficiently handle large volumes of passengers, as now occurs in Curitiba, Brazil;Quito, Ecuador;and Bogotá, Colombia. Alternatively, access can be provided at key stops, serving passengers with disabilities, using "mini-platforms "with a bridge stored on and deployed from the bus, or affixed to the platform.

A special case, which would especially benefit from research and demonstration projects, is that of providing platform access to smaller vehicles such as vans, shared ride fixed- route taxis, or motor rickshaws. The low floors of such vehicles could lend themselves to less expensive smaller platforms at key stops. In some systems, relatively minor modifications to the interior of small vehicles would make them accessible to passengers who remain seated in their wheelchairs while riding, or, failing this, at least to passengers who could transfer to a regular seat while folding their wheelchairs.

b) *Low-floor buses* (very popular in Europe and increasingly around the world) require a fairly well-maintained road infrastructure, without large potholes, high protruding speed bumps, or very sharp changes in grade (e. g., from steep incline to flat surface) . Under favorable conditions, all passengers -including those using wheelchairs-can quickly board and alight using ramps and/or direct access from high sidewalks. In addition to their heavy use in Europe and increasingly in North America, a thousand or more low- floor buses operate in Hong Kong and in Buenos Aires, with smaller numbers in other cities in developing regions.

c) *High-floor lift-equipped buses:* Unlike low-floor buses or high-floor buses using wayside platforms, which exhibit "universal design "serving all passengers, lift-equipped buses provide a specialized elevator primarily for wheelchair users. This feature especially lends itself to situations where neither low-floor buses nor platform access is possible. This can occur where there are bad road conditions or a dense urban environment that makes it difficult to install platforms. This approach may be especially appropriate to serve heavily traveled routes, but capital and maintenance costs for the lifts can be an obstacle.

d) Forming policies Forming policies is a related area, which permit and train transit personnel to manually assist wheelchair users to board and alight from transit vehicles even when such vehicles are not technically accessible. While this is generally not done in North America and Europe, for a variety of good reasons, cultural differences in other countries may at times make this possible in some situations.

5) *Service routes* generally run on fixed routes that pass by key sites. Service routes are heavily used in Sweden and are found at times in the USA, Mexico, Colombia, Japan, South Africa, and other countries. Typically, service routes use small buses. Fares tend to be more expensive per trip than "main line "bus transport but may be less expensive than door-to-door service. Service routes can either serve all passengers, or primarily those with disabilities and their families or assistants. Recent service route start-ups in developing countries need to be monitored to determine their sustainability.

6) *Door to door services*

Called "paratransit service "in the USA, door-to-door services using vans or mini-buses are very heavily used in Western Europe and North America. Many systems are found in Japan and Australia. Larger public systems of approximately 100 vehicles are found in São Paulo, Brazil, and Hong Kong, China. Smaller systems are found in some South African cities: Kuala Lumpur, Malaysia;Curitiba, Brazil, and elsewhere. Such systems generally exhibit a higher cost per trip than other modes.

One way to address cost concerns is the use of ramped or lift-equipped taxis. Costa Rica has taken the lead in the developing world by mandating that 10%of its taxi fleet be accessible to passengers using wheelchairs. There are some interesting examples of accessible taxis based on the concept of the London cab. These taxis are accessible, with wide doors, spacious interiors and low floors.

It should be noted that large bus and rail systems, no matter how accessible to most persons most persons most with disabilities, will not be able to serve all persons with disabilities. There will always all persons with disabilities. There will always all be a need for some type of door-to-door transportation for those with functional problems that simply make it impossible to use bus and rail transport. The almost universal absence of door-to-door systems in poorer countries, and the resulting invisibility of those who most need such services, should not be taken as evidence to the contrary. Cross-disability NGOs generally are of special help to transportation planners and agencies in advocating for door-to-door transport to supplement fixed route transportation.

7) *Motor rickshaws and other vehicles* somewhat smaller than vans deserve a great deal of study. Inclusive design features on such vehicles may be inexpensive and enhance access to fleets ranging into ten thousand or more vehicles in urban areas in countries such as India.

8) Access features can also be developed for *non-motorized vehicles,* including cycle rickshaws. Initial research has been done on access to cycle rickshaws in India.

9) Another area in need of study is access to *small boats on rural waterways small boats on rural waterways* around the world. While access to larger ferries and large ships is well understood, little has been done by way of advocacy or research concerning small boats. Practitioners in Costa Rica have shown interest in investigating this important subject.

10) *Airport* access is of course extremely important but is beyond the scope of this short Airport access is of course extremely important but is beyond the scope of this short Airport paper. However, it can be said that new airports in major cities around the world are increasingly being constructed with an array of access features.

11) *Personal transportation:* Another area largely beyond the scope of this report is access to personal transportation, including wheelchairs and private cars that normally do not fall under the head of "public transportation. "Yet personal mobility, gained by many through the use of canes, crutches, walkers, calipers, and manual or powered wheelchairs, is essential for access to transit stops.

    Since the start of the automobile industry, cars have been adapted to meet the needs of people with mobility impairments. Cars were first adapted at special workshops so that people with mobility disabilities could drive using their hands. Today, cars can even be adapted at the production line to meet the needs of different people. For people who need more advanced adaptations, manufacturers can customize the accessibility of the car. Technological advancements have made it possible for even people with severe mobility impairments to drive a car through mechanisms such as voice control or sip and blow methods.

    In many countries hand-propelled tricycles substitute for wheelchairs and, to some extent, for cars. Hand propelled tricycles can be produced, repaired and maintained at a reasonable cost at bicycle factories or local mechanic shops.

12) *New technology,* often under the heading of Intelligent Transportation Systems (ITS), creates both problems

and possibilities for passengers with disabilities. As such technology becomes less expensive, wayfinding systems may assist blind or visually impaired passengers to navigate increasingly complex transport environments. Small easy-to-understand handheld equipment such as palm computers can assist people with cognitive disabilities by giving them step-by-step advice that simplifies complex travel. Yet complex information on screens can be difficult for people with cognitive disabilities to understand.

Inclusive Operating Practices

When operated in a highly unsafe manner, public transportation may cause far more than 10%of the population to "become disabled "in terms of the ability of older persons, children, many women, and all those with even the most modest mobility concerns to safely board, ride and alight from buses, jitneys, and other transport vehicles .

To address this situation, a number of steps can be taken. These include:

1) Establish regulatory mechanisms to enforce safe vehicle operation by private and especially informal sector transit operators. Positive and negative reinforcements are needed to encourage safety and courtesy to all passengers. To date, the global trend toward privatization of transport services in developing countries has tended to decrease accessibility due to a lack of proper regulation of transportation providers. Especially where governments are too weak to regulate informal sector transportation providers, inaccessible service is generally the result.
2) Provide sensitivity training to transit personnel (including bus drivers and fare collectors) so that

they will have direct experience of what it is like to use a wheelchair or crutches for mobility, to board a bus when blind, etc.

3) Require that buses and jitneys come to a complete stop at bus stops and remain stopped until passengers have entered and positioned themselves for their ride.
4) Require drivers to call out key stops and require audible announcements at transit terminals, as an aid to passengers who are blind or partially sighted.
5) Disaggregate data on bus accidents where possible to gain public support for key safety practices related, e. g., to injuries while trying to board a moving vehicle, injuries. while crossing traffic lanes to get to a vehicle, or on-board injuries due to bad driving. Elders are far more likely to suffer severe injuries during a fall or accident than are other passengers suffering the same fall or accident, but specific data in each country will assist in quantifying this problem.
6) Explore increased employment of women as potentially safer bus drivers.
7) Consider alternatives to paying drivers "per passenger, "to remove the major incentive for unsafe operation.

Accessible social service transportation had its beginnings in door-to-door services in wealthier countries, where agencies needed to bring clients to their facilities for their program services. Accessible public transport was initiated in Sweden and other Scandinavian countries and quickly followed by initial steps toward such transport in other western European countries and in North America. The Swedish "service route "concept has been copied in other regions, as has the use of low-floor buses and trams (first initiated in Germany) and ramped taxis (first used on a large scale in the United Kingdom) . It can be generally stated that western European and North American nations are now well on their way toward achieving accessible public transportation.

In the developing world, the European and North American models were especially copied in Latin America, usually beginning with pedestrian infrastructure projects such as curb cuts and ramps to public buildings, followed by modifications in building codes and the initiation of pilot projects involving both city-operated and especially concessioned (private sector operated) transportation systems. Currently, most major Latin American cities have a program of pedestrian access, especially involving the installation of curb ramps at key sites and along key pedestrian corridors. Major programs to make rail and bus terminals accessible are under way in some parts of Brazil and Argentina.

Latin American cities with a subway or metro system generally have at least a dozen stations already fitted with access features for passengers with disabilities. First steps toward access for wheelchair users to large buses have been taken in Buenos Aires, while Mexico City has deployed in excess of 50 lift-equipped buses on major routes. More specialized service routes (aimed at passengers with disabilities) are found in a Mexican and a Colombian city, while some Brazilian cities have initiated door-to-door services. National and municipal legislation mandates access to transport in a number of countries. A distinctive and highly important Latin American contribution is the universal design of bus rapid transit systems.

While the late 1990's saw significant gains in Latin America, the early years of the current decade are witnessing rapid change in Asia and the Pacific. Japan and Australia have taken a lead in national legislation mandating inclusive transport systems. Hong. Kong has become a model for the rest of Asia with its "family of accessible services " ranging from accessible rail and low-floor bus routes to service routes and door-to-door service. Access to commuter rail and subway systems is found in most Japanese cities and at some key stations in some cities in China, Korea, Thailand, Singapore, and India. First steps in the use of low-floor buses are planned in India. Initial deployment of service routes as well as door-to-door services are found in Tokyo while a small door to door service was recently started in Kuala Lumpur.

Advocacy is moving ahead, with "access audits "recently reported in India, Cambodia, Laos, and Thailand. An AEI guide has been published in Chinese and Japanese versions, with other versions planned by NGOs in Malaysia, Indonesia, and India. A key bus corridor has become more accessible in Pune, India, as part of the DFID-sponsored project referenced above.

South Africa is definitely the lead country in Africa in terms of initiating accessible transport projects. Prototype lift-equipped or low-floor buses exist or are planned in Johannesburg and other cities. Plans call for access features when 120, 000 fixed route "taxis "are recapitalized. A 17-vehicle door-to-door system now operates in Cape Town. Pedestrian infrastructure is beginning to be modified to enhance access for pedestrians. CSIR Transportek in Pretoria, South Africa, is coordinating demonstration projects to enhance pedestrian access in Malawi and Mozambique and to demonstrate the use of wayside platforms to assist wheelchair users to board buses in Pretoria, as part of the DFID-sponsored project referenced above.

First steps toward accessible transportation have also been taken in central and eastern Europe. As very partial survey of the region notes that a high percentage of Warsaw, Poland's bus fleet is now low-floor and accessible via ramps. Railroad stations in the Czech Republic and Hungary are becoming more accessible, as are airports in Romania. In Russia, accessible rail service is reported between Moscow and Nizhniy Novgorod; a service route has been initiated in the northern city of Archangelsk; and the ECMT has signed a protocol with the Russian Transport Ministry to share knowledge and skills based on western European experience in this field. Projects are also reported in Croatia, Bulgaria, and elsewhere. Disabled persons in Russia often receive government subsidies to purchase specialized automobiles.

Many countries have national legislation requiring some level of access to transportation. Other countries have established less formal guidelines. All countries need detailed regulations and work plans to implement and monitor compliance with such legislation and guidelines. Readers are especially referred to the discussion of policy frameworks in the inception report of the DFID project, Enhanced Accessibility for People with Disabilities Living in Urban Areas.

5

Monitoring with the Handicapped

In the early part of this century, handicapped people were isolated and protected from the cruelty of society, for their own survival, or simply to exclude them and deny them their right to a full life. In the light of this, Scouting...decided to take some of its programmes to hospitals and other institutions. To a large extent, Scout associations saw handicapped people as a problem, as people who needed a special programme". "For many years, Extension Scouting was the term applied to this service. It was Scouting for the handicapped, rather than Scouting with handicapped people. Thi s type of Scouting was more a service activity than a joint activity shared by handicapped and non-handicapped persons". At that time, Extension Scouting was largely "...ordinary Scouting for young people in hospitals, orphanages and rehabilitation centres".

Period between 1922, the date of the first World Scout Conference (then called the International Scout Conference), and 1968, when the World Scout Bureau moved from Ottawa to Geneva, all historical evidence shows that Scout associations considered it their duty to recruit as many Scouts as possible, in every walk of life, including children and young people with handicaps, either confined in specialised institutions and therefore belonging to special troops or packs, or as part of regular units.

Two changes takes place in the period between 1968-1993. First of all, changes in Scouting itself, and secondly, changes in the social environment.

Changes in Scouting: Three important decisions were taken by the World Scout Conference and the World Scout Committee at their meetings in Seattle in August 1967: to accept the "Report on World Scouting" prepared by Dr Laszlo Nagy as an independent researcher, and to make it the basis for the reorganisation of the Movement; to move the world headquarters from Ottawa to Geneva; and to strengthen the staff of the World Scout Bureau. As a result of those changes, the nature of the activities undertaken and the volume and substance of the documentation available since the Bureau was established in Geneva is significantly different from the previous situation.

Societal changes: "Society's general attitude towards the physically and the mentally handicapped has changed significantly, especially over the last 20 years, and this has influenced the very concept of Extension Scouting". Different societies have gradually realised that disabled people do not necessarily have to spend their lives in institutions and that it is important both for them and for society at large to recognise their abilities and to integrate them into society by allowing them to participate in the lives of their communities.

This progressive change in attitude has come about as a result of the converging effect of several factors, notably:

— Technological and scientific progress, which has liberated the physically and mentally disabled to a certain extent.

— The increasing number of disabled people. As already seen, the most optimistic statistics indicate that some 10% of the world's population is disabled (and) the more the methods of analysing disabilities are improved, the greater the number of disabled persons becomes.

— The raising of national awareness was conducive to a higher profile of this question on the international scene.

Consequently, 1981 was declared the "International Year of the Disabled", which in turn considerably raised international awareness of this issue.

For historical as well as for educational reasons, the World Scout Jamborees deserve special attention: traditionally, they have been an important occasion in the Movement to share experiences through educational games and activities, to generate new ideas and to give new impetus to old ideas, sharing means, techniques and skills with young people from all over the world.

In this respect, the introduction of the "Global Development Village" (GDV) has been an important innovation in the history of World Scout Jamborees. The GDV has been a true springboard, in which thousands of people have taken part and whose activities have been disseminated throughout the world, first through the example and enthusiasm of those present, and secondly through publications of very different types.

The first Global Development Village was held during the 17th World Scout Jamboree in Korea in August 1991. This innovative feature was devised to help Scouts become more aware of health, development and environmental problems in the world and to encourage them to play a greater role in making the world a better place. As part of it, many awareness activities were held, including "exhibition and activities relating to handicap" introduced by Belgium. Notable among them was a team game designed to help participants understand what it is like to be visually impaired. With their eyes covered, opposing teams played with a ball containing a bell and had to try and score goals.

Building on the experience and enthusiasm generated by the Global Development Village in Korea, the 18th World Scout Jamboree, held in the Netherlands in August 1995, included a more ambitious set of activities, divided into five areas: educational programme, environmental programme, health programme, travel around the world and human rights.

The activities concerning disability and handicap were organised in several workshops within the health programme, under the general heading of "Scouting for everyone". Notable among them were: "Adapt your games and rooms for the disabled", "Riding a wheelchair track", "Adapting a building or sports field", "Making a construction drawing: adapted club building" and "Sensitisation to handicap". Two points, common to most activities, are worth mentioning: the importance of catering for different types of handicaps: wheelchair basketball, blindfolded obstacle course, signal game for deaf participants and a game for spastic participants, all forming part of the same workshop; and the concern of the organisers to allow participants to disseminate the content of the workshops in a back-home situation: every workshop had a small booklet in English and French describing the objectives of the activities, the content, and an explanation of some of the games played.

The 19th World Scout Jamboree was held in Chile from 26 December 1998 to 6 January 1999. It was a historical Jamboree for many reasons, most particularly because it took place in Latin America for the first time in the history of the Scout Movement. From the point of view of Scouting with the disabled, it was also a milestone.

Taking into account that most of the victims of such mines are civilians, and that many of them are young people of Scout age, Scouting could not remain indifferent to this tragedy. In 1997, a group of leaders from the Geneva Scout Association decided that they could take action to make more young people aware of the problem. They developed a simulation game which used one of the fundamental aspects of the Scout method: learning by doing.

After several tests, the game was fully developed. Thanks to their geographical proximity to the World Scout Bureau and the links of friendship established, they shared the idea with members of the World Scout Bureau, and what started as a local project became world-wide. Indeed, at the World Scout Jamboree, the game was one of the more significant features of the Global Development Village. The stand, managed jointly by Handicap International and the Geneva Scouts, was very strategically located and attracted the attention of thousands of participants. After a brief introduction, Scouts went through the different steps of the game, trying to step lightly through a "minefield" to avoid setting off electronic explosions.

Also during the Jamboree, on 3 January 1999, an Agreement of Cooperation was signed between the World Organization of the Scout Movement and Handicap International. The signature was followed by a press conference. One of the key aspects of this agreement was the production and distribution of an educational kit entitled "Together, we can make a mine-free earth". It includes: a booklet which describes the awareness game, with all the necessary information for running the game with a group of young people; a video cassette, two posters giving information on antipersonnel landmines, and concrete ideas for sensitising and taking action with young people. The kit was distributed to each Jamboree contingent and, immediately after the Jamboree, was circulated to all National Scout Associations.

In this way, Scouting has joined the many forces in the international community united in the "International campaign to ban landmines" . Why is this involvement so important? From the point of view of Scouting, obviously the most important aspect is the educational value and the creation of awareness among young people. But there are other aspects to be taken into account.

The Landmines Convention was signed on 1 December 1997 and entered into force on 1 March 1999. According to the most recent information available, out of the 136 countries which signed the convention, 89 have ratified it and 47 have still to do so. But 12 countries are still opposed to it, and 42 "unknown or undecided". It is therefore very important that the international community retains a deep interest in the subject, and that the civilian world is mobilised if the overall objective of the total disappearance of landmines is to be reached in the coming years.

The evolution of Scouting with the disabled over the past 25 years, which goes along the same lines as the general philosophy of the "Year" and the "Decade" of Disabled Persons, can be summarised as follows:

1. Projection of a positive image of people with disabilities, putting the emphasis on what they can do and not on their handicaps. The portrayal of people with disabilities in written material, photographs and illustrations should encourage a sense of interdependence and solidarity, not dependence and pity.
2. Sensitisation of non-disabled people to the problem of people with disabilities.
3. Linked with point No. 2 above is the importance of giving both disabled and non-disabled children and

young people a better understanding of each others' needs, thereby contributing to the integration of disabled people with others in society.

4. Conceptual and practical integration of disability prevention and rehabilitation in the field of health, particularly in the field of Primary Health Care.
5. Emphasis on the need to have a key person - or better still, a team responsible for Scouting with the disabled and to obtain the support of all the leaders of a National Scout Association, helping those leaders to pass from a receptive attitude to action in favour of integration.

The efforts towards the early prevention and rehabilitation of disabled people should be part, inasmuch as possible, of the general approach to Primary Health Care. This is valid both for conceptual and for practical reasons, in order to ensure the best use of the resources available. The field is wide open for Scouting action, both in industrialised and in developing countries. Following are few ideas based on the experience of many National Scout Associations and on the work of other NGOs.

— "Reaching the unreached": Scouting can play a very important role because of its vast network of groups and units at grassroots level, reaching both urban and rural areas, affluent neighbourhoods and under-privileged inner-city areas.
— Early stimulation and early detection of disability: In many countries, as part of the Primary Health Care approach, teams of community women have been recruited to make weekly visits to homes with children.

On the basis of early detection, an intervention programme tailor-made to each child is prepared and the "...community aides demonstrate step-by-step to the parents the activities to be undertaken for their child's development". This approach has two advantages: first, the principal agents for carrying out the training of each disabled child are the parents themselves and second, it has been found "...that these community aides, who range from barely literate to 7th-grade education, can also be taught the skills necessary for testing and curriculum planning". Scouts are well equipped to fulfil this role and, as experience has shown, with appropriate training they can become "health animators" in their respective communities, particularly in remote rural areas where access to medical care is difficult and expensive.

Primary prevention: Many of these "first-level prevention measures" are the most efficient and cost-effective measures for avoiding impairments and, as experience has shown, Scouts of different age groups, can be involved in all of them. A few examples:

— vaccination, facilitate access to clean water and hygiene education in order to prevent communicable diseases;

— education in traffic behaviour in order to prevent road accidents;

— community education, improvement of housing and home installations, in order to prevent accidents in the home;

— community (and especially youth) education concerning smoking, alcohol, and drug abuse in order to provoke changes in attitude and behaviour;

— introduction of new agricultural varieties and changes in farming output in order to improve nutrition in the community, coupled with nutrition education;

— redesign of cooking stoves, use of less dangerous fuel and community education in this field in order to avoid burns and other accidents. The list is endless.

As a general rule, one can say that in all matters belonging to daily family life, Scouts can make a very relevant contribution. The document "The disability process and intervention levels"has been used as a source for enumerating problems and possible measures.

Second-level and third-level prevention: "Once an impairment is apparent, intervention can be directed towards the prevention of the development of disabilities..." This is called "second-level prevention". "Once disabilities are present and irreversible, the transition into handicap may be prevented by therapeutic measures...by training in self-care activities...the provision of technical aids...vocational rehabilitation training...social training aimed at specific groups (such as the blind or the deaf)... and provision of education and suitable jobs for those with functional limitations..." . This is called "third-level prevention".

To the extent that those two levels involve community-based rehabilitation measures, Scouts can be involved in several ways.

— First of all, by providing technical aids for the disabled, such as simple legs made in the community with local material (wood, rubber, leather, etc), or crutches made locally.

— In second place, in the whole community education field: helping train children in self-care activities, prevention and treatment of river blindness, and so on.

— Thirdly, in the general effort of information and education of the public in order to improve community and family attitudes towards disabled persons and make their integration into normal life as easy as possible, i.e. the elimination of physical barriers, and other measures of this type.

— And, last but not least, direct work with disabled people themselves, which is of utmost importance "...since the patient has often lost his motivation to break a pattern of already established dependency...". In these situations,

Scouting can provide (in the words of Baden-Powell) the necessary incentive "...to gain hope and strength...". Acting in this way, Scouting can prevent the appearance of psychological disturbances following a somatic condition

"Data from many countries and regions verify that at least one-tenth of all children are born with, or acquire, impairments – physical, mental or sensory – that will interfere with their capacities for normal development unless some special assistance and attention is provided. This is a minimum estimate. The numbers can be much greater, ranging up to 15% or 20% of all children, depending on the conditions included, the definitions of disability used, the age of the child population studied, and other factors."

"Using the conservative estimate that one child in every ten is disabled and on the basis of population figures from 1975...

— Of 1.4 billion children under the age of 15 years, 140 million were disabled. Approximately 80%, or 120 million, of these children live in the developing world...

— On the basis of current population projections, there will be at least 190 million disabled children in the world by the year 2000, at least 150 million in developing countries.

"In addition, the presence of a child with an impairment or disability may produce the following consequences on the family: "...the use of the time and energy of the family members, strained relationships between parents, complications and distortions in the development of the siblings, and mental health implications...". A United Nations Expert Group Meeting on socio-economic aspects of rehabilitation concluded that "when these effects are taken into account, and on the basis of the average family size, the proportion of the population affected by disability could be at least 25 per cent".

The statistics above were recorded on the occasion of the International Year of Disabled Persons. In the past 20 years, both the definition of what a "disabled person" is and the way statistics on the subject are compiled have undergone important changes. To avoid entering into overly sophisticated medical terminology - it is important to mention two aspects:

First of all, the trend in recent years is to record diseases or medical conditions in a separate way. Three cases in point:

— For visual disability (including cataract-related, glaucoma-related, etc.), the overall figure is 179 million in the world.

— For hearing loss (41 or more decibels), the estimates of 1997 give a figure of 123 million people world-wide.

— For chronic rheumatic diseases, the figures for 1995 were: 40 million people in the USA alone, and the projection for 2020 is 60 million persons.

There is, however, a second factor which also plays a role. More and more, both from the medical and social points of view, ageing is considered as a "...normal dynamic process...not as a disease" and therefore "...disabling conditions which become more common with increasing age..." (such as circulatory diseases or degenerative disorders) are considered and treated in a specific way and therefore recorded in a separate way.

Impairment, Disability and Handicap

To keep pace with international terminology, it is

important to distinguish between impairment, disability and handicap. The following definitions were published by the World Health Organization in 1980and are now widely accepted. "In the context of health experience... impairment is any loss or abnormality of psychological, physiological or anatomical structure or function."In other words, an impairment is the loss of an ability or function because part of the body is defective or missing. An eye that does not see, a leg that is missing, a brain that has a defective memory: these are all forms of impairment.

"In the context of health experience...a disability is any restriction or lack (resulting from an impairment) of ability to perform an activity in the manner or within the range considered normal for a human being."In other words, it is a lack of ability to perform a function that most other people can perform. Disabilities may be difficulties in seeing, walking, hearing, thinking, speaking and other ordinary human abilities. "In the context of health experience... a handicap is a disadvantage for a given individual, resulting from an impairment or a disability, that limits or prevents the fulfilment of a role that is normal (depending on age, sex, and social and cultural factors) for that individual."

In other words, a handicap is the limitation of a disabled person's ability to lead a regular and normal life. It is important to note that "A disability becomes a handicap when society's attitudes and physical obstacles make it difficult to do what is expected in life. People in a wheelchair become handicapped when stairs block them from entering buildings. A blind girl becomes handicapped in reading when she is n¬t taught to read Braille".

As a result of this distinction between disability and handicap, as the WHO Report points out ,"a person may be handicapped in one group and not in another - time, place, status and role are all contributing". "One can be impaired without being disabled, and disabled without being handicapped." The external environment, such as an absence of physical barriers or family support, can mediate an impairment and not result in a handicap."

Prevention, Rehabilitation and Integration

Many impairments are preventable. They are not decreed by fate, but are the result of living conditions that can and should be modified. In most cases, the prevention of impairments does not require expensive medical skills and facilities with complex equipment. At the list of causative factors, it is easy to understand that it is up to everyone to make the effort to prevent diseases and accidents, be they in the home, at school, at the working place or on the roads.

In this respect, it is important to underline the concept of primary health care, which is fundamental for preventing impairments. Primary health care aims to educate, support and encourage people to take responsibility for their health. When people assume responsibility for their own health, they become more independent and self-reliant, better able to live richer and fuller lives and to participate meaningfully in the lives of their communities.

Rehabilitation is the combined and co-ordinated use of medical, social, educational and vocational measures for training or retraining the individual to the highest possible level of functional ability. "Rehabilitation is a comprehensive process. It is based upon the realisation that the handicapped person must achieve emotional and social adjustment to his or her particular circumstances and environment, and that all of the needs of the individual must be seen in the context of his or her relationship to the community."

Rehabilitation implies a number of measures to be

taken to minimise disability. It does not always have to be administered by highly qualified personnel in institutions with sophisticated technology. The majority can be reached by trained volunteers using low-cost technology. However, it is a sad fact that the majority of the world's population still do not have access to rehabilitation. It has been estimated that 90% of the resources used for rehabilitation are spent on assisting only 20% of those in need. That means that 80% of those who urgently need rehabilitation receive little or no assistance. They live in deprived areas of industrialised and developing countries and their number is increasing.

Integration is the third stage in the process of combating the impairmentdisability-handicap sequence. It is achieved "when the degree of participation in the mainstream of community life that a disabled person seeks is attained". In order to achieve the full integration of a disabled person in community life, a number of measures have to be taken. The person may need rehabilitative aids, equipment (a wheelchair or an artificial limb, etc), the removal of architectural barriers so that they can have access to schools, libraries, museums, shops or restaurants, the availability of publications in Braille for the blind or sub-titles on television for the deaf, and so on. This is what is known as physical or functional integration.

However, social integration is the most difficult aspect to achieve. It requires an increasing awareness and a change of attitude on the part of the community as a whole. In many places, the integration of disabled people in social life is denied by the limitations of poverty, ignorance and fear. Widespread misconceptions about the origin and nature of certain disabilities are still prevalent in many societies. A conscious effort of education is therefore needed.

Health and Disability

The International Year for Disabled Persons in 1981

was a catalyst for crystallising the evolution that has taken place over the last decades. This evolution puts the emphasis on the following trends:

— A growing awareness of the causative elements in the process of impairment leading to disability and disability leading to handicap.

— An increasing awareness of the social, political and economic factors that have a bearing on that process.

— An increasing awareness of the social consequences of handicap.

— And, as a result of the three above-mentioned trends, a less "medical-only" approach to treatment, with the emphasis placed on community prevention and treatment.

As could have been expected, those changes have been linked in a causal relationship with the increasing awareness of the rights of handicapped people to live - to the maximum extent possible - fully human and independent lives and their right to participate meaningfully in the lives of their communities. Therefore, the change has been from segregation to integration, from dependency to autonomy and selfrealisation as independent human beings. The paternalistic and "assistive" approach has progressively given way to a participative and supportive approach which is widely recognised today not only as the most effective course of action but also as the most compatible with the basic human rights of disabled people themselves.

Participative and Supportive Approach

Self-reliance and autonomy: "One of the most common features of the relationship between parents and their retarded child is overprotection. Study after study has shown that parents of such children tend to overprotect the child, doing for him what the child could easily be taught to do for himself. This may occur because the mother finds it easier to feed, bathe or dress the child than to teach the child to do these things independently. In other cases, however, the reason for the overprotection may be psychological, involving the parents' fear that anything that might happen to the child would be the last straw on their own burden of guilt."

Essential role of the family: "The family is the most important instrument for the preservation of the normal child development process, and its capabilities to deal with the problems of impairment must be strengthened and supported."

Community participation and integration: This is a rule which applies to school as well as to other forms of community participation and integration: put the child (or the person) in a situation as near as possible to the "normal" situation. Prof. Edgerton says about special classes: "...after each retarded child has been assessed, he should be placed in a program that is as close to regular classroom education as his personal needs and abilities permit. These programs should be designed so that retarded children can be integrated into regular education in a way that is beneficial for retarded and non-retarded children alike.

Furthermore, the needs and abilities of retarded children should be reassessed frequently to assure that every child is receiving the best possible education in terms of his or her changing needs and characteristics". And Dr P. E. Mandl confirms: " The vast majority of locomotor and sensory impairments would today be less handicapping for the adult if, instead of concentrating on the child's impairment, the family's and the community's efforts were directed in such a way as to ensure to the extent possible the same development process as that of normal children".

Efforts of prevention and rehabilitation should be included in the Primary Health Care policy: This policy was adopted by the World Health Organization (WHO) and UNICEF at the Alma-Ata Conference in 1978. It recognises that, in terms of policy definition and implementation, it is ... important to keep the integrated approach, which is at the same time "less expensive, more equitable, and more effective than institution-based approaches". "Many needed forms of ...prevention and rehabilitation...can be rendered through the appropriate application of resources already available to many of the families and communities in developing countries.

A modest enrichment of training programmes for basic health, welfare, education, and vocational services can expand their coverage to include children with disabilities". One case in point concerning this issue is the prevention and treatment of xerophtalmia, better known as nutritional blindness, due to a lack of vitamin A. Once the problem is identified in a country and an appropriate strategy designed, it can be integrated into the health and nutrition system with a high degree of cost-effectiveness, as it is not necessary to establish any new delivery system to operate the programme.

Emphasis on prevention rather than on rehabilitation: Given the scarcity of resources, the emphasis should be on prevention rather than on rehabilitation, even though none of these dimensions can be neglected. This policy applies to the general efforts in the field of health and has guided Primary Health Care philosophy and action for many years. It is particularly appropriate for developing countries since "...one should on the long-term basis try to give priority to the approaches that have the best cost/effectiveness ratio". Some examples: "extend vaccination against poliomyelitis rather than extending rehabilitation services for those already crippled by polio, invest funds in the prevention of blindness rather than extending special education and sheltered workshops for the blind...".

Poverty and Disability

Different research studies carried out in the last decades - both in industrialised and developing countries - have shown that "...the incidence of impairment differs by social class and by country.

Therefore it is not a coincidence that the relative numbers of impairments and of multiple impairments increases more than proportionally as one descends the ladder of poverty. Malnutrition, an unhealthy environment, the absence of clean drinking water, the presence of endemic diseases, the lack of access to basic notions of hygiene, and the lack of means to apply them in daily life are among the factors contributing to many impairments".

"...a comparison of statistics for Third World and industrialised countries reveal that in 1975 three-fourths of the disabled lived in Third World countries". And Prof. Mandl ventured the forecast that: "In the year 2000, this gap will increase even further if the present trends continue, that is, if traditional theories of economic development continue to dominate, with their irreversible inequality in the distribution of income. Four-fifths of the disabled will then belong to the developing countries". It is sad to assess that, in spite of the undeniable progress made in the past 20 years in many fields concerning health, the situation prevailing today, at the dawn of the third millennium, is far from satisfactory.

The World Health Organization devoted its annual report of 1995 to discussing the disparities between industrialised and developing countries. Its conclusion: "Poverty is ... the main cause of low life expectancy, handicap, disability and starvation, and it is a major factor in mental illness, stress, suicide, family disintegration and substance abuse". The World Health Report of 1998 confirms that trend. In the Message from the Director General, together with many positive and encouraging signs, he writes: "Tragically...while average life expectancy has been increasing throughout the 20th century, 3 out of 4 people in the least developed countries today are dying before the age of 50 - the global life expectancy figure of half a century ago".

The same confirmation can be found in the UNICEF Report "The Progress of Nations 1999" concerning the difference between a child born in an industrialised country and a child born in Africa, where "...half the children...(are) already suffering from illnesses caused by unsafe drinking water, poor sanitation and a degraded environment, it is almost certain that constant bouts of preveritable diseases will sap the child's overall health...(and) his physical and mental development is likely to be stunted by malnutrition..."

War and Disability

It has been estimated that approximately 145 armed conflicts have occurred between the end of the Second World War and 1990, the year that is roughly considered to be the end of the "Cold War". At the present time, according to UNICEF figures, "Over 40 armed conflicts currently claim children's lives, most of them in developing countries. In the past decade, more than 1.5 million children have been killed, more than 4 million handicapped, 12 million have been left homeless, more than 1 million orphaned and an estimated 10 million have suffered psychological trauma".

The relationship between war and disability for the civilian population, and most especially for women and children, is complex and farreaching. A report prepared in 1990 by UNICEF and Rehabilitation International entitled "Relief and rehabilitation of traumatised children in war situations" indicates that "...approximately 500,000 children were wounded or physically disabled every year". But there are other consequences which are equally important:

1. War and civil unrest often destroy the existing infrastructures , including essential welfare, health and rehabilitation services, which especially affect the disabled population. As a result, there is a steep decline in the standard of those services.
2. In addition, particularly after conflicts, widespread foodproduction shortages, hunger and malnutrition are common in developing countries, with a particularly heavy impact on the lessprivileged, including the disabled.
3. To this should be added the psychosocial trauma provoked by those conflicts. "Such stress-induced emotional shock especially affected children, who were denied the security needed for their natural development...affecting around 10 million children every year...", according to UNICEF sources. It (has been) confirmed that "...armed conflicts caused feelings of sadness and anxiety and that the children affected demonstrated behavioural disorders of various levels of intensity. This was especially true for child combatants aged under 15, who were sometimes forcibly abducted to serve in the armed forces, and for displaced and refugee children , who suffered the additional trauma of being uprooted from their homes for resettlement".
4. It has also been demonstrated that the number of unaccompanied children and orphans increases as a consequence of war and civil unrest.
5. Finally, if situations of war are stressful for everybody involved, they are particularly harmful for mentally disabled persons, who are in special need of tranquillity, affection and environmental stability.

The Declaration adopted by the Heads of State and Heads of Government at the end of the "World Summit for Children" held in New York in 1990 acknowledged this terrible situation by saying: "No. 4. Each day, countless children around the world are exposed to dangers that hamper their growth and development. They suffer immensely as casualties of war and violence; as victims of racial discrimination, apartheid, aggression, foreign occupation and annexation; as refugees and displaced children, forced to abandon their homes and their roots; as disabled; or as victims of neglect, cruelty and exploitation". At the same time, a new and extremely harmful pattern has developed over the last decades: the dissemination of landmines. In military language, they are called "anti-personnel" devices, but they mainly affect the civilian population.

Influence and Attitudes of Other People

The attitudes and behaviour of society in general towards persons with an impairment can be of primary importance in the process leading to permanent disability or, in contrast, to rehabilitation measures. Perhaps the best example is that of deafness and hearing impairment, as illustrated by Susan R. Hammerman, a specialist from Rehabilitation International. She states: " For generations, the myth of mutism has been united with concepts of deafness; in some languages the word to describe a deaf person carries the double meaning of speechlessness, and in some instances stupidity as well. It is not difficult to understand the aura of hopelessness which surrounds deafness in such circumstances and the fact that family members assume their deaf child incapable of speech".What are the facts, as proved by medical science?

1. "Mutism, the inability to utter sound, is a very rare condition indeed, just as is the total inability to hear any sound. Most deaf people have some degree of

residual hearing, particularly in the lower sound frequencies, which with training they can learn to use in understanding the sounds of the world around them, as well as in understanding and producing speech".

2. "The critical period for auditory stimuli is generally considered to be until 8 months of age, and the sensitive period extends until 18 months of age".
3. "Language learning peaks for a child at 3 to 4 years of age (and) considerable research documents the relationship of language development to cognition".
4. Therefore, "..the earlier the hearing-impaired child is identified and the earlier remedial measures are instituted, the greater is the likelihood of successful learning".
5. As a consequence of the early detection, "...hearing aids and auditory training can be of benefit to almost all deaf and hearing-impaired people".

However, the tragic reality is that the majority of hearing-impaired children live in developing countries and lack access to any type of rehabilitative assistance. This dramatic picture has been illustrated by research carried out by Rehabilitation International: "Their families receive no information about their conditions whatsoever; there is no place for them to turn for advice as to what they might do to improve the situation of their children.

The result is that the parents have no expectations that anything can be done to improve the life of their child, seeking only a cure for his or her condition; the child, after years deprived of sound and other forms of social and educational stimulation, may be less emotionally mature than his or her brothers and sisters, less able to cope with new and strange situations, perhaps being grouped with other children considered to be slow or retarded, and worst of all, brought for attention too late -at a time in life well past the critical learning periods for language, speech and sound discrimination". This is perhaps one of the most clear examples of how an initial impairment can be transformed into a permanent disability and handicap through lack of knowledge, incorrect assumptions, lack of early detection and stimulation, and the absence of appropriate and timely rehabilitation measures.

Literacy and Disability awareness Training Programme

Literacy is a very important issue for people with disabilities. Many people with disabilities do not have the opportunity to become adequately educated and either cannot read or write or have low literacy skills. Our society is defined and functions by the written word. When people have trouble reading and writing they have difficulty participating fully in society. They don't have the opportunity to voice their opinions. It is difficult to find and keep a job. Many people who have low literacy skills live in poverty. Many people with disabilities are not employed and live in poverty because of a number of systemic societal barriers. Not being able to read or write at a functional literate level is one more strike against them.

The mission of Independent Living is, "to promote and enable the progressive process of citizens with disabilities to take responsibility for the development and management of personal and community resources". This means that people with disabilities should be able to participate as fully as they want in their respective communities. Without literacy skills consumers are not a ble to participate. If Independent Living Resource Centres are to achieve their goal of enabling people with disabilities to live independently within their respective communities, then literacy must be a priority. ILRCs must be committed to reaching out to people with disabilities who have low literacy skills. Centres must be committed to promoting literacy programs within their communities that include people with disabilities.

When seeking the proper literacy education programs, literacy workers need to be aware of the barriers facing persons with disabilities as well as general disability issues. There are many definitions of literacy. Literacy means different things to different people. People's experiences help them to develop their own definition of literacy. For some people literacy is being able to read the newspaper. Another person may think that reading street signs means that a person is literate. Still, other people may feel that they are not computer literate. Literacy is a personal matter.

For most people, the word literacy means reading the alphabet. Literacy can also mean reading Blissymbols, Braille, symbols, numbers, signs, communication boards and countless other forms of communication. The United Nations Economic, Scientific and Cultural Organization (UNESCO) defined literacy in terms of basic literacy and functional literacy, According to UNESCO, a person has basic literacy skills if they can, "read and write a short simple statement on their everyday life".

If a person has a low writing and reading level then they have basic literacy skills. According to the 1990 Canadian Census, 7% of Canadians cannot read, and 9% of Canadians can only read basic words. Functionally literate people can use reading and writing skills to work and live in their community. The UNESCO definition, developed by William S. Gray, states that a person is functionally literate when they have, "acquired the knowledge and skills in reading and writing which enables the individual to engage in all those activities in which literacy is normally assumed in their culture or group." In other words, functional literacy means that a person can get by on a daily basis without too much trouble.

Many people accept that the completion and understanding of grade nine is the minimum level of functional literacy. In Canada, there are over three million people who have not finished grade nine. Most jobs require more than a grade nine education and in most jobs you do have to use reading and writing skills.

In Broken Words, the Southam Survey found that the following tasks can easily be completed by people who are functionally literate,

— Read and understand the right dosage from an ordinary bottle of cough syrup (10% of Canadian residents cannot do this)

— From 6 road signs, pick out the sign which warns of a traffic light ahead (13% of Canadian residents cannot do this)

— Circle the long distance charges on a telephone bill (29% of Canadian residents cannot do this)

— Figure out the change from $3.00 if you order soup (33% of Canadian residents cannot do this)

— Find a store in the Yellow Pages (50% of Canadian residents cannot do this)

The Canadian Census tried to measure the percentage of Canadians who are not functionally literate. Statistics Canada used the UNESCO measurement of functional literacy which is the completion of grade nine level of education. The Census reported that 24% of Canadians have completed less than a grade nine level of education. As well they reported that 7% of the Canadian population cannot read or write. When the Census looked specifically at people with disabilities within the population, it found that 38.2% have not completed a grade nine level of education and 66% of developmentally disabled individuals are functionally illiterate.

Keep in mind that while these statistics are useful to gain a national perspective they may not represent the population of a particular community. Remember that while the Canadian Census looks at the number of-people out of 100 that fit into a particular category, the Independent Living Resource Centre must deal with individuals and each individual's situation is unique.

Barriers to Literacy

There are many reasons why the numbers of people with disabilities who are do not read at a functional literacy level are so high. Unfortunately, there are numerous barriers which prevent people from becoming literate or improving their literacy skills. Often a person is confronted with a combination of barriers. An individual acting alone can have great difficulty overcoming these barriers. ILRCs can become involved in helping to remove these barriers from literacy programs within the community. The first step is to recognize that these barriers exist.

There are physical barriers to learning which exist for people with disabilities. The most obvious physical barrier is a building that is inaccessible. In some cases the building may be accessible but activities that take place outside the classroom are held in places that are inaccessible. Books, computers and other resources may be kept out of reach of a consumer.

A barrier to learning that exists for many people are family responsibilities. Some literacy programs offer child care at the program for children of students in adult literacy classes. There are also adult students who are the primary caregiver for their elderly parents. If they are unable to get someone to help with this responsibility then they are not able to leave home to go to school. Many people, in most cases women, have additional family responsibilities that act as a barrier to returning to school or entering a tutor program. There are few literacy programs that offer attendant care services. An attendant assists with the personal needs of the consumer, if asked to do so by the consumer. The attendant may assist with feeding, toileting, note-taking and page turning.

In many cities and rural areas there is inadequate public transportation for consumers. Where transportation does exists it can be expensive. There are literacy programs that offer transportation to and from the literacy classes. However, these shuttle buses may not be accessible. There are barriers to learning which are based on community attitudes. People may label consumers and, wrongly, believe that consumers can not learn. Society is lacking relevant information about people with disabilities.

Many tutors express a fear of working with a consumer. The tutors believe that they do not have the skills to teach a person with a disability and that they lack relevant information. This barrier is often the most difficult to overcome for people with disabilities who wish to gain literacy skills. It is much easier to build a ramp or renovate a washroom than to change someone's attitude.

Community barriers to increasing an individual's literacy level may also include access to resources. Literacy programs may not have access to large type materials and alternative format materials. There are technological aids that can assist a consumer in increasing his or her literacy level. These include computer programs which can translate Blissymbols into English, page turners, book stands, resources to take notes and TTYITTD (telephone device for the deaf).

Another barrier is the personal barriers that many people face when going back to school. For people who have a low literacy level, school (if they had the opportunity to attend) may have been a bad experience.

People may have been labelled or told that they would never learn. People may have been segregated into special classes and not had the same opportunity to learn to read as their peers. For these and countless other reasons people may be afraid to go back to school.

Communication Barriers

For some people with disabilities overcoming these barriers is only the beginning. For people who are deaf or non-verbal, finding an adequate literacy program is the next hurdle. Communication is a basic component of literacy and people who are deaf or non-verbal communicate by methods other than speaking and hearing. Therefore, gaining literacy skills becomes particularly difficult.

Communication is a necessity for full participation in this society. Many people who communicate by methods other than speaking and hearing are isolated from mainstream society. The basic tool that literacy teachers use, communication by speaking and hearing, cannot be used. This issue warrants further discussion.

Literacy and People who are Deaf, Deafened, Hearing Impaired and Hard-of-Hearing Deaf means a person born with a "profound hearing loss". Most people who are deaf go to special schools and use American sign language (ASL) or langue des signes Quebecoise in Quebec (LSQ) to communicate. These people make up the "deaf community".

People who lose their hearing after they learn primary language skills are called Deafened. Their needs depend on when they lost their hearing and how much of their hearing they lost. Deafened people may learn ASLJLSQ and become part of the deaf community. Other Deafened people will use hearing aids and other aids to help them hear and speak. Hearing impairment is any type of hearing loss. Some people want to be called hearing impaired instead of deaf. These people probably don't use sign language.

It is also important to know that one third of people with hearing loss have another disability. Many people with hearing loss have trouble speaking and they may have trouble reading and writing. Most adult deaf people read at a grade 3-5 level. There are different explanations on why this occurs. Some people think that if deaf people had better training in speaking and hearing they would be able to read and write better. This is called the oral view.

Some people think that if deaf people were taught Sign Language in the school system they would be able to read and write better. They think deaf people are not taught enough language skills when they are young. Other people think that deaf people have trouble reading and writing because they can't hear themselves read. These people think that language skills are learned by hearing and speaking and you have to have language skills to learn to read and write. Many people are trying to find out why deaf people have trouble reading and writing. Probably each of the views is partially correct. An awareness of all of the views is important.

Most deaf people will use writing as a way to communicate on a daily basis to write short notes to ask and answer questions. If they cannot lip -read then they will read notes. Low literacy skills are a barrier to communication for people who rely on writing and reading notes. Adult deaf people who use Sign Language and have trouble reading and writing need to be able to communicate to participate fully in society. To talk to deaf people on the phone a TDD/TDY (telephone device for the deaf) is used. To talk to people who are deaf face -to-face a sign language interpreter is needed. If you don't have a TDD/TDY then the 1-800 Bell telephone operator can provide assistance. It is important to know about local deaf clubs and the local chapter of the Canadian Association of the Deaf (CAD). All provinces have one or more programs to help deaf adults read and write.

In the classes, deaf adults learn to read and write by learning more Sign Language. The language used in these classes is ALS\LSQ.There is another kind of sign language called Signed English or Manually Coded English, but it is very limited. Many teachers and professionals like this kind of sign language. The deaf community prefers ASL. People who are deaf learn by methods different from those used by people who can hear. Trying to use the same methods may make people who are deaf feel inadequate because they may have difficulty learning in this manner. New ways of teaching deaf people in Canada to learn to read and write are being developed.

The inability to communicate effectively through speech occurs for a wide range of reasons. This can include persons with a physical disability, a developmental disability, or people who have had a stroke. The nature and degree of speech difficulty will vary from person to person. Many people who cannot communicate through speech have been denied the opportunity to learn how to read and write. They are often not accepted in mainstream schools. Many teachers or literacy workers feel they are not qualified to teach people who are non-verbal. To have effective communication there must be at least two participants, a sender and a receiver.

People who are non-verbal have ways of communicating; however, many people do not understand the methods used. For example, a person may use gestures such as blinking or looking up or down to communicate common messages such as "yes" or "no". There are a number of devices that a person who is non -verbal can use to help communicate. These include Communication

Boards which feature a variety of written or graphic symbols representing words, ideas, or phrases. Bliss is a well known communication system which uses graphic images.

A person using a Communication Board points to a picture, phrase, or series of letters and the reader must interpret the message out loud. There are a variety of electronic communication devices which have an electronic voice and are known as Alternative Augmentative Communication Systems. They may use graphics, pictures, words or a regular keyboard. There are a number of computer programs that have speech synthesizers. A learner may need to have literacy skills to use the program. However computer programs can be used to further develop literacy skills.

It is important that an instructor or tutor become familiar with the particular communication system a non-verbal learner uses. It is also important to remember that communication by the methods described above wilt be slower than communicating by speaking. Patience on the part of both the learner and instructor is necessary.

How can Independent Living Resource Centres assist people who do not read or write or have low literacy skills? The first step is identification. Many people who cannot read or write or have low literacy skills will not identify themselves. A person who has difficulty reading or writing will have created compensation strategies in order to participate in the community. Often people with low reading and writing skills have developed an excellent memory.

If you suspect that someone has low reading skills, do not confront them directly. People try to hide their low reading skills. Many people are embarrassed and reluctant to talk about their reading level and their learning experiences. By bringing the issue up directly with a person they may be intimidated and not return to your centre. If you have a good rapport with a consumer, who you suspect does not read or write well, you may decide to talk about upgrading options. At this point it is important to supply information without being judgemental. Be sure to listen carefully to all decisions made by a consumer. Be positive and reassuring. Making the decision to go back to school or to enter a pre - employment program is a major decision. It can be quite an emotional experience for an adult. The following are signs of a low level or non reader:

— "forgets their glasses" at home
— spends too much, or not enough time looking at written materials
— detailed, written instructions are followed incorrectly
— misses appointments or arrives at the wrong time
— information is from a friend, boss or T.V., not from a newspaper or magazine
— memorizes tasks rather than writing them down
— asks several times for oral instructions to be repeated
— pieces of paper are stuffed into pockets, person says, "I'll read them later"
— watches what is said, not what is written
— asks other people to fill out forms, returns forms later
— has difficulty with public transportation (street signs, bus numbers)
— watches others before beginning an assignment

If you think that someone may have low reading and writing skills you may decide to offer information. Remember that the person has probably spent a great deal of energy hiding their literacy skill level. People who are supported and encouraged may choose to enter an adult education program. The decision belongs to the individual.

Your role should take on a supportive capacity. Once a person has decided that they wish to enter an adult education program they may come to the Centre for information.

Before referring any person to a literacy program, volunteers or staff of-the Centre should conduct research into the literacy programs offered in their community: What programs are available in the community? What type of clientele are served? Are the organizations aware of the differing needs of people with disabilities? What approach does the organization take to teaching literacy skills? The staff at the ILRC must always keep in mind the requirements and preferences of the individual.

The Independent Living Resource Centres (ILRC) provide a service to citizens with disabilities within the community. In order to serve the community the Centres must clearly communicate information. Therefore consumers will all have equal access to the information. The Centres should provide a comfortable non-intimidating environment. A good way to do this is to conduct a literacy assessment of the Independent Living Resource Centre. When the assessment is complete follow up with changes. The Centre should have a policy to only produce materials in Clear Language.

Clear Language

Clear Language may also be called: plain writing, plain English, clear writing or readability. Using Clear Language will make written work easier to understand. Using Clear Language makes materials more comfortable to read for all readers. People who have difficulty with written materials will be able to read Clear Language documents easier than documents written in fancy language. People who are good readers will not be questioning what the writer really means to say.

The material that is written in Clear Language is not dull or childish. It does not insult the reader. Rather, Clear Language is direct and focuses on relevant information. When readers look at written work, the first thing they notice is the layout. A document, pamphlet or newsletter that is written in Clear Language will have:

— white space - space where there is no graphics or text

— relevant graphics and illustrations

— simple and clear design

— larger rather than smaller type size

— dark type on light paper (the best choice is black print on white paper)

— no more than 3 type styles

— justification on the left side only

— no words that are hyphenated

Well organized information on a page will increase the clarity of a document. An organized page is easy to follow and understand. An organized document will have:

— one idea for each sentence

— one idea for each paragraph

— short sentences, no longer that 25 words

— titles and spaces to direct the reader

— important information at the beginning of a paragraph

— enough information

Clear Language uses words that are common and familiar. Be sure to choose words that do not exclude the reader.

Designing a Disability Awareness Workshop

Several stages to be followed are suggested when designing a Disability Awareness Workshop. This is true whether the workshop is for two hours, a full day or a two day session. These steps are important to follow because they assist the facilitator in having a clear understanding of what occurs during the sessions and why it is occurring.

It is vital that the participants have ownership over their own learning process. The Program Design Model ensures that the participants have ownership in the whole process, starting with the Needs Assessment. It is important that the needs are identified by the participants. The original idea may come from the Centre or another source, but the participants must be able to say, "Yes, I am interested in learning about that." If the participants are not interested, or do not identify this as a need, then the workshop might not be successful.

The Program Design should be initiated two months before the workshop date. The steps of the Program Design are:

— Needs Assessment
— Setting Objective
— Planning
— Implementing
— Processing
— Evaluation

Needs Assessment:A Needs Assessment is conducted to find out if there is a need or desire for a particular service, in this case a Disability Awareness Workshop for literacy workers. There are several ways to carry out a Needs Assessment. The method that is chosen will depend on the size of the group, the structure of the group, the location and other resources that are available. Some methods for gathering information for a Needs Assessment are:

— personal interviews
— group interviews
— questionnaires

— group discussions

— knowledge and skill tests

— self-interest and self-identified

The following is an example of a Needs Assessment Questionnaire completed by a literacy program. A blank copy of this Needs Assessment follows the completed one. This assessment questionnaire could be photocopied or used as a guideline when developing one.

Objective Setting: Once the needs have been identified, the Objective can be set. The Objective is what is hoped to be achieved by providing the workshop. This will clarify the desired outcome of the workshop. This statement should be clear, concise and specific. The Objective Statement must also be realistic. There can be more than one Objective to the Workshop.

Examples of Objectives are:

— To increase the literacy instructors' understanding of issues facing people with disabilities.

— To identify resources in the community that literacy instructors can access.

Planning: During the planning phase the workshop activities are designed. When completed, the activities will ensure that the Objective(s) is met. There are three phases in the planning process.

— *Planning the workshop activities*: This may include brainstorming about resources, speakers and audio - visual aids. Determine how much time will be allocated to each activity. Decide how people will be arranged in the room. Think through the clear instructions that you will give to the participants. Test the activities with a co-worker.

— *Planning the learning*: Design questions to get people to think about what they have learned. Design methods which will ensure feedback.

— *Panning the Evaluation*: The Evaluation is essential. From a well designed Evaluation, improvements can be made for the next workshop. Decide how you will carry out the evaluation. It could be a written questionnaire, verbal response or a discussion.

Implementing: At this point the workshop is conducted. Remember:

— The workshop is based on an identified need

— The activities are designed to meet the Objectives

— Trust the planning process

— Be flexible, anything can happen to change the plan, but remember the objectives

Processing: This step assists participants to learn from the experience. Questions that are designed to make people think about what they have learned will be a good starting ground for discussion. Be aware of the group dynamics and the needs of the group as well as the Learning Objectives. This will ensure that the group stays on track.

Evaluation: There are two reasons for doing an Evaluation. The Evaluation will give structured feedback to the facilitators of the group. The Evaluation will also tell if the workshop achieved the Objective and met the Needs of the participants.

6

Guidance and Counselling for Disabled Persons

School counsellors, regular classroom teachers, school support personnel as well as community therapists and counsellors may all eventually deal with individuals who have a disability. With the focus on mainstreaming physically and mentally disabled students into the regular classroom whenever appropriate and possible, classroom teachers and school counsellors who have had no special education training are brought face to face with individuals with disabilities. This encounter may challenge some attitudes which the teacher, counsellor and support staff may never had to give thought to until it happens. This section focuses on some attitudinal and psychological harriers which are placed in the way of the student with a disability, and offers some solutions.

The presence of a physical disability certainly means that an individual must deal with special concerns and problems because of the disability, and that the environment must often be altered so that the individual has the best opportunity possible to function normally. An individual with a disability may have learned to cope well with the problems caused by the disability if help is needed it may be due to other problems from other sources.

A disability can be defined as an inability to perform a certain task. Some individuals cannot walk, some cannot talk, some cannot see—and there are tasks associated with each ability that those individuals cannot perform.

A handicap is not so easily defined; poverty can be handicap, lack of education can be a handicap. Handicaps have more to do with the environment than the individual. In an adjusted environment a person with a disability has no handicap.

These definitions are somewhat interchangeable, and for the sake of not repeating the same word over and over again, one is often used in place of the other. Yet, there is much truth to the two definitions which help define our attitude toward disability.

Attitudes and Psychological Behavior

Attitude and the use of language which reflects our attitudes may be a bigger burden than the individual's physical disability. Anyone who will be dealing with an individual with a disability must first come to understand what their own attitude towards disability is, where it came from and how to deal with the attitude in a more positive manner.

Language reflects how we think, and the use of language has effect on attitude; in this paper I have made every effort to reflect a positive image of disability. The phrase "person with a disability" focuses on the person, first, who has a disability second. Phrases like "confined to a wheelchair" seem negative beside "uses a wheelchair for mobility", and the wholesale term "the disabled" is much less personal and individual than "people who have disabilities". The use of the more positive and personal description reflects our concern with the person.

Attitudes may be thought of as positive or negative emotional reactions to an object, accompanied by specific beliefs. People hold many attitudes toward a wide range of topics, in varying intensities. The strength of the attitude often depends on early learning experiences, available factual information, influence of significant others and the beliefs of the larger community.

Less than a decade ago, researchers were concluding "that more than 504 of the people surveyed express slightly positive attitudes toward disabled people" and "research demonstrates generally negative and stereotypical attitudes from the general public toward the disabled". Since then, individuals like Terry Fox and Rick Hansen have positively affected the world view of what persons with disabilities can accomplish. As well, the media and government have paid attention, generally, to language used to describe the person with a disability. Such changes have come about through the efforts of the disabled themselves; legislation concerning education and employment also has effect on the behavior of the system.

The general view of the person with a disability is less intelligent, less happy, less likable than a "normal" person. Such negative attitudes are usually based on myth, false assumptions and stereotypes. Stereotypical views of people with disabilities are that the person is different, which contributes to social isolation.

Self Concept

Self concept is created largely through our interaction with others. The feedback we receive from those with whom we interact give us a picture of ourselves as cheerful, shy, friendly, etc. Some of this feedback comes from the non-verbal messages we receive, such as facial expression, and body language. Society' expectations of us shape our behavior. Many individuals with disabilities learn early in life that they have a negative role in this society. They have received negative feedback about their worth, both verbally and non-verbally. Their response is often passivity, rigid thinking, and failure to take part in life — because the expectations placed on the individual with a disability are negative.

Negative attitude can be more debilitating and damaging to a person than the physical disability itself. School aged youth, who are involved in the development of self identity, learning social skills as well as academic growth are most susceptible to devaluation by their peers and adults around them. When a child's interaction is limited to their family that experience may be supportive and non-threatening. Because the environment has been supportive, they may not perceive themselves as disabled; as the child's world grows larger, the generally negative attitude that society holds towards disability has its effect on the individual.

Rejection by peers has a profound negative effect on self confidence and self esteem. Avoidance by peers and teachers, coupled with lowered expectations by adults about them all hamper motivation to achieve and participate.

Peer Attitude

The first and major influence on the child is the family, the next most important environment is school. When the child with a disability enters the regular classroom, it may be their first non-family contact, as well as their first experience in a non-special classroom filled with able bodied peers.

The initial response, on both sides, may be apprehension due to an unfamiliar situation. Students with disabilities may be isolated or rejection by their peers, and in general, the more visible the handicap, the more rejection and isolation. Because children are generally concerned with physical skills and activities, perhaps being unable to take part means, to the student's pears, that the child is incapable of any activity.

Educator Attitude

The effect of teacher attitude has been well studied, but the effect of counselor attitude has received less attention. We know from research that teacher attitude has considerable impact on students; eye contact and conscious or unconscious positive reinforcement all effect how students respond. The expectation of the teacher has positive or negative effect on the student; the child with a disability is no different in their responses to their teacher. If a teacher has fears, holds stereotypes about disability, or has lowered expectations of a student who has a disability, these are conveyed to the student, who responds with apathy, lowered self-expectations and a feeling of helplessness.

Thirty years ago, handicapped individuals in a regular school system were viewed as different and unable to meet regular goals in school. Rules, then, were changed for the person with a disability. The advent of the '60s and '70s saw less emphasis on special education, especially separate education, and the beginning of legislation regarding mainstreaming physically disabled children into regular school.

Simply legislating the rights of handicapped individuals to receive education alongside their able bodied peers does not take care of the problems which plague regular classroom teachers. Lack of preparation time, overcrowded classes and inadequate time schedules are problems for all teachers, but the addition of a student with a disability into the classroom intensifies the problems with time and discipline all teachers have.

Regular classroom teachers, unlike special education teachers, rarely have exposure to students with disabilities. Any introduction to disabilities may have been through texts which present stereotypical views of disabilities as "problems". The text may focus on low intellect, low achievement and disruptive behavior of special students with disabilities; such labeling and stereotyping may lead regular teachers to believe that students with disabilities will be difficult to teach. This may result in lowered expectations in many areas, including social skills. If a student has been previously labeled, reduced expectations may be the result.

When a teacher is faced with a student with a disability, that teacher must have a willingness to accept such a student into their classroom. Teacher's educational backgrounds and knowledge about disabilities is a factor in development of positive attitudes. In-service training to develop teacher skills are seen by regular classroom teachers as useful, and in-service training has a positive impact on attitude change.

Counsellor attitudes to Disability

We can assume that counsellors and teachers, like other humans, have both negative and positive attitudes towards disability, and have had both negative and positive experiences. A counsellor or teacher who will be dealing with students with disabilities must examine their attitudes closely prior to contact. Honorable intentions to help will be useless if the unspoken attitude is negative, or one of pity or dismay. The unspoken attitude is more likely to be conveyed clearly through body language, actions and non-verbal communication.

The job of teaching positive attitude to a student's peers cannot leave the counselor or teacher unaffected. If a teacher or counsellor is gathering together accurate information about specific disabilities, they come to know more and more about how negative attitude affects the person with the disability. In fact, any school personnel who deals with a student with a disability can be perceived as a role model for all students and the task of a role model is a serious one.

Attitude is a major factor in dealing successfully with a student with a disability. Not only must the counsellor or teacher come to terms with their personal attitude toward disability, but they must also foster a positive environment which would allow change in negative attitude. This may be done by direct intervention through programming, workshops and in-servicing of fellow professionals. Such programs and in-services would focus on overcoming negative attitudes and may be presented to the student's peers, teachers, counsellors, administrators and school support staff.

Making Attitude Changes

Two general means of changing negative attitudes according to Lomhana are contact with persons with disabilities and the dissemination of accurate information about specific disabilities. Interaction between persons who have disabilities and non-disabled people is vital to reverse the strongly entrenched social stereotypes. The differences are minimized when disabled and able bodied people interact; anxiety and fears on both sides lessen. Exposure through such organized events as panel discussion with panelists who are disabled but active and independent can do much to educate the able bodied about the day to day barriers faced by persons with disabilities.

Contact is most effective when prolonged and on a personal, interactive level. A creative counsellor or teacher can find many well designed programs available through the school system to foster positive contact, or can approach individuals and associations in the community to help them do so.

Information

Accurate, clear information about specific disabilities can decrease anxiety and increase awareness. Teachers and counsellors may become less fearful of dealing with disabilities when supported by access to accurate information. Myths and misinformation can be dispelled and confidence can be fostered. Personal information about the experience of the person with a disability can also point out that human problems are all the same and that people with disabilities and able bodied people are more alike than different. Adolescent and adult literature written about or by persons with disability can be used as a resource to educate and change attitude.

Contact Plus Information

To foster the most positive environment for changing negative attitude to positive, a combination of contact and information is best. A program or in-service which includes information plus personal contact with persons with disability, such as a speaker or a visit by a person with a disability, makes for a lasting change of attitude.

Counselor Role in Attitude Change

It is often the school counselor's job to provide in-service training and information about disability attitudes and resources for the classroom teacher. If the classroom teachers feel competent and well supported, they may be more willing to accept students with disabilities and have a more positive attitude toward disability in general. Attitudes are complex. because of the influence that attitudes have on the individual, counsellors as well as teachers need to be ready to foster positive attitudes toward persons with disabilities.

In an ideal society, all would accept one another despite differences; but we are not yet in an ideal society. Negative attitudes exist, and are often thoughtlessly promoted and expressed. They have a profound effect on the individual. Some attitudes which are negative are often not overly expressed, but are evident in negative behavior.

It is often the action rather than the word which carries the message.

Counsellors, teachers, and other educational support personnel need to understand and come to terms with their own attitudes regarding disability. To be able to deal effectively with persons with disabilities, the counsellor and teacher needs to realize that their attitudes will come through to the student with a disability in both verbal and non-verbal ways. Teachers and counsellors need to have a clear understanding of various disabilities, what the effect of the disability may have on the person, and at the same time know that individuals with disabilities have common human needs and are more alike than different.

As well as understanding and coming to terms with their own personal attitude, the effective counsellor and teacher must have an understanding of how individuals with disabilities, and their families, cope with life with a handicap.

Myths and Misconceptions

All humans have basic needs of security, affection, belonging and achievement. There are two myths surrounding disability that most counsellors, teachers and the general public have come to believe. The first myth is that the existence of a disability makes the person with the disability different from able bodied people. The second myth is that having a disability makes all persons with disabilities the same. Neither is true, though there are certain differences in how people cope with the environment when a disability is present, and there are certainty common experiences among people who have similar disabilities. To counsel persons with disabilities and be helpful, teachers and school counsellors will have to identify the true counselling needs of students with disabilities.

Counseling Needs

Many persons with disabilities successfully come to terms with the disability, particularly those with conditions which began at birth. Their counselling needs will center around normal developmental concerns which students in their age group may normally have. Other students with disabilities may have issues which are generated because of the presence of a disability, such as issues about body image, self concept and attitudes of others towards them. They may have family problems due to the disability which are more 'debilitating' than the physical handicap.

Personal Adjustment to Disability

Personal adjustment to disability is closely linked to the reactions of the student's parents, family members and society at large. Adjustment and acceptance to disability is affected by the way society adjusts and accepts the person who has a disability.

The person with a disability needs to see the disability as a part of them, not the whole. Handicapping conditions can overwhelm the entire self concept; when this happens, the person often develops unnecessary psychological dependence on others, feelings of depression, loss of motivation, and a feeling of powerlessness. The disability becomes the focus of the individual's life, their whole identity. The disability becomes the reason they cannot achieve, are not loved, do not belong. The focus of counselling may be, in this case, to help the individual identify all the other things they are, their strengths, and take the emphasis off the disability.

Ignoring the Disability

At the other end of the Spectrum from the disability being the total focus of the person's life, the individual may deny the existence of the disability. They desire to he "just like everyone else". Plans and dreams are made without taking into account the effect of the disability. No coping strategies can be developed if the disability is denied, and constant failures to accomplish what has been planned lead to frustration, anger and unnecessary problems and delays. The individual who denies the existence of a disability, or denies the severity of it often places themselves in situations which are destined for failure. The focus of counselling in this case may be to help the individual find their true limitations and match their interests and skills with ability.

Coping or Not?

When does the counsellor know that an individual is coping well with a disability? There are some positive signs that tell a counsellor whether or not an individual is coping positively with life, according to Roesseler and Bolton (1978), in their text "Psychosocial Adjustment to Disability".

Signs of Coping:

1. The individual's values enlarge to encompass more than their personal disability and its effect on them.
2. The effects of the disability are contained and the individual is open to learning new skills to help overcome their limitations.
3. The disability is seen as an inconvenience, and is not seen as devaluing the person's worth.
4. Other values are more important than physical perfection; kindness, wisdom, effort are seen as important.
5. The individual realizes that not all life is determined by disability.
6. Individuals stop comparing themselves with outside sources and look to inward assets and begin to develop them

Counsellors and teachers who deal with individuals with disabilities should also be sensitive to signs that a person is not coping positively with their disability. Any individual with a disability, considering all that they may have to deal with on a daily basis, may on occasion succumb to feeling of being overwhelmed and cannot cope for a short period of time. Some individuals may be completely overcome by the feeling of not being able to cope, and there are some signals which suggest that the individual is not coping well.

Signs of not coping:

1. Individuals act as if the disability did not exist, and no effort is made to accommodate for the disability.
2. Normal standards are idolized.
3. What an individual can accomplish, what they physically can do, is ignored. New skills are not accepted as valuable.
4. Deficiencies are compensated for by exaggerated striving. This puts extra stress on the individual to overachieve in some specific area — and this is often encouraged and praised by adults as being good.

Counselor Role in Personal Adjustment

Counsellors and teachers can he supportive to the individual as the person with a disability evaluates themselves. Counsellors can challenge the student at the appropriate developmental level and teachers can provide success oriented training. The most important thing to remember is that the person is an individual and that needs are individual. One of the most difficult thoughts to keep in mind is that the person with a disability has human needs and has a right to choose wrongly, a right to fail and a right to suffer.

Right to Choose

Like all human beings, people with disabilities have

the right to decide what is right for them, and when the environment is supportive they also may have their own manner of doing things. This idea may cause friction between the individual and the helpers when the non-disabled feels the need to impose their ways of functioning on the person with the disability. Counsellors and teachers must be ready to broaden their view of how things are done and be ready to accept the individual's way of accomplishing the task.

Counsellors, teachers and parents are more effective when they remember that the individual with a disability also has the right to honest information about their condition, about their ability to do and achieve. False praise, false hope and false dreams may do more damage than good. Honesty about the disability and its effects does more than pretense about what the disability is and what its limitations may be.

Implicit in all counselling is the belief that the individual has the right and ability to determine the course of their life. The counsellor or teacher must have respect for the individual's feelings and allow them responsibility for their own actions. Fostering independence rather than dependence is the key to the individual's success as they take part in living their life.

Factors Affected by Disability

Following are the factors affected by disability:

Maturity

Students with physical handicaps may be generally less mature than non-handicapped students. This may be due to social isolation and opportunity to interact with peers of the same age.

Relationships

Persons with disabilities may have more problems establishing social relationships. This may be due to social isolation as well, but may also be affected by society's view of what qualities a person should have.

Emotions

Children with disabilities experience greater anxiety, conflict and defensiveness, and may he more inhibited than non-handicapped children. This, in part, may be due to their experience with negative attitudes of peers and significant others.

Knowing about specific disabilities is important for the counselor or teacher since characteristics of specific disabilities can limit a person's physical or academic ability, and directly effect the individual's self concept and body image. Some general assumptions may be made about specific disabilities, which can serve as a starting point to counselling. Identifying such things as methods of positive or negative coping skills may help the counsellor, but it is best to keep in mind that it is the existence of the disability which has the greater impact than the type or severity of the physical involvement.

Learned Helplessness

A problem which counsellors and teachers should be alerted to is the possibility that the individual with a disability is overcome with a feeling of helplessness. This syndrome is a theory of Martin Seligman. Seligman's basic theory is that the experience of not being able to control the environment, or learning that events are uncontrollable, leads to a psychological state of helplessness, which may not be related to the real ability of the individual. If a person comes to believe that his or her actions will not affect the environment, the likelihood that they will even attempt a response decreases, and the attitude will become "Why bother? It won't make any difference what I do." If actions have no effect, the next logical step is to cease all action.

If a child learns early in life that outcomes are independent of their response or request, they stop responding and it is difficult in later life to attempt to control situations. The syndrome of learned helplessness has effect on cognitive growth and may cause effective disturbances — the child may seem non-responsive, uninterested in life around them and dull.

The feeling of helplessness is self perpetuating. Anxiety, frustration or fear is the result. If the feelings of no control persist, depression may be the end result. Learned helplessness undermines motivation and retards the ability to perceive success. Seligman believes that motivation and emotion are influenced by environment. A child whose environment does not respond to their needs comes to believe in their own helplessness. Being helpless in one situation leads to the feeling of helplessness in another situation — feelings of learned helplessness are frequently transferred to other settings.

This learned helplessness has behaviors which a counsellor or teacher may observe. Individuals, and their families, may have been in countless situations in which they have no choices, in which their desires have no effect on the outcome. As a result, they have learned to react with helplessness and this may transfer to situations in which decisions must be made or action must be taken.

Symptoms of Learned Helplessness.

1. Few voluntary responses, only answers to direct inquiries.
2. Negative thinking and difficulty learning how to act to effect the outcome.
3. Passivity in all situations.
4. Increase of all of the above over time.
5. Depressed appetite, sexual interest, less socialization, lack of self care, no desire to put out any energy.

6. Physiological changes such as weight loss or gain.

Seligman feels that learned helplessness has its roots in infant development for the child with a disability. When an infant's environment responds, the child has a sense of mastery The helplessness syndrome can result from separation from mother, from stimulus deprivation due to isolation, or from a combination of these things. Individuals experiencing reactions to grief and loss may also exhibit symptoms of the helplessness syndrome.

To overcome the feelings of helplessness, children need warning clues about coming events, such as physically painful treatments, or parent's departure. The child needs to predict events; children can deal with unpleasant events and cope better if they are given a warning and an honest explanation.

What a counsellor or teacher may interpret as apathy on the part of the student with a disability may be more attributed to the helplessness syndrome; what may seem like an inability to learn may be the effect of this syndrome as well.

Adolescent Issues

Though development is effected by disability at each age, adolescents and their families have some special additional problems. Adolescence is the time when individuals are attempting to gain their independence from family and establish their future identity.

Disability as an Excuse

An adolescent may come to use their disability as an excuse to avoid social contact and school. They may become ashamed of their disability, ashamed of being different. They may retreat into a world of home, hospital, or other safe institutions. They may even refuse medication or treatment to bring about a health crisis, so they may regain their safe haven through hospitalization.

Physiotherapy may be refused as well, because of its focus on the disability. This is often done to avoid the critical stares of peers, the questions or comments about the disability.

Attitudes of Others

The opinion of others is important to adolescents. They form their view of self through comments and attitudes of others. The differences of having a disability, using a wheelchair, having problems of muscle control, often stigmatizes the individual, giving rise to feelings of shame. The move from a neighborhood school into a less personal selling of high school can be a devastating experience. Teachers, counsellors, school support staff and parents can help the young adolescent make the transition with support, encouragement and care. Older adolescents may need special attention, helping them find out about themselves, their disability and what they can rather than can't do.

Defense Mechanisms

An adolescent will develop various and personally individual methods of coping with the attitudes of others and their own acceptance or nonacceptance of their disability. Defense mechanisms, methods of making reality more bearable, may include:

— Denial

— Testing Limits

— Challenging Behavior

— Anger

— Regression

— Withdrawal

— Depression

Denial: Adolescents who are physically disabled may use denial as a protection against the devastating emotional effects of disability. Spinal cord injured individuals may refuse to believe that their condition is permanent and refuse to deal with the reality of the paralysis. At this stage, they may refuse to do daily self care, refuse physical treatments.

Denial can be a mechanism of escape — escaping the fear of death or disfigurement. Denial may be, at times, an effective and necessary coping strategy. Care should be taken when asking an individual to face reality. Too soon or too blunt an approach may leave an individual unable to cope with reality "all at once". Rather, strategies which introduce the reality of situation gently may allow for adjustment and gradual acceptance.

Testing Limits: The Stage of adolescence is the time of testing of the limit of abilities, as well as limits set by parent and schools.

Challenging Behavior: The adolescent with a disability may carry this time of testing to the extreme. The individual may attempt things which are impossible and even put themselves in danger. They may refuse medications or supportive medical treatments and actively challenge decisions made by parents.

Anger: Adolescents with a disability may have unexpressed anger and rage at their situation and may act out physically or verbally to teachers, parents, peers or siblings. They may resort to sarcasm and name calling; their rage at their own helplessness and their embarrassment at being disabled and different may be expressed in verbal or physical abuse of others.

Regression: Pain due to disability, dependency on others for daily living tasks, and the obvious physical differences due to disability may combine to make an adolescent with a disability use regression as a coping strategy. It may he easier to retreat to an earlier age than struggle with interdependence. The individual with a disability may lack social skills, and not be used to risk taking; they may seek to be cared for and accept many parents' attempts to keep them dependent and "secure".

The normal adolescent at this stage is achieving more physical and emotional independence from parents; the physically disabled adolescent may be struggling to achieve emotional independence while needing physical dependence. Parents play an immeasurably important role in helping the physically disabled adolescent achieve a realistic, healthy balance between physical dependency and emotional independence.

Withdrawal: Choosing to drop out of school or enter into a very restricted but secure environment, such as a special school or sheltered workshop, may allow an individual a way of withdrawing which is acceptable. They may have little interest in anything, little energy to do even simple, daily routines.

Parents and teachers may accept or even encourage this to protect the individual from stigmatization, feeling that it would be cruel to allow the individual to be faced with a challenge they may fail.

Depression: Times of mild depression may not be uncommon during adolescence. An individual with a disability may have bouts of severe depression.

While focusing on the plans for the future, adolescents may suffer from feelings of loss, and need a time to grieve for a loss of a 'normal future'. Long term depression, including resignation and apathy, may require professional intervention. The individual may speak of suicide. Such threats should be taken seriously. Pat responses such as "you'll get over it", "it's not so bad", "you're not as bad off as some" are not helpful or realistic. The truth is that the disability exists, and it causes problems for the individual, it won't go away. Rather than platitudes, adolescents need alternate coping strategies.

The opposite of challenging behavior, depressive behavior, may occur. Adolescents with a severe disability may feel hopeless and refuse all outside help. The loneliness, boredom and isolation associated with disability may lead to substance abuse, to help them escape a seemingly hopeless reality. Drug abuse may be easy, as the availability of pain medication or anxiety-lessening drugs may be high through prescription misuse.

7

Role of UN in Mainstreaming Disabled

Over the course of the United Nations' first half century, people with disabilities have gone from passively accepting whatever was made available to them to actively asserting strength and confidence in their own abilities to lead self-reliant and independent lives. The following brief history shows how the United Nations' efforts have helped to bring about this transformation.

During 1945 - 1955, its first decade of work in the field of disability, the United Nations promoted a welfare perspective of disability. Concern for the disabled was expressed in the establishment of mechanisms and the development of programmes suitable for dealing with disability issues. Beginning with the promotion of the rights of people with physical disabilities, such as the blind, it concentrated on disability prevention and rehabilitation. The United Nations Secretariat, the Economic and Social Council and its subsidiary organ, the Social Commission, were the principal bodies dealing with disability issues.

In 1950, the Social Commission considered two reports, "Social rehabilitation of the physically handicapped" and "Social rehabilitation of the blind". At the same session, the Social Commission also examined a report by the International Programme for the Welfare of the Blind, which recommended education, rehabilitation, training and employment of the visually handicapped. Later, the Economic and Social Council agreed to establish programmes of rehabilitation for the physically disabled and for the prevention and treatment of blindness.

A conference was convened in Geneva from 26 February to 3 March 1950 to discuss coordination among the specialized agencies in the field of rehabilitation of the disabled. It was attended by the United Nations Secretariat, the ILO, WHO, UNESCO, the International Refugee Organization (IRO), and UNICEF. It led to agreement on the need to establish international standards for the education, treatment, training and placement of disabled persons, with particular emphasis on the needs of the blind in underdeveloped areas.

The focus of the United Nations on disability issues shifted in the late 1950s from a welfare perspective to one of social welfare. A reevaluation of policy in the 1960s led to de-institutionalization and spurred a demand for fuller participation by disabled persons in an integrated society. Operational activities in the field of disability changed through implementation of various United Nations programmes on prevention and rehabilitation. Technical advice was offered to Governments through advisory missions, personnel training workshops and the establishment or improvement of demonstration centres. Information was exchanged through study groups and teaching fellowships and scholarships.

A public information campaign was launched by the United Nations through regular distribution of publications in the newly emerging field of disability policy. The first of a set of works entitled Rehabilitation of the Handicapped was published in the Social Welfare Information series. This special issue outlined the international programme for the rehabilitation of handicapped persons and highlighted programmes, books and films on rehabilitation. In 1956, the International Social Service Review was founded, one of whose objectives was to raise awareness of disability issues and emphasize rehabilitation programmes around the world.

While early United Nations activities supported the rights of persons with disabilities to receive welfare and public services, initially little attention was paid to societal obstacles that might be created by those goals. Starting in the late 1960s, attitudes began shifting towards a new social model for dealing with disability. The Declaration on Social Progress and Development, adopted on 11 December 1969, affirmed the fundamental freedoms and principles set forth in the Charter of the United Nations and emphasized the need to protect the rights and welfare of the disabled and the physically and mentally handicapped.

The 1970s marked a new approach to disability. The concept of human rights for disabled persons began to become more accepted internationally. Two major declarations on the disabled were adopted by the General Assembly in the new decade. The Declaration on the Rights of Mentally Retarded Persons of 20 December 1971, provided a framework for protecting rights through national and international action.

The Declaration stated that mentally retarded persons had, to the degree feasible, the same rights as other human beings, including a right to proper medical care and education, to economic security, to a qualified guardian, as required, to protection from exploitation and to access to legal procedures. The Declaration stated that, if possible, mentally retarded persons should live with their families or with foster parents and should participate in various aspects of community life. Essentially, the Declaration paved the way for future comprehensive sets of principles, which would eventually seek to integrate persons with disabilities into society.

The Declaration on the Rights of Disabled Persons, adopted by the General Assembly on 9 December 1975, encouraged national and international protection of the rights of the disabled. Recognition was given to the fact that disabled persons were entitled to the same political and civil rights as others, including measures necessary to enable them to become self-sufficient. The Declaration reiterated the rights of disabled persons to education, medical services, and placement service. It further recognized their right to economic and social security, to employment, to live with their families, to participate in social and creative events, to be protected against all exploitation, abuse or degrading behaviour, and to avail themselves of legal aid.

Realizing the need to promote the full participation of the disabled in the social life and development of their societies, on 16 December 1976, the General Assembly declared the year 1981 International Year of Disabled Persons (IYDP), stipulating that it be devoted to integrating disabled persons fully into society.

The International Year of Disabled Persons, 1981, was celebrated with numerous programmes, research projects, policy innovations and recommendations. Many conferences and symposiums were held during the Year, including the First Founding Congress of Disabled People International, held in Singapore from 30 November to 6 December. The Trust Fund for the International Year, established in 1977, collected over $510,000 in contributions from member States.

In 1982, the General Assembly took a major step towards ensuring effective follow-up to the International Year by adopting, on 3 December 1982, the World Programme of Action concerning Disabled Persons. The Programme restructured disability policy into three distinct areas: prevention; rehabilitation; and equalization of opportunities.

Implementation of the Programme of Action, using multisectoral and multidisciplinary approaches, was addressed by the General Assembly on 3 December 1982 and 22 November 1983. In a broad sense, implementation would entail long-term strategies integrated into national policies for socio-economic development, preventive activities that would include development and use of technology for the prevention of disablement, and legislation eliminating discrimination regarding access to facilities, social security, education and employment. At the international level, Governments were requested to cooperate with each other, the United Nations and non-governmental organizations.

Together, the Programme and the International Year had launched a new era—one that would seek to define "handicapped" as the relationship between persons with disabilities and their environment. It was imperative that the barriers created by society to full participation by persons with disabilities be removed.

The proclamation in December 1982 of the United Nations Decade of Disabled Persons prompted a flurry of activity designed to improve the situation and status of the disabled. Emphasis was placed on raising new financial resources, improving education and employment opportunities for the disabled, and increasing their participation in the life of their communities and country.

The Sub-Commission on Prevention of Discrimination and Protection of Minorities had included disabled persons in international human rights discourse since its establishment. In 1984, it appointed Leandro Despouy of Argentina as Special Rapporteur to study the connection between human rights violations, violations of fundamental human freedoms and disability. He was to report biannually to the Sub-Commission on the particular human rights situation of disabled persons. His final report in which he recommended the establishment of an international ombudsman was submitted in 1991.

The General Assembly endorsed a continued focus on the objectives of the World Programme of Action with regard to equalization of opportunities for the disabled. The Trust Fund for the International Year of Disabled Persons was to be used to support innovative projects in new and emerging areas regarding disabled persons. With $1.1 million dispersed for 51 projects throughout the world between 1980 and 1985, there was much increased visibility and support for promotional activities, organizations concerned with disability, data collection, research and training.

At this juncture, the United Nations also took itself to task, with the General Assembly noting that persons with disabilities would enjoy the same rights to employment as all other qualified citizens and that the United Nations itself would declare employment opportunities open to all persons, regardless of sex, religion, ethnic origin or disability. In August 1987, a mid-decade review of the United Nations Decade of Disabled persons was conducted at a global meeting of experts in Stockholm, Sweden. The meeting recommended the importance of recognizing the rights of persons with disabilities after the Decade. Since the pace of progress during the first five years had not been as fast as initially expected, the experts agreed that the disability issues should be further addressed within a wider interdisciplinary context—namely, a comprehensive well-coordinated information and evaluation campaign; establishment of a data base on disability; and creation of technical cooperation programmes.

Publication in 1989 of the Tallinn Guidelines for Action on Human Resources Development in the Field of Disability encouraged recognition of disabled persons as agents of their own destiny rather than as dependent objects of Governments. With independence and full integration as goals, the Guidelines encouraged educating disabled persons within the regular school system, in particular, and promoting the teaching of skills to render the disabled economically viable. The Guidelines suggest that training of the disabled should include independent socialization and self-help skills to prepare them for independent living. International development agencies and intergovernmental and regional organizations were encouraged to work together in training the disabled for optimum human resource development.

On 17 December 1991, the General Assembly adopted the Principles for the Protection of Persons with Mental Illness and for the Improvement of Mental Health Care. The twenty-five principles define fundamental freedoms and basic rights. They deal with, inter alia, the right to life in the community, the determination of mental illness, provisions for admission to treatment facilities, and the conditions of mental health facilities. They serve as a guide to Governments, specialized agencies and regional and international organizations, helping them facilitate investigation into problems affecting the application of fundamental freedoms and basic human rights for persons with mental illness. On 16 December 1992, the General Assembly appealed to Governments to observe 3 December of each year as International Day of Disabled Persons. The Assembly further summarized the goals of the United Nations regarding disability and asked the Secretary-General to move from consciousness-raising to action, placing the Organization in a catalytic leadership role which would place disability issues on the agendas of future world conferences. In the same year, the Economic and Social Council endorsed the proclamation of 1993-2002 as Asian and Pacific Decade of Disabled Persons, a decision taken by the Economic and Social Commission of Asia and the Pacific, in order effectively to implement the World Programme of Action in the Asian and Pacific region.

On 20 December 1993 the General Assembly adopted the Standard Rules on the Equalization of Opportunities for Persons with Disabilities. The Rules serve as an instrument by which policy makers can form technical and human rights cooperation within and among States, and between international organizations and governmental agencies. The Rules include a monitoring mechanism to support their implementation. They call for the appointment of a Special Rapporteur who would establish a direct dialogue between Member States, local non-governmental organizations and other intergovernmental bodies in order to implement the Standard Rules. In 1994, Mr. Bengt Lindqvist was appointed Special Rapporteur on Disability of the Commission for Social Development by the Secretary-General.

Recent Developments

The five most recent United Nations world conferences have emphasized the need for a "society for all", advocating the participation of all citizens, including persons with disabilities, in every sphere of society. In 1992, the Rio de Janeiro Conference on Environment and Development encouraged Governments to give more attention to "demographic trends and factors ... that have a critical influence on consumption patterns, production, lifestyles and long-term sustainability." Other conferences advocated social initiatives for people with disabilities to improve health care, universal education, elimination or reduction of violent conflict and a lessening of the poverty rate for the disabled population, all of which are key themes in promoting equalization for persons with disabilities. The Rio document mirrors this trend and dedicates an entire section of the final report to "strengthening the role of major groups."

The World Conference on Human Rights, held in Vienna in 1993, reconsidered universally recognized human rights instruments in the light of contemporary issues and produced a Programme of Action to guide human rights efforts forward in light of today's realities. The Conference recognized that "all human rights and fundamental freedoms are universal and thus unreservedly include persons with disabilities." The Vienna Conference recognized that any discrimination, intentional or unintentional, against persons with disabilities is per se a violation of human rights.

The International Conference on Population and Development, held in Cairo in 1994, recognized the importance of the equalization of opportunities for people with disabilities. The objectives endorsed by the Conference included "ensuring realization of rights...and participation in all aspects of social, economic, and cultural life ...to create, improve, and develop necessary conditions...[to] ensure equal opportunities ...and dignity [while] promot[ing] self-reliance" of persons with disabilities.

During March 1995, the United Nations held the World Summit for Social Development in Copenhagen, Denmark. The Summit adopted the Copenhagen Declaration on Social Development and the Programme of Action of the World Summit for Social Development. .

The Declaration attempts to respond to the material and spiritual needs of individuals, their families and communities. It stipulates that economic development, social development and environmental protection are interdependent and mutually reinforcing components of sustainable development, and it cites disadvantaged groups such as disabled persons as deserving special attention. "Social development and social justice cannot be attained in the absence of peace and security or in the absence of respect for all human rights and fundamental freedoms."

The Platform for Action, adopted by the Fourth World Conference on Women stipulates areas of special concern and recognizes that barriers to full equality for women can include factors such as their disability. Concerns relating to disability are also raised in the Beijing Declaration when the parties to the Conference commit to "intensifying efforts to ensure equal enjoyment of all human rights and fundamental freedoms for all women and girls who face multiple barriers to their empowerment and advancement because of factors such as...disability."

The recent work of other organs has focused on the special needs of children with disabilities. UNICEF worked with UNHCR and the United Nations Centre on Human Rights to study the impact of armed conflict on children, as mandated by the General Assembly. During the World Summit for Social Development, a workshop on the rights of children with disabilities was organized by UNICEF and Rehabilitation International, a non-governmental organization.

The Statistical Division of the United Nations Secretariat, having noted the lack of sufficient, accurate and up-to-date information on the topic of disability, continues to undertake methodological work and gather relevant information. To date, it has published the International Disability Statistics Data Base , the Disability Statistics Compendium , and the Manual for the Development of Statistical Information on Disability Programmes and Policies. The Division is currently preparing for publication the Guidelines and Principals for the Development of Impairment, Disability, and Handicap Statistics. Publication of a Handbook on Census and Survey Methods for Development of Impairment, Disability, and Handicap Statistics is planned by the Division.

The Department of Humanitarian Affairs, United Nations Secretariat, reports that at least 250,000 anti-personnel mine victims worldwide require prostheses. The figure increases at a rate of 800 per month. In 1997, anti-personnel mines were responsible for creating a marginalized group of disabled persons and their dependants in 68 countries, four times as many as in 1994. Currently, at the grassroots level, clearance programmes continue to be undertaken with the assistance of the Mine Clearance Unit of the Department of Humanitarian Affairs.

The regional commissions have pursued a number of assistance projects for the disabled in recent years. The Economic Commission for Europe (ECE), through its project on rehabilitation engineering, has conducted workshops in various countries to analyse the current status of rehabilitation services, technical aids, the mobility of persons with disabilities, and the market potential for rehabilitation according to the needs of people with disabilities. Housing for the disabled and improvements in the living conditions of the elderly and the disabled are also on the ECE agenda.

The Economic and Social Commission for Asia and the Pacific (ESCAP) has established a trust fund to promote the Decade of Disabled Persons in the Asia and Pacific Areaz. From 1983 to 1992, during the United Nations Decade, ESCAP organized training workshops on managing self-help organizations, conducting surveys, and preparing technical guidelines and hosting regional conferences for non-governmental organizations. The Economic and Social Commission for Western Asia (ESCWA) works in several countries still recovering from armed conflicts and in others where resources and services for people with disabilities continue to be scarce.

In collaboration with the member States of the Arab Gulf Fund for the United Nations Development Organizations (AGFUND), the United Nations Voluntary Fund on Disability has financed projects and programmes for disabled persons around the world. The Economic Commission for Africa (ECA) created the African Rehabilitation Institute with assistance from the Organization of African Unity (OAU).

Conceived in 1980 during the African Regional Conference on the International Year of Disabled Persons, the Institute works for the development of regional programmes for the socio-economic integration of disabled persons in Africa. The Economic Commission for Latin America and the Caribbean (ECLAC) has focussed its efforts on recovery from recent armed conflicts in the area, financial constraints and the elimination of negative cultural images of disabled persons still frequently perpetuated.

Clearly, the achievement of global human rights for all citizens is a matter of securing justice. While Governments as well as individual citizens bear a moral responsibility toward this goal, it should be "common sense" for civil society to recognize the human resource potential in all of its members. It is imperative that planners remain sensitive to the disability dimension early and throughout the development process.

One of the major development goals of the United Nations continues to be promoting the quality of life of the world's disadvantaged, including people with disabilities. One of the most significant issues still to be addressed is the accessibility of the disabled to new and emerging information technologies through computer literacy.

United Nations Global Programme On Disability

The UN Programme on Disability is the lead programme on disability within the United Nations System. It is housed in the Division for Social Policy and Development at the Department of Economic and Social Affairs of the UN Secretariat. The mandate of the Programme stems from the World Programme of Action concerning Disabled Persons adopted by the United Nations in 1982 and the Standard Rules on Equalization of Opportunities for Persons with Disabilities adopted in 1994. The major objectives of the Programme are the following:

1. to support the full and effective participation of persons with disabilities in social life and development;
2. to advance the rights and protect the dignity of persons with disabilities and;
3. to promote equal access to employment, education, information, goods and services.

The UN Programme on Disability also serves as substantive secretariat for the General Assembly Ad Hoc Committee on a comprehensive and integral international convention to promote and protect the rights and dignity of persons with disabilities.

United Nations Voluntary Fund on Disability

The Fund was established pursuant to General Assembly resolution 32/133, in connection with preparations for the 1981 International Year of Disabled Persons. The General Assembly decided in its resolution 40/31 that the Fund would be renamed the Voluntary Fund for the United Nations Decade of Disabled Persons, and that its resources would support catalytic and innovative action to implement further the World Programme of Action concerning Disabled Persons. By its resolution 47/88, the General Assembly decided that the Fund would continue in the period beyond the Decade as the United Nations Voluntary Fund on Disability, and that its terms of reference would include support for action to achieve the target of a "Society for all" by the year 2010, as endorsed by the General Assembly in its resolution 45/91.

The United Nations provides support to organizations for persons with disabilities in their activities through the UN Voluntary Fund on Disability. Funding priority is targeted to building the capacity of non-governmental organizations to take part in the making of the Convention and its future implementation. The Fund also provide small grants to support catalytic and innovative action, which will promote greater awareness of disability issues and exchanges of knowledge and experience and promote wide dissemination of appropriate disability technologies.

Following the adoption of resolution 57/229 by the General Assembly, a sub-account of the United Nations Voluntary Fund on Disability was created to receive contributions that have been earmarked for the participation of non-governmental organizations and experts from developing countries, in particular from the least developed countries in the work of the Ad Hoc Committee on a Comprehensive and Integral International Convention on the Protection and Promotion of the Rights and Dignity of Persons with Disabilities.

The Standard Rules on the Equalization of Opportunities for Persons with Disabilities

Introduction

Background and current needs

There are persons with disabilities in all parts of the world and at all levels in every society. The number of persons with disabilities in the world is large and is growing.

Both the causes and the consequences of disability vary throughout the world. Those variations are the result of different socio-economic circumstances and of the different provisions that States make for the well-being of their citizens.

Present disability policy is the result of developments over the past 200 years. In many ways it reflects the general living conditions and social and economic policies of different times. In the disability field, however, there are also many specific circumstances that have influenced the living conditions of persons with disabilities. Ignorance, neglect, superstition and fear are social factors that throughout the history of disability have isolated persons with disabilities and delayed their development.

Over the years disability policy developed from elementary care at institutions to education for children with disabilities and rehabilitation for persons who became disabled during adult life. Through education and rehabilitation, persons with disabilities became more active and a driving force in the further development of disability policy. Organizations of persons with disabilities, their families and advocates were formed, which advocated better conditions for persons with disabilities. After the Second World War the concepts of integration and normalization were introduced, which reflected a growing awareness of the capabilities of persons with disabilities.

Towards the end of the 1960s organizations of persons with disabilities in some countries started to formulate a new concept of disability. That new concept indicated the close connection between the limitation experienced by individuals with disabilities, the design and structure of their environments and the attitude of the general population. At the same time the problems of disability in developing countries were more and more highlighted. In some of those countries the percentage of the population with disabilities was estimated to be very high and, for the most part, persons with disabilities were extremely poor.

Previous international action

The rights of persons with disabilities have been the subject of much attention in the United Nations and other international organizations over a long period of time. The most important outcome of the International Year of Disabled Persons, 1981, was the World Programme of Action concerning Disabled Persons, adopted by the General Assembly by its resolution 37/52 of 3 December 1982. The Year and the World Programme of Action provided a strong impetus for progress in the field. They both emphasized the right of persons with disabilities to the same opportunities as other citizens and to an equal share in the improvements in living conditions resulting from economic and social development. There also, for the first time, handicap was defined as a function of the relationship between persons with disabilities and their environment.

The Global Meeting of Experts to Review the Implementation of the World Programme of Action concerning Disabled Persons at the Mid-Point of the United Nations Decade of Disabled Persons was held at Stockholm in 1987. It was suggested at the Meeting that a guiding philosophy should be developed to indicate the priorities for action in the years ahead. The basis of that philosophy should be the recognition of the rights of persons with disabilities.

Consequently, the Meeting recommended that the General Assembly convene a special conference to draft an international convention on the elimination of all forms of discrimination against persons with disabilities, to be ratified by States by the end of the Decade.

A draft outline of the convention was prepared by Italy and presented to the General Assembly at its forty-second session. Further presentations concerning a draft convention were made by Sweden at the forty-fourth session of the Assembly. However, on both occasions, no consensus could be reached on the suitability of such a convention. In the opinion of many representatives, existing human rights documents seemed to guarantee persons with disabilities the same rights as other persons.

Towards standard rules

Guided by the deliberations in the General Assembly, the Economic and Social Council, at its first regular session of 1990, finally agreed to concentrate on the elaboration of an international instrument of a different kind. By its resolution 1990/26 of 24 May 1990, the Council authorized the Commission for Social Development to consider, at its thirty-second session, the establishment of an ad hoc open-ended working group of government experts, funded by voluntary contributions, to elaborate standard rules on the equalization of opportunities for disabled children, youth and adults, in close collaboration with the specialized agencies, other intergovernmental bodies and non-governmental organizations, especially organizations of disabled persons. The Council also requested the Commission to finalize the text of those rules for consideration in 1993 and for submission to the General Assembly at its forty-eighth session.

The subsequent discussions in the Third Committee of the General Assembly at the forty-fifth session showed that there was wide support for the new initiative to elaborate standard rules on the equalization of opportunities for persons with disabilities.

At the thirty-second session of the Commission for Social Development, the initiative for standard rules received the support of a large number of representatives and discussions led to the adoption of resolution 32/2 of 20 February 1991, in which the Commission decided to establish an ad hoc open-ended working group in accordance with Economic and Social Council resolution 1990/26.

Purpose and content of the Standard Rules on the Equalization of Opportunities for Persons with Disabilities

The Standard Rules on the Equalization of Opportunities for Persons with Disabilities have been developed on the basis of the experience gained during the United Nations Decade of Disabled Persons (1983-1992). The International Bill of Human Rights, comprising the Universal Declaration of Human Rights, the International Covenant on Economic, Social and Cultural Rights and the International Covenant on Civil and Political Rights, the Convention on the Rights of the Child and the Convention on the Elimination of All Forms of Discrimination against Women, as well as the World Programme of Action concerning Disabled Persons, constitute the political and moral foundation for the Rules.

Although the Rules are not compulsory, they can become international customary rules when they are applied by a great number of States with the intention of respecting a rule in international law. They imply a strong moral and political commitment on behalf of States to take action for the equalization of opportunities for persons with disabilities. Important principles for responsibility, action and cooperation are indicated. Areas of decisive importance for the quality of life and for the achievement of full participation and equality are pointed out. The Rules offer an instrument for policy-making and action to persons with disabilities and their organizations. They provide a basis for technical and economic cooperation among States, the United Nations and other international organizations.

The purpose of the Rules is to ensure that girls, boys, women and men with disabilities, as members of their societies, may exercise the same rights and obligations as others. In all societies of the world there are still obstacles preventing persons with disabilities from exercising their rights and freedoms and making it difficult for them to participate fully in the activities of their societies. It is the responsibility of States to take appropriate action to remove such obstacles. Persons with disabilities and their organizations should play an active role as partners in this process. The equalization of opportunities for persons with disabilities is an essential contribution in the general and worldwide effort to mobilize human resources. Special attention may need to be directed towards groups such as women, children, the elderly, the poor, migrant workers, persons with dual or multiple disabilities, indigenous people and ethnic minorities. In addition, there are a large number of refugees with disabilities who have special needs requiring attention.

Fundamental concepts in disability policy

The concepts set out below appear throughout the Rules. They are essentially built on the concepts in the World Programme of Action concerning Disabled Persons. In some cases they reflect the development that has taken place during the United Nations Decade of Disabled Persons.

Disability and handicap: The term "disability" summarizes a great number of different functional limitations occurring in any population in any country of the world. People may be disabled by physical, intellectual or sensory impairment, medical conditions or mental illness. Such impairments, conditions or illnesses may be permanent or transitory in nature.

The term "handicap" means the loss or limitation of opportunities to take part in the life of the community on an equal level with others. It describes the encounter between the person with a disability and the environment. The purpose of this term is to emphasize the focus on the shortcomings in the environment and in many organized activities in society, for example, information, communication and education, which prevent persons with disabilities from participating on equal terms.

The use of the two terms "disability" and "handicap", as defined in paragraphs 17 and 18 above, should be seen in the light of modern disability history. During the 1970s there was a strong reaction among representatives of organizations of persons with disabilities and professionals in the field of disability against the terminology of the time. The terms "disability" and "handicap" were often used in an unclear and confusing way, which gave poor guidance for policy-making and for political action. The terminology reflected a medical and diagnostic approach, which ignored the imperfections and deficiencies of the surrounding society.

In 1980, the World Health Organization adopted an international classification of impairments, disabilities and handicaps, which suggested a more precise and at the same time relativistic approach. The International Classification of Impairments, Disabilities, and Handicaps

11/ makes a clear distinction between "impairment", "disability" and "handicap". It has been extensively used in areas such as rehabilitation, education, statistics, policy, legislation, demography, sociology, economics and anthropology. Some users have expressed concern that the Classification, in its definition of the term "handicap", may still be considered too medical and too centred on the individual, and may not adequately clarify the interaction between societal conditions or expectations and the abilities of the individual. Those concerns, and others expressed by users during the 12 years since its publication, will be addressed in forthcoming revisions of the Classification.

As a result of experience gained in the implementation of the World Programme of Action and of the general discussion that took place during the United Nations Decade of Disabled Persons, there was a deepening of knowledge and extension of understanding concerning disability issues and the terminology used. Current terminology recognizes the necessity of addressing both the individual needs (such as rehabilitation and technical aids) and the shortcomings of the society (various obstacles for participation).

Prevention: The term "prevention" means action aimed at preventing the occurrence of physical, intellectual, psychiatric or sensory impairments (primary prevention) or at preventing impairments from causing a permanent functional limitation or disability (secondary prevention). Prevention may include many different types of action, such as primary health care, prenatal and postnatal care, education in nutrition, immunization campaigns against communicable diseases, measures to control endemic diseases, safety regulations, programmes for the prevention of accidents in different environments, including adaptation of workplaces to prevent occupational disabilities and diseases, and prevention of disability resulting from pollution of the environment or armed conflict.

Rehabilitation: The term "rehabilitation" refers to a process aimed at enabling persons with disabilities to reach and maintain their optimal physical, sensory, intellectual, psychiatric and/or social functional levels, thus providing them with the tools to change their lives towards a higher level of independence. Rehabilitation may include measures to provide and/or restore functions, or compensate for the loss or absence of a function or for a functional limitation. The rehabilitation process does not involve initial medical care. It includes a wide range of measures and activities from more basic and general rehabilitation to goal-oriented activities, for instance vocational rehabilitation.

Equalization of opportunities: The term "equalization of opportunities" means the process through which the various systems of society and the environment, such as services, activities, information and documentation, are made available to all, particularly to persons with disabilities.

The principle of equal rights implies that the needs of each and every individual are of equal importance, that those needs must be made the basis for the planning of societies and that all resources must be employed in such a way as to ensure that every individual has equal opportunity for participation.

Persons with disabilities are members of society and have the right to remain within their local communities. They should receive the support they need within the ordinary structures of education, health, employment and social services.

As persons with disabilities achieve equal rights, they should also have equal obligations. As those rights are being achieved, societies should raise their expectations of persons with disabilities. As part of the process of equal opportunities, provision should be made to assist persons with disabilities to assume their full responsibility as members of society.

Preamble

States,

Mindful of the pledge made, under the Charter of the United Nations, to take joint and separate action in cooperation with the Organization to promote higher standards of living, full employment, and conditions of economic and social progress and development,

Reaffirming the commitment to human rights and fundamental freedoms, social justice and the dignity and worth of the human person proclaimed in the Charter,

Recalling in particular the international standards on human rights, which have been laid down in the Universal Declaration of Human Rights, the International Covenant on Economic, Social and Cultural Rights and the International Covenant on Civil and Political Rights,

Underlining that those instruments proclaim that the rights recognized therein should be ensured equally to all individuals without discrimination,

Recalling the Convention on the Rights of the Child, which prohibits discrimination on the basis of disability and requires special measures to ensure the rights of children with disabilities, and the International Convention on the Protection of the Rights of All Migrant Workers and Members of Their Families, which provides for some protective measures against disability,

Recalling also the provisions in the Convention on the Elimination of All Forms of Discrimination against Women to ensure the rights of girls and women with disabilities,

Having regard to the Declaration on the Rights of

Disabled Persons, the Declaration on the Rights of Mentally Retarded Persons, the Declaration on Social Progress and Development, the Principles for the Protection of Persons with Mental Illness and for the Improvement of Mental Health Care and other relevant instruments adopted by the General Assembly,

Also having regard to the relevant conventions and recommendations adopted by the International Labour Organisation, with particular reference to participation in employment without discrimination for persons with disabilities,

Mindful of the relevant recommendations and work of the United Nations Educational, Scientific and Cultural Organization, in particular the World Declaration on Education for All, the World Health Organization, the United Nations Children's Fund and other concerned organizations,

Having regard to the commitment made by States concerning the protection of the environment,

Mindful of the devastation caused by armed conflict and deploring the use of scarce resources in the production of weapons,

Recognizing that the World Programme of Action concerning Disabled Persons and the definition therein of equalization of opportunities represent earnest ambitions on the part of the international community to render those various international instruments and recommendations of practical and concrete significance,

Acknowledging that the objective of the United Nations Decade of Disabled Persons (1983-1992) to implement the World Programme of Action is still valid and requires urgent and continued action,

Recalling that the World Programme of Action is based on concepts that are equally valid in developing and industrialized countries,

Convinced that intensified efforts are needed to achieve the full and equal enjoyment of human rights and participation in society by persons with disabilities,

Re-emphasizing that persons with disabilities, and their parents, guardians, advocates and organizations, must be active partners with States in the planning and implementation of all measures affecting their civil, political, economic, social and cultural rights,

In pursuance of Economic and Social Council resolution 1990/26, and basing themselves on the specific measures required for the attainment by persons with disabilities of equality with others, enumerated in detail in the World Programme of Action,

Have adopted the Standard Rules on the Equalization of Opportunities for Persons with Disabilities outlined below, in order:

— To stress that all action in the field of disability presupposes adequate knowledge and experience of the conditions and special needs of persons with disabilities;

— To emphasize that the process through which every aspect of societal organization is made accessible to all is a basic objective of socio-economic development;

— To outline crucial aspects of social policies in the field of disability, including, as appropriate, the active encouragement of technical and economic cooperation;

— To provide models for the political decision-making process required for the attainment of equal opportunities, bearing in mind the widely differing technical and economic levels, the fact that the process must reflect keen understanding of the cultural context within which it takes place and the crucial role of persons with disabilities in it;

— To propose national mechanisms for close collaboration among States, the organs of the United Nations system, other intergovernmental bodies and organizations of persons with disabilities;

— To propose an effective machinery for monitoring the process by which States seek to attain the equalization of opportunities for persons with disabilities.

I. Preconditions for Equal Participation

Rule 1. Awareness-raising

States should take action to raise awareness in society about persons with disabilities, their rights, their needs, their potential and their contribution.

— States should ensure that responsible authorities distribute up-to-date information on available programmes and services to persons with disabilities, their families, professionals in the field and the general public. Information to persons with disabilities should be presented in accessible form.

— States should initiate and support information campaigns concerning persons with disabilities and disability policies, conveying the message that persons with disabilities are citizens with the same rights and obligations as others, thus justifying measures to remove all obstacles to full participation.

— States should encourage the portrayal of persons with disabilities by the mass media in a positive way; organizations of persons with disabilities should be consulted on this matter.

— States should ensure that public education programmes reflect in all their aspects the principle of full participation and equality.

— States should invite persons with disabilities and their families and organizations to participate in public education programmes concerning disability matters.

— States should encourage enterprises in the private sector to include disability issues in all aspects of their activity.

— States should initiate and promote programmes aimed at raising the level of awareness of persons with disabilities concerning their rights and potential. Increased self-reliance and empowerment will assist persons with disabilities to take advantage of the opportunities available to them.

— Awareness-raising should be an important part of the education of children with disabilities and in rehabilitation programmes. Persons with disabilities could also assist one another in awareness-raising through the activities of their own organizations.

— Awareness-raising should be part of the education of all children and should be a component of teacher-training courses and training of all professionals.

Rule 2. Medical care

States should ensure the provision of effective medical care to persons with disabilities.

— States should work towards the provision of programmes run by multidisciplinary teams of professionals for early detection, assessment and treatment of impairment. This could prevent, reduce or eliminate disabling effects. Such programmes should ensure the full participation of persons with disabilities and their families at the individual level, and of organizations of persons with disabilities at the planning and evaluation level.

— Local community workers should be trained to participate in areas such as early detection of impairments, the provision of primary assistance and referral to appropriate services.

— States should ensure that persons with disabilities, particularly infants and children, are provided with the same level of medical care within the same system as other members of society.

— States should ensure that all medical and paramedical personnel are adequately trained and equipped to give medical care to persons with disabilities and that they have access to relevant treatment methods and technology.

— States should ensure that medical, paramedical and related personnel are adequately trained so that they do not give inappropriate advice to parents, thus restricting options for their children. This training should be an ongoing process and should be based on the latest information available.

— States should ensure that persons with disabilities are provided with any regular treatment and medicines they may need to preserve or improve their level of functioning.

Rule 3. Rehabilitation

Rehabilitation is a fundamental concept in disability policy and is defined above in the introduction.

States should ensure the provision of rehabilitation services to persons with disabilities in order for them to reach and sustain their optimum level of independence and functioning.

— States should develop national rehabilitation programmes for all groups of persons with disabilities. Such programmes should be based on the actual individual needs of persons with disabilities and on the principles of full participation and equality.

— Such programmes should include a wide range of activities, such as basic skills training to improve or compensate for an affected function, counselling of persons with disabilities and their families, developing self-reliance, and occasional services such as assessment and guidance.

- All persons with disabilities, including persons with severe and/or multiple disabilities, who require rehabilitation should have access to it.
- Persons with disabilities and their families should be able to participate in the design and organization of rehabilitation services concerning themselves.
- All rehabilitation services should be available in the local community where the person with disabilities lives. However, in some instances, in order to attain a certain training objective, special time-limited rehabilitation courses may be organized, where appropriate, in residential form.
- Persons with disabilities and their families should be encouraged to involve themselves in rehabilitation, for instance as trained teachers, instructors or counsellors.
- States should draw upon the expertise of organizations of persons with disabilities when formulating or evaluating rehabilitation programmes.

Rule 4. Support services

States should ensure the development and supply of support services, including assistive devices for persons with disabilities, to assist them to increase their level of independence in their daily living and to exercise their rights.

- States should ensure the provision of assistive devices and equipment, personal assistance and interpreter services, according to the needs of persons with disabilities, as important measures to achieve the equalization of opportunities.

— States should support the development, production, distribution and servicing of assistive devices and equipment and the dissemination of knowledge about them.

— To achieve this, generally available technical know-how should be utilized. In States where high-technology industry is available, it should be fully utilized to improve the standard and effectiveness of assistive devices and equipment. It is important to stimulate the development and production of simple and inexpensive devices, using local material and local production facilities when possible. Persons with disabilities themselves could be involved in the production of those devices.

— States should recognize that all persons with disabilities who need assistive devices should have access to them as appropriate, including financial accessibility. This may mean that assistive devices and equipment should be provided free of charge or at such a low price that persons with disabilities or their families can afford to buy them.

— In rehabilitation programmes for the provision of assistive devices and equipment, States should consider the special requirements of girls and boys with disabilities concerning the design, durability and age-appropriateness of assistive devices and equipment.

— States should support the development and provision of personal assistance programmes and interpretation services, especially for persons with severe and/or multiple disabilities. Such programmes would increase the level of participation of persons with disabilities in everyday life at home, at work, in school and during leisure-time activities.

— Personal assistance programmes should be designed in such a way that the persons with disabilities using the programmes have a decisive influence on the way in which the programmes are delivered.

II. Target Areas for Equal Participation

Rule 5. Accessibility

States should recognize the overall importance of accessibility in the process of the equalization of opportunities in all spheres of society. For persons with disabilities of any kind, States should (a) introduce programmes of action to make the physical environment accessible; and (b) undertake measures to provide access to information and communication.

— Access to the physical environment

— States should initiate measures to remove the obstacles to participation in the physical environment. Such measures should be to develop standards and guidelines and to consider enacting legislation to ensure accessibility to various areas in society, such as housing, buildings, public transport services and other means of transportation, streets and other outdoor environments.

— States should ensure that architects, construction engineers and others who are professionally involved in the design and construction of the physical environment have access to adequate information on disability policy and measures to achieve accessibility.

— Accessibility requirements should be included in the design and construction of the physical environment from the beginning of the designing process.

— Organizations of persons with disabilities should be consulted when standards and norms for accessibility are being developed. They should also be involved locally from the initial planning stage when public construction projects are being designed, thus ensuring maximum accessibility.

— Access to information and communication

— Persons with disabilities and, where appropriate, their families and advocates should have access to full information on diagnosis, rights and available services and programmes, at all stages. Such information should be presented in forms accessible to persons with disabilities.

— States should develop strategies to make information services and documentation accessible for different groups of persons with disabilities. Braille, tape services, large print and other appropriate technologies should be used to provide access to written information and documentation for persons with visual impairments. Similarly, appropriate technologies should be used to provide access to spoken information for persons with auditory impairments or comprehension difficulties.

— Consideration should be given to the use of sign language in the education of deaf children, in their families and communities. Sign language interpretation services should also be provided to facilitate the communication between deaf persons and others.

— Consideration should also be given to the needs of people with other communication disabilities.

— States should encourage the media, especially television, radio and newspapers, to make their services accessible.

— States should ensure that new computerized information and service systems offered to the general public are either made initially accessible or are adapted to be made accessible to persons with disabilities.

— Organizations of persons with disabilities should be consulted when measures to make information services accessible are being developed.

Rule 6. Education

States should recognize the principle of equal primary, secondary and tertiary educational opportunities for children, youth and adults with disabilities, in integrated settings. They should ensure that the education of persons with disabilities is an integral part of the educational system.

— General educational authorities are responsible for the education of persons with disabilities in integrated settings. Education for persons with disabilities should form an integral part of national educational planning, curriculum development and school organization.

— Education in mainstream schools presupposes the provision of interpreter and other appropriate support services. Adequate accessibility and support services, designed to meet the needs of persons with different disabilities, should be provided.

— Parent groups and organizations of persons with disabilities should be involved in the education process at all levels.

— In States where education is compulsory it should be provided to girls and boys with all kinds and all levels of disabilities, including the most severe.

— Special attention should be given in the following areas:

— Very young children with disabilities;

— Pre-school children with disabilities;

— Adults with disabilities, particularly women.

— To accommodate educational provisions for persons with disabilities in the mainstream, States should:

— Have a clearly stated policy, understood and accepted at the school level and by the wider community;

— Allow for curriculum flexibility, addition and adaptation;

— Provide for quality materials, ongoing teacher training and support teachers.

— Integrated education and community-based programmes should be seen as complementary approaches in providing cost-effective education and training for persons with disabilities. National community-based programmes should encourage communities to use and develop their resources to provide local education to persons with disabilities.

— In situations where the general school system does not yet adequately meet the needs of all persons with disabilities, special education may be considered. It should be aimed at preparing students for education in the general school system. The quality of such education should reflect the same standards and ambitions as general education and should be closely linked to it. At a minimum, students with disabilities should be afforded the same portion of educational resources as students without disabilities. States should aim for the gradual integration of special education services into mainstream education. It is acknowledged that in some instances special education may currently be considered to be the most appropriate form of education for some students with disabilities.

— Owing to the particular communication needs of deaf

and deaf/blind persons, their education may be more suitably provided in schools for such persons or special classes and units in mainstream schools. At the initial stage, in particular, special attention needs to be focused on culturally sensitive instruction that will result in effective communication skills and maximum independence for people who are deaf or deaf/blind.

Rule 7. Employment

States should recognize the principle that persons with disabilities must be empowered to exercise their human rights, particularly in the field of employment. In both rural and urban areas they must have equal opportunities for productive and gainful employment in the labour market.

— Laws and regulations in the employment field must not discriminate against persons with disabilities and must not raise obstacles to their employment.

— States should actively support the integration of persons with disabilities into open employment. This active support could occur through a variety of measures, such as vocational training, incentive-oriented quota schemes, reserved or designated employment, loans or grants for small business, exclusive contracts or priority production rights, tax concessions, contract compliance or other technical or financial assistance to enterprises employing workers with disabilities. States should also encourage employers to make reasonable adjustments to accommodate persons with disabilities.

— States' action programmes should include:

— Measures to design and adapt workplaces and work premises in such a way that they become accessible to persons with different disabilities;

— Support for the use of new technologies and the development and production of assistive devices, tools and equipment and measures to facilitate access to such devices and equipment for persons with disabilities to enable them to gain and maintain employment;

— Provision of appropriate training and placement and ongoing support such as personal assistance and interpreter services.

— States should initiate and support public awareness-raising campaigns designed to overcome negative attitudes and prejudices concerning workers with disabilities.

— In their capacity as employers, States should create favourable conditions for the employment of persons with disabilities in the public sector.

— States, workers' organizations and employers should cooperate to ensure equitable recruitment and promotion policies, employment conditions, rates of pay, measures to improve the work environment in order to prevent injuries and impairments and measures for the rehabilitation of employees who have sustained employment-related injuries.

— The aim should always be for persons with disabilities to obtain employment in the open labour market. For persons with disabilities whose needs cannot be met in open employment, small units of sheltered or supported employment may be an alternative. It is important that the quality of such programmes be assessed in terms of their relevance and sufficiency in providing opportunities for persons with disabilities to gain employment in the labour market.

— Measures should be taken to include persons with disabilities in training and employment programmes in the private and informal sectors.

— States, workers' organizations and employers should cooperate with organizations of persons with disabilities concerning all measures to create training and employment opportunities, including flexible hours, part-time work, job-sharing, self-employment and attendant care for persons with disabilities.

Rule 8. Income maintenance and social security

States are responsible for the provision of social security and income maintenance for persons with disabilities.

— States should ensure the provision of adequate income support to persons with disabilities who, owing to disability or disability-related factors, have temporarily lost or received a reduction in their income or have been denied employment opportunities. States should ensure that the provision of support takes into account the costs frequently incurred by persons with disabilities and their families as a result of the disability.

— In countries where social security, social insurance or other social welfare schemes exist or are being developed for the general population, States should ensure that such systems do not exclude or discriminate against persons with disabilities.

— States should also ensure the provision of income support and social security protection to individuals who undertake the care of a person with a disability.

— Social security systems should include incentives to restore the income-earning capacity of persons with disabilities. Such systems should provide or contribute to the organization, development and financing of vocational training. They should also assist with placement services.

— Social security programmes should also provide incentives for persons with disabilities to seek employment in order to establish or re-establish their income-earning capacity.

— Income support should be maintained as long as the disabling conditions remain in a manner that does not discourage persons with disabilities from seeking employment. It should only be reduced or terminated when persons with disabilities achieve adequate and secure income.

— States, in countries where social security is to a large extent provided by the private sector, should encourage local communities, welfare organizations and families to develop self-help measures and incentives for employment or employment-related activities for persons with disabilities.

Rule 9. Family life and personal integrity

States should promote the full participation of persons with disabilities in family life. They should promote their right to personal integrity and ensure that laws do not discriminate against persons with disabilities with respect to sexual relationships, marriage and parenthood.

— Persons with disabilities should be enabled to live with their families. States should encourage the inclusion in family counselling of appropriate modules regarding disability and its effects on family life. Respite-care and attendant-care services should be made available to families which include a person with disabilities. States should remove all unnecessary obstacles to persons who want to foster or adopt a child or adult with disabilities.

— Persons with disabilities must not be denied the opportunity to experience their sexuality, have sexual relationships and experience parenthood. Taking into account that persons with disabilities may experience difficulties in getting married and setting up a family, States should encourage the availability of appropriate counselling. Persons with disabilities must have the same access as others to family-planning methods, as well as to information in accessible form on the sexual functioning of their bodies.

— States should promote measures to change negative attitudes towards marriage, sexuality and parenthood of persons with disabilities, especially of girls and women with disabilities, which still prevail in society. The media should be encouraged to play an important role in removing such negative attitudes.

— Persons with disabilities and their families need to be fully informed about taking precautions against sexual and other forms of abuse. Persons with disabilities are particularly vulnerable to abuse in the family, community or institutions and need to be educated on how to avoid the occurrence of abuse, recognize when abuse has occurred and report on such acts.

Rule 10. Culture

States will ensure that persons with disabilities are integrated into and can participate in cultural activities on an equal basis.

— States should ensure that persons with disabilities have the opportunity to utilize their creative, artistic and intellectual potential, not only for their own benefit, but also for the enrichment of their community, be they in urban or rural areas. Examples of such activities are dance, music, literature, theatre, plastic arts, painting and sculpture. Particularly in developing countries, emphasis should be placed on traditional and contemporary art forms, such as puppetry, recitation and story-telling.

— States should promote the accessibility to and availability of places for cultural performances and services, such as theatres, museums, cinemas and libraries, to persons with disabilities.

— States should initiate the development and use of special technical arrangements to make literature, films and theatre accessible to persons with disabilities.

Rule 11. Recreation and sports

States will take measures to ensure that persons with disabilities have equal opportunities for recreation and sports.

— States should initiate measures to make places for recreation and sports, hotels, beaches, sports arenas, gym halls, etc., accessible to persons with disabilities. Such measures should encompass support for staff in recreation and sports programmes, including projects to develop methods of accessibility, and participation, information and training programmes.

— Tourist authorities, travel agencies, hotels, voluntary organizations and others involved in organizing recreational activities or travel opportunities should offer their services to all, taking into account the special needs of persons with disabilities. Suitable training should be provided to assist that process.

— Sports organizations should be encouraged to develop opportunities for participation by persons with disabilities in sports activities. In some cases, accessibility measures could be enough to open up opportunities for participation. In other cases, special arrangements or special games would be needed. States should support the participation of persons with disabilities in national and international events.

— Persons with disabilities participating in sports activities should have access to instruction and training of the same quality as other participants.

— Organizers of sports and recreation should consult with organizations of persons with disabilities when developing their services for persons with disabilities.

Rule 12. Religion

States will encourage measures for equal participation by persons with disabilities in the religious life of their communities.

— States should encourage, in consultation with religious authorities, measures to eliminate discrimination and make religious activities accessible to persons with disabilities.

— States should encourage the distribution of information on disability matters to religious institutions and organizations. States should also encourage religious authorities to include information on disability policies in the training for religious professions, as well as in religious education programmes.

— They should also encourage the accessibility of religious literature to persons with sensory impairments.

— States and/or religious organizations should consult with organizations of persons with disabilities when developing measures for equal participation in religious activities.

III. Implementation Measures

Rule 13. Information and research

States assume the ultimate responsibility for the

collection and dissemination of information on the living conditions of persons with disabilities and promote comprehensive research on all aspects, including obstacles that affect the lives of persons with disabilities.

— States should, at regular intervals, collect gender-specific statistics and other information concerning the living conditions of persons with disabilities. Such data collection could be conducted in conjunction with national censuses and household surveys and could be undertaken in close collaboration, inter alia, with universities, research institutes and organizations of persons with disabilities. The data collection should include questions on programmes and services and their use.

— States should consider establishing a data bank on disability, which would include statistics on available services and programmes as well as on the different groups of persons with disabilities. They should bear in mind the need to protect individual privacy and personal integrity.

— States should initiate and support programmes of research on social, economic and participation issues that affect the lives of persons with disabilities and their families. Such research should include studies on the causes, types and frequencies of disabilities, the availability and efficacy of existing programmes and the need for development and evaluation of services and support measures.

— States should develop and adopt terminology and criteria for the conduct of national surveys, in cooperation with organizations of persons with disabilities.

— States should facilitate the participation of persons with disabilities in data collection and research. To undertake such research States should particularly encourage the recruitment of qualified persons with disabilities.

— States should support the exchange of research findings and experiences.

— States should take measures to disseminate information and knowledge on disability to all political and administration levels within national, regional and local spheres.

Rule 14. Policy-making and planning

States will ensure that disability aspects are included in all relevant policy-making and national planning.

— States should initiate and plan adequate policies for persons with disabilities at the national level, and stimulate and support action at regional and local levels.

— States should involve organizations of persons with disabilities in all decision-making relating to plans and programmes concerning persons with disabilities or affecting their economic and social status.

— The needs and concerns of persons with disabilities should be incorporated into general development plans and not be treated separately.

— The ultimate responsibility of States for the situation of persons with disabilities does not relieve others of their responsibility. Anyone in charge of services, activities or the provision of information in society should be encouraged to accept responsibility for making such programmes available to persons with disabilities.

— States should facilitate the development by local communities of programmes and measures for persons with disabilities. One way of doing this could be to develop manuals or check-lists and provide training programmes for local staff.

Rule 15. Legislation

States have a responsibility to create the legal bases for measures to achieve the objectives of full participation and equality for persons with disabilities.

— National legislation, embodying the rights and obligations of citizens, should include the rights and obligations of persons with disabilities. States are under an obligation to enable persons with disabilities to exercise their rights, including their human, civil and political rights, on an equal basis with other citizens. States must ensure that organizations of persons with disabilities are involved in the development of national legislation concerning the rights of persons with disabilities, as well as in the ongoing evaluation of that legislation.

— Legislative action may be needed to remove conditions that may adversely affect the lives of persons with disabilities, including harassment and victimization. Any discriminatory provisions against persons with disabilities must be eliminated. National legislation should provide for appropriate sanctions in case of violations of the principles of non-discrimination.

— National legislation concerning persons with disabilities may appear in two different forms. The rights and obligations may be incorporated in general legislation or contained in special legislation. Special legislation for persons with disabilities may be established in several ways:

— By enacting separate legislation, dealing exclusively with disability matters;

— By including disability matters within legislation on particular topics;

— By mentioning persons with disabilities specifically in the texts that serve to interpret existing legislation.

— A combination of those different approaches might be desirable. Affirmative action provisions may also be considered.

— States may consider establishing formal statutory complaints mechanisms in order to protect the interests of persons with disabilities.

Rule 16. Economic policies

States have the financial responsibility for national programmes and measures to create equal opportunities for persons with disabilities.

— States should include disability matters in the regular budgets of all national, regional and local government bodies.

— States, non-governmental organizations and other interested bodies should interact to determine the most effective ways of supporting projects and measures relevant to persons with disabilities.

— States should consider the use of economic measures (loans, tax exemptions, earmarked grants, special funds, and so on) to stimulate and support equal participation by persons with disabilities in society.

— In many States it may be advisable to establish a disability development fund, which could support various pilot projects and self-help programmes at the grass-roots level.

Rule 17. Coordination of work

States are responsible for the establishment and strengthening of national coordinating committees, or similar bodies, to serve as a national focal point on disability matters.

— The national coordinating committee or similar bodies should be permanent and based on legal as well as appropriate administrative regulation.

— A combination of representatives of private and public organizations is most likely to achieve an intersectoral and multidisciplinary composition. Representatives could be drawn from concerned government ministries, organizations of persons with disabilities and non-governmental organizations.

— Organizations of persons with disabilities should have considerable influence in the national coordinating committee in order to ensure proper feedback of their concerns.

— The national coordinating committee should be provided with sufficient autonomy and resources to fulfil its responsibilities in relation to its decision-making capacities. It should report to the highest governmental level.

Rule 18. Organizations of persons with disabilities

States should recognize the right of the organizations of persons with disabilities to represent persons with disabilities at national, regional and local levels. States should also recognize the advisory role of organizations of persons with disabilities in decision-making on disability matters.

— States should encourage and support economically and in other ways the formation and strengthening of organizations of persons with disabilities, family members and/or advocates. States should recognize that those organizations have a role to play in the development of disability policy.

— States should establish ongoing communication with organizations of persons with disabilities and ensure their participation in the development of government policies.

— The role of organizations of persons with disabilities could be to identify needs and priorities, to participate in the planning, implementation and evaluation of services and measures concerning the lives of persons with disabilities, and to contribute to public awareness and to advocate change.

— As instruments of self-help, organizations of persons with disabilities provide and promote opportunities for the development of skills in various fields, mutual support among members and information sharing.

— Organizations of persons with disabilities could perform their advisory role in many different ways such as having permanent representation on boards of government-funded agencies, serving on public commissions and providing expert knowledge on different projects.

— The advisory role of organizations of persons with disabilities should be ongoing in order to develop and deepen the exchange of views and information between the State and the organizations.

— Organizations should be permanently represented on the national coordinating committee or similar bodies.

— The role of local organizations of persons with disabilities should be developed and strengthened to ensure that they influence matters at the community level.

Rule 19. Personnel training

States are responsible for ensuring the adequate training of personnel, at all levels, involved in the planning and provision of programmes and services concerning persons with disabilities.

— States should ensure that all authorities providing services in the disability field give adequate training to their personnel.

— In the training of professionals in the disability field, as well as in the provision of information on disability in general training programmes, the principle of full participation and equality should be appropriately reflected.

— States should develop training programmes in consultation with organizations of persons with disabilities, and persons with disabilities should be involved as teachers, instructors or advisers in staff training programmes.

— The training of community workers is of great strategic importance, particularly in developing countries. It should involve persons with disabilities and include the development of appropriate values, competence and technologies as well as skills which can be practised by persons with disabilities, their parents, families and members of the community.

Rule 20. National monitoring and evaluation of disability programmes in the implementation of the Rules

States are responsible for the continuous monitoring and evaluation of the implementation of national programmes and services concerning the equalization of opportunities for persons with disabilities.

— States should periodically and systematically evaluate national disability programmes and disseminate both the bases and the results of the evaluations.

— States should develop and adopt terminology and criteria for the evaluation of disability-related programmes and services.

— Such criteria and terminology should be developed in close cooperation with organizations of persons with disabilities from the earliest conceptual and planning stages.

— States should participate in international cooperation

in order to develop common standards for national evaluation in the disability field. States should encourage national coordinating committees to participate also.

— The evaluation of various programmes in the disability field should be built in at the planning stage, so that the overall efficacy in fulfilling their policy objectives can be evaluated.

Rule 21. Technical and economic cooperation

States, both industrialized and developing, have the responsibility to cooperate in and take measures for the improvement of the living conditions of persons with disabilities in developing countries.

— Measures to achieve the equalization of opportunities of persons with disabilities, including refugees with disabilities, should be integrated into general development programmes.

— Such measures must be integrated into all forms of technical and economic cooperation, bilateral and multilateral, governmental and non-governmental. States should bring up disability issues in discussions on such cooperation with their counterparts.

— When planning and reviewing programmes of technical and economic cooperation, special attention should be given to the effects of such programmes on the situation of persons with disabilities. It is of the utmost importance that persons with disabilities and their organizations are consulted on any development projects designed for persons with disabilities. They should be directly involved in the development, implementation and evaluation of such projects.

— Priority areas for technical and economic cooperation should include:

- The development of human resources through the development of skills, abilities and potentials of persons with disabilities and the initiation of employment-generating activities for and of persons with disabilities;
- The development and dissemination of appropriate disability-related technologies and know-how.
- States are also encouraged to support the formation and strengthening of organizations of persons with disabilities.
- States should take measures to improve the knowledge of disability issues among staff involved at all levels in the administration of technical and economic cooperation programmes.

Rule 22. International cooperation

States will participate actively in international cooperation concerning policies for the equalization of opportunities for persons with disabilities.

- Within the United Nations, the specialized agencies and other concerned intergovernmental organizations, States should participate in the development of disability policy.
- Whenever appropriate, States should introduce disability aspects in general negotiations concerning standards, information exchange, development programmes, etc.
- States should encourage and support the exchange of knowledge and experience among:
- Non-governmental organizations concerned with disability issues;
- Research institutions and individual researchers involved in disability issues;

— Representatives of field programmes and of professional groups in the disability field;
— Organizations of persons with disabilities;
— National coordinating committees.
— States should ensure that the United Nations and the specialized agencies, as well as all intergovernmental and interparliamentary bodies, at global and regional levels, include in their work the global and regional organizations of persons with disabilities.

IV. Monitoring Mechanism

The purpose of a monitoring mechanism is to further the effective implementation of the Rules. It will assist each State in assessing its level of implementation of the Rules and in measuring its progress. The monitoring should identify obstacles and suggest suitable measures that would contribute to the successful implementation of the Rules. The monitoring mechanism will recognize the economic, social and cultural features existing in individual States. An important element should also be the provision of advisory services and the exchange of experience and information between States.

The Rules shall be monitored within the framework of the sessions of the Commission for Social Development. A Special Rapporteur with relevant and extensive experience in disability issues and international organizations shall be appointed, if necessary, funded by extrabudgetary resources, for three years to monitor the implementation of the Rules.

International organizations of persons with disabilities having consultative status with the Economic and Social Council and organizations representing persons with disabilities who have not yet formed their own organizations should be invited to create among themselves a panel of experts, on which organizations of persons with disabilities shall have a majority, taking into account the different kinds of disabilities and necessary equitable geographical distribution, to be consulted by the Special Rapporteur and, when appropriate, by the Secretariat.

The panel of experts will be encouraged by the Special Rapporteur to review, advise and provide feedback and suggestions on the promotion, implementation and monitoring of the Rules.

The Special Rapporteur shall send a set of questions to States, entities within the United Nations system, and intergovernmental and non-governmental organizations, including organizations of persons with disabilities. The set of questions should address implementation plans for the Rules in States. The questions should be selective in nature and cover a number of specific rules for in-depth evaluation. In preparing the questions the Special Rapporteur should consult with the panel of experts and the Secretariat.

The Special Rapporteur shall seek to establish a direct dialogue not only with States but also with local non-governmental organizations, seeking their views and comments on any information intended to be included in the reports. The Special Rapporteur shall provide advisory services on the implementation and monitoring of the Rules and assistance in the preparation of replies to the sets of questions.

The Department for Policy Coordination and Sustainable Development of the Secretariat, as the United Nations focal point on disability issues, the United Nations Development Programme and other entities and mechanisms within the United Nations system, such as the regional commissions and specialized agencies and inter-agency meetings, shall cooperate with the Special Rapporteur in the implementation and monitoring of the Rules at the national level.

The Special Rapporteur, assisted by the Secretariat, shall prepare reports for submission to the Commission for Social Development at its thirty-fourth and thirty-fifth sessions. In preparing such reports, the Rapporteur should consult with the panel of experts.

States should encourage national coordinating committees or similar bodies to participate in implementation and monitoring. As the focal points on disability matters at the national level, they should be encouraged to establish procedures to coordinate the monitoring of the Rules. Organizations of persons with disabilities should be encouraged to be actively involved in the monitoring of the process at all levels.

Should extrabudgetary resources be identified, one or more positions of interregional adviser on the Rules should be created to provide direct services to States, including:

- The organization of national and regional training seminars on the content of the Rules;
- The development of guidelines to assist in strategies for implementation of the Rules;
- Dissemination of information about best practices concerning implementation of the Rules.

At its thirty-fourth session, the Commission for Social Development should establish an open-ended working group to examine the Special Rapporteur's report and make recommendations on how to improve the application of the Rules. In examining the Special Rapporteur's report, the Commission, through its open-ended working group, shall consult international organizations of persons with disabilities and specialized agencies, in accordance with rules 71 and 76 of the rules of procedure of the functional commissions of the Economic and Social Council.

At its session following the end of the Special Rapporteur's mandate, the Commission should examine the possibility of either renewing that mandate, appointing a new Special Rapporteur or considering another monitoring mechanism, and should make appropriate recommendations to the Economic and Social Council.

States should be encouraged to contribute to the United Nations Voluntary Fund on Disability in order to further the implementation of the Rules.

World Programme of Action Concerning Disabled Persons

The General Assembly,

Recalling its resolutions 31/123 of 16 December 1976 by which it proclaimed the year 1981 International Year of Disabled Persons, 32/133 of 16 December 1977 by which it established the Advisory Committee for the International Year of Disabled Persons, 33/170 of 20 December 1978, 34/154 of 17 December 1979 in which it, inter alia, decided to expand the theme of the International Year of Disabled Persons to "Full participation and equality", 35/133 of 11 December 1980 and 36/77 of 8 December 1981,

Deeply concerned that no less than five hundred million persons are estimated to suffer from disability of one form or another, of whom four hundred million are estimated to be in developing countries,

Reiterating the continuing need to promote the realization of the right of disabled persons to participate fully in the social life and development of their societies and to enjoy living conditions equal to those of other citizens, as well as to share equally in the improvements in living conditions resulting from social and economic development,

Recognizing that the International Year of Disabled Persons contributed to the acceptance by the community of the right of disabled persons to participate fully in the social life and development of their societies and to enjoy living conditions equal to those of their fellow citizens,

Convinced that the International Year of Disabled Persons gave a genuine and meaningful impetus to activities related to equalization of opportunities for disabled persons, as well as prevention and rehabilitation at all levels,

Expressing its satisfaction with the efforts of Member States during the International Year of Disabled Persons to improve the conditions and well-being of disabled persons and their willingness to involve disabled persons and their organizations in all matters of concern to them,

Also expressing its satisfaction with the initiatives taken by the specialized agencies and other organizations of the United Nations system, non-governmental organizations and, in particular, organizations of disabled persons,

Taking note of the emergence of organizations of disabled persons in all parts of the world and their positive influence on the image and condition of persons with a disability,

Having considered the Vienna Affirmative Action Plan adopted by the World Symposium of Experts on Technical Co-operation among Developing Countries and Technical Assistance in Disability Prevention and Rehabilitation,

Expressing its appreciation to the Advisory Committee for the International Year of Disabled Persons for the work it has done,

Having considered the report of the Advisory Committee for the International Year of Disabled Persons on its fourth session and its proposal for a World Programme of Action concerning Disabled Persons,

Desirous of ensuring an effective follow-up to the International Year of Disabled Persons and aware that if this is to be achieved Member

States, organs, organizations and agencies of the United Nations system, non-governmental organizations and organizations of disabled persons must therefore be encouraged to continue the activities already undertaken and to initiate new programmes and activities,

Stressing that the primary responsibility for promoting effective measures for prevention of disability, rehabilitation and the realization of the goals of "full participation" of disabled persons in social life and development and of "equality" rests with individual countries and that international action should be directed to assist and support national efforts in this regard,

1. Adopts the World Programme of Action concerning Disabled Persons, as set forth in recommendation 1 (IV) of the annex to the report of the Advisory Committee for the International Year of Disabled Persons at its fourth session;
2. Calls upon all Member States, all relevant non-governmental organizations and organizations of disabled persons and, through a reallocation of existing resources, calls also upon all organs, organizations and agencies of the United Nations system to ensure early implementation of the World Programme of Action concerning disabled persons;
3. Decides to evaluate at its forty-second session, with the help of the Secretary-General, the implementation of the World Programme of Action concerning Disabled Persons.

8

Distribution of Disabled Persons by Type of Disability (India/States/Union Territories/Districts 2001)

Distribution of Disabled Persons by Type of Disabilty and Residence (in %)

India/States/Union	*T/R/U*	*Total disabled population*	*In seeing*	*In speech*	*In hearing*	*In move-ment*	*Mental*
1	*2*	*3*	*4*	*5*	*6*	*7*	*8*
INDIA	T	21906769	48.5	7.5	5.8	27.9	10.3
	R	16388382	48.0	7.6	6.2	28.4	9.7
	U	5518387	50.0	7.2	4.3	26.3	12.1
JAMMU &	T	302670	69.0	5.6	4.7	12.5	8.2
KASHMIR	R	229718	66.4	6.1	5.1	14.2	8.3
	U	72952	77.1	4.1	3.3	7.5	8.1
Kupwara	T	20809	66.5	5.9	5.1	13.7	8.8
	R	19821	65.8	6.0	5.2	14.1	8.8
	U	988	79.6	3.8	2.3	5.8	8.5
Baramula	T	45152	75.3	4.1	2.4	9.0	9.1
	R	37013	73.8	4.4	2.7	9.9	9.3
	U	8139	82.2	2.7	1.5	5.0	8.6

Contd.

Contd.

1	2	3	4	5	6	7	8
Srinagar	T	34844	77.1	4.0	3.7	7.1	8.2
	R	7255	71.0	5.1	3.3	13.2	7.5
	U	27589	78.7	3.7	3.8	5.4	8.3
Badgam	T	15316	66.1	6.1	5.4	13.8	8.6
	R	13574	65.5	6.3	5.1	14.4	8.7
	U	1742	70.7	4.8.	7.4	9.5	7.6
Pulwama	T	16003	66.9	6.0	4.7	13.9	8.5
	R	14375	66.5	6.1	4.7	14.1	8.7
	U	1628	70.5	5.4	4.7	12.4	7.1
Anantnag	T	30781	67.8	6.1	5.1	12.6	8.5
	R	26813	67.1	6.2	5.4	12.8	8.5
	U	3968	72.2	5.1	3.4	11.0	8.2
Leh (Ladakh)	T	2717	53.9	7.1	10.5	21.2	7.2
	R	2228	49.9	7.3	11.9	23.1	7.8
	U	489	72.2	6.3	4.3	12.7	4.5
Kargil	T	2892	55.8	7.8	8.2	16.5	11.8
	R	2577	53.1	8.0	9.0	17.6	12.3
	U	315	78.1	6.0	1.6	7.0	7.3
Doda	T	22743	59.0	8.5	7.2	18.7	6.6
	R	21527	58.1	8.7	7.5	19.1	6.6
	U	1216	74.2	5.4	1.6	12.0	6.8
Udhampur	T	22183	65.8	6.8	6.1	14.3	7.0
	R	19137	64.6	6.9	6.4	15.0	7.1
	U	3046	73.7	5.7	4.1	9.8	6.7
Punch	T	14130	65.9	5.7	5.4	16.6	6.4
	R	13118	65.0	5.8	5.6	17.1	6.5
	U	1012	78.5	4.1	2.6	9.8	5.1
Rajauri	T	15119	67.3	5.9	4.8	15.5	6.5
	R	14409	67.3	5.9	4.9	15.6	6.3
	U	710	67.2	6.1	3.7	12.7	10.4
Jammu	T	47514	72.8	4.6	3.5	10.5	8.6
	R	26969	69.5	5.1	4.0	12.1	9.2
	U	20545	77.0	4.0	2.8	8.3	7.8

Contd.

Contd.

1	2	3	4	5	6	7	8
Kathua	T	12467	57.5	7.8	7.3	17.9	9.6
	R	10902	57.0	8.0	7.7	18.2	9.1
	U	1565	60.5	6.2	4.8	15.7	12.8
HIMACHAL PRADESH	T	155950	41.1	8.2	9.8	29.8	11.1
	R	144756	40.2	8.3	10.2	30.4	11.0
	U	11194	53.5	6.9	4.6	23.0	12.0
Chamba	T	11394	48.0	8.6	10.3	24.2	8.9
	R	10378	45.8	9.0	11.0	25.2	9.0
	U	1016	70.9	4.6	3.1	13.1	8.3
Kangra	T	31238	35.6	8.8	9.8	32.0	13.7
	R	30051	35.1	8.9	10.0	32.3	13.7
	U	1187	47.8	8.2	6.1	24.9	13.1
Lahul & Spiti	T	766	59.8	5.7	9.5	18.7	6.3
	R	766	59.8	5.7	9.5	18.7	6.3
	U	0	0.0	0.0	0.0	0.0	0.0
Kullu	T	9786	43.8	10.4	14.4	23.5	7.8
	R	9337	43.8	10.5	14.8	23.4	7.5
	U	449	45.2	8.5	5.6	25.8	14.9
Mandi	T	24214	38.3	8.3	11.0	31.8	10.5
	R	22809	37.7	8.3	11.3	32.2	10.5
	U	1405	47.1	9.1	6.4	26.4	11.0
Hamirpur	T	13292	44.7	6.1	6.9	30.1	12.3
	R	12363	43.6	6.2	7.0	30.8	12.4
	U	929	59.1	5.1	4.5	20.5	10.9
Una	T	11172	37.5	7.5	5.7	35.7	13.6
	R	10439	38.1	7.5	5.7	35.5	13.3
	U	733	29.5	7.6	6.7	38.3	17.9
Bilaspur	T	11528	36.9	7.0	8.4	35.9	11.8
	R	11035	37.0	7.0	8.5	35.8	11.6
	U	493	34.1	7.3	4.5	39.4	14.8
Solan	T	11563	37.8	7.2	7.4	35.8	11.8
	R	10456	37.4	7.3	7.6	36.2	11.5
	U	1107	41.4	6.0	5.8	32.3	14.5

Contd.

Contd.

1	2	3	4	5	6	7	8
Sirmaur	T	13728	44.8	7.9	10.6	26.8	9.9
	R	12916	45.4	7.9	11.0	26.5	9.2
	U	812	35.2	7.5	4.7	32.4	20.2
Shimla	T	14675	49.1	9.2	11.0	21.7	9.0
	R	11612	43.4	9.9	13.2	24.3	9.3
	U	3063	70.6	6.4	2.7	12.1	8.2
Kinnaur	T	2594	53.8	9.1	15.4	18.2	3.5
	R	2594	53.8	9.1	15.4	18.2	3.5
	U	0	0.0	0.0	0.0	0.0	0.0
PUNJAB	T	424523	40.2	5.4	4.1	35.3	15.0
	R	297018	37.9	5.4	4.3	37.9	14.5
	U	127505	45.7	5.3	3.6	29.1	16.3
Gurdaspur	T	32454	35.8	6.6	4.2	35.2	18.2
	R	25355	35.5	6.6	4.1	36.3	17.5
	U	7099	36.9	6.6	4.3	31.2	21.0
Amritsar	T	45921	30.7	5.6	3.8	42.2	17.6
	R	29417	28.8	5.5	3.6	46.2	15.8
	U	16504	34.1	5.9	4.0	35.1	20.8
Kapurthala	T	12386	40.0	5.8	3.6	34.1	16.4
	R	8613	38.2	6.0	3.8	36.0	16.0
	U	3773	44.2	5.4	3.0	29.9	17.5
Jalandhar	T	28787	37.9	5.9	5.1	32.6	18.5
	R	17654	38.1	5.6	4.9	34.4	16.9
	U	11133	37.5	6.4	5.3	29.7	21.0
Hoshiarpur	T	22464	30.5	7.6	4.7	38.1	19.1
	R	18767	29.8	7.8	4.8	38.6	19.0
	U	3697	33.8	6.4	4.0	35.9	19.8
Nawanshahr *	T	12978	47.4	4.6	3.7	32.4	12.0
	R	11443	46.7	4.6	3.8	33.0	12.0
	U	1535	52.6	4.7	3.1	27.4	12.3
Rupnagar	T	20909	46.2	5.2	4.0	30.0	14.7
	R	15661	45.3	5.1	4.2	30.9	14.5
	U	5248	48.8	5.5	3.3	27.3	15.2

Contd.

Contd.

1	2	3	4	5	6	7	8
Fatehgarh Sahib *	T	15131	61.8	3.6	3.1	21.5	10.0
	R	11719	62.1	3.6	3.1	21.7	9.4
	U	3412	60.7	3.8	3.0	20.6	11.8
Ludhiana	T	57623	54.6	4.2	3.0	24.3	13.9
	R	26139	47.6	4.4	3.5	30.4	14.1
	U	31484	60.5	4.1	2.5	19.2	13.7
Moga *	T	20788	43.0	4.2	4.2	37.1	11.5
	R	16357	39.7	4.4	4.6	39.9	11.5
	U	4431	55.1	3.6	2.6	26.9	11.8
Firozpur	T	27649	25.6	6.5	5.0	48.3	14.6
	R	21189	24.4	6.6	5.1	50.1	13.7
	U	6460	29.7	6.1	4.5	42.2	17.5
Muktsar *	T	14967	36.8	5.1	4.3	41.1	12.7
	R	11628	37.8	4.9	4.4	40.8	12.0
	U	3339	33.3	5.6	3.7	42.2	15.1
Faridkot	T	10009	35.0	4.9	4.3	42.9	12.8
	R	6929	32.0	5.0	4.6	45.3	13.2
	U	3080	42.0	4.9	3.6	37.5	12.0
Bathinda	T	20997	38.1	5.8	4.7	37.9	13.5
	R	16023	38.6	5.6	5.0	38.1	12.8
	U	4974	36.4	6.5	4.0	37.3	15.7
Mansa *	T	13458	33.4	5.1	5.7	43.2	12.7
	R	11194	33.3	4.8	5.9	43.9	12.1
	U	2264	33.7	6.4	4.9	39.6	15.5
Sangrur	T	41541	46.9	4.5	3.7	32.1	12.8
	R	30459	44.0	4.5	4.0	34.3	13.2
	U	11082	54.7	4.7	3.0	26.1	11.6
Patiala	T	26461	33.2	5.8	4.7	39.3	17.0
	R	18471	31.2	5.6	4.7	42.1	16.4
	U	7990	37.8	6.3	4.7	32.8	18.4
Chandigarh	T	15538	54.2	5.7	3.9	24.6	11.6
	R	1656	57.5	6.0	3.7	22.9	9.8
	U	13882	53.8	5.6	3.9	24.8	11.8

Contd.

Contd.

1	2	3	4	5	6	7	8
UTTARANCHAL	T	194769	44.0	8.6	8.2	29.0	10.2
	R	154829	43.1	8.8	9.1	29.2	9.7
	U	39940	47.2	7.9	4.8	28.0	12.0
Uttarkashi	T	7978	37.0	10.5	12.4	32.3	7.8
	R	7527	36.9	10.5	12.6	32.2	7.8
	U	451	37.7	8.9	9.8	34.8	8.9
Chamoli	T	10030	44.1	9.6	10.3	27.4	8.6
	R	8999	42.9	9.6	10.8	28.1	8.7
	U	1031	54.6	9.8	6.0	21.5	8.1
Rudraprayag *	T	6618	56.3	7.7	8.9	21.3	5.9
	R	6565	56.2	7.7	8.9	21.3	5.9
	U	53	67.9	1.9	5.7	17.0	7.5
Tehri Garhwal	T	16514	41.9	8.6	11.2	28.8	9.4
	R	15415	41.1	8.7	11.7	29.1	9.5
	U	1099	53.8	8.0	4.4	25.1	8.7
Dehradun	T	24360	42.6	9.0	6.3	29.3	12.8
	R	12634	42.7	9.7	7.5	29.1	11.0
	U	11726	42.4	8.3	5.0	29.5	14.8
Garhwal	T	18534	44.5	8.0	10.4	26.0	11.1
	R	17186	44.9	7.7	10.7	25.6	11.1
	U	1348	39.2	11.6	6.2	31.2	11.9
Pithoragarh	T	10247	33.2	11.3	12.3	32.0	11.2
	R	9387	32.5	11.5	12.9	31.9	11.2
	U	860	41.2	9.8	5.3	32.2	11.5
Bageshwar	T	6292	44.5	8.6	8.3	28.7	9.8
	R	6167	44.7	8.5	8.4	28.6	9.9
	U	125	36.8	12.8	6.4	35.2	8.8
Almora	T	13934	40.0	8.7	10.0	28.5	12.9
	R	13055	39.2	8.9	10.4	28.7	12.8
	U	879	51.2	5.2	4.6	24.5	14.6
Champawat	T	5701	45.1	7.9	9.7	27.4	9.8
	R	5023	45.3	8.2	10.2	26.6	9.8
	U	678	44.2	5.9	6.5	33.8	9.6

Contd.

Contd.

1	2	3	4	5	6	7	8
Nainital	T	15572	36.1	10.3	9.5	31.7	12.4
	R	11320	33.9	10.6	10.9	32.5	12.1
	U	4252	42.1	9.4	5.9	29.8	12.9
Udham Singh	T	27833	48.7	7.1	4.8	30.3	9.1
Nagar *	R	19678	48.7	7.0	5.0	30.7	8.6
	U	8155	48.7	7.5	4.2	29.2	10.3
Hardwar	T	31156	49.8	7.7	4.9	29.0	8.7
	R	21873	47.6	8.3	5.2	31.1	7.8
	U	9283	54.9	6.4	4.0	24.0	10.7
HARYANA	T	455040	44.3	5.5	6.1	33.3	10.9
	R	339792	43.6	5.4	6.5	34.3	10.1
	U	115248	46.1	5.7	4.8	30.2	13.3
Panchkula *	T	9740	47.4	6.6	5.4	27.8	12.8
	R	5799	44.9	6.9	5.6	29.6	13.0
	U	3941	51.1	6.2	5.0	25.1	12.6
Ambala	T	20380	40.7	6.5	4.8	33.3	14.7
	R	13922	40.5	6.4	5.1	33.9	14.1
	U	6458	41.2	6.6	4.3	31.9	16.1
Yamunanagar	T	22573	42.8	6.0	5.6	31.3	14.3
	R	14790	41.7	6.3	6.2	32.8	13.1
	U	7783	45.0	5.4	4.4	28.5	16.7
Kurukshetra	T	20431	44.7	4.9	4.8	33.1	12.5
	R	16116	45.7	4.7	5.2	32.7	11.7
	U	4315	41.0	5.9	3.3	34.5	15.3
Kaithal	T	20422	34.4	6.0	6.8	42.2	10.6
	R	17145	34.5	5.9	6.8	42.7	10.2
	U	3277	34.1	7.0	6.7	39.3	12.8
Karnal	T	27411	40.5	5.2	5.7	36.9	11.7
	R	20662	38.9	5.4	6.1	38.3	11.3
	U	6749	45.5	4.8	4.2	32.4	13.2
Panipat	T	18601	43.8	5.6	5.1	33.9	11.5
	R	11730	42.2	5.6	5.5	36.2	10.6
	U	6871	46.6	5.6	4.5	30.1	13.2

Contd.

Contd.

1	2	3	4	5	6	7	8
Sonipat	T	30949	52.4	5.1	4.9	28.3	9.3
	R	22982	51.2	5.2	5.2	29.7	8.7
	U	7967	55.6	4.9	4.0	24.5	11.0
Jind	T	31107	48.9	4.6	5.4	32.2	8.9
	R	25680	48.7	4.5	5.7	32.7	8.3
	U	5427	49.5	4.7	3.9	30.1	11.7
Fatehabad *	T	25624	54.4	4.3	5.0	27.9	8.4
	R	21765	54.0	4.2	5.3	28.4	8.1
	U	3859	56.4	4.6	3.4	25.4	10.1
Sirsa	T	34312	55.0	4.6	4.8	26.9	8.7
	R	25998	55.0	4.5	5.0	27.2	8.3
	U	8314	54.8	5.0	4.2	26.0	10.0
Hisar	T	32304	42.1	5.5	6.5	34.4	11.4
	R	23965	41.4	5.6	6.7	35.8	10.6
	U	8339	44.2	5.3	5.9	30.6	13.9
Bhiwani	T	27864	38.2	6.3	8.1	35.8	11.6
	R	23302	38.9	6.2	8.6	35.3	11.0
	U	4562	34.8	6.4	5.7	38.3	14.8
Rohtak	T	15864	34.9	6.4	6.7	38.3	13.8
	R	10209	33.1	6.2	7.1	41.7	11.8
	U	5655	38.0	6.8	5.8	32.1	17.3
Jhajjar *	T	16110	37.2	6.0	8.0	37.3	11.5
	R	13178	37.0	5.9	7.9	38.3	11.0
	U	2932	38.4	6.6	8.4	32.6	14.1
Mahendragarh	T	18912	40.6	5.5	8.5	36.3	9.2
	R	16818	40.5	5.5	9.0	36.0	9.0
	U	2094	41.0	5.0	4.3	39.0	10.8
Rewari	T	15208	41.6	5.4	7.4	34.1	11.4
	R	12778	40.9	5.4	7.8	35.1	10.8
	U	2430	45.6	5.6	5.3	29.0	14.6
Gurgaon	T	29744	40.6	6.3	7.5	35.4	10.1
	R	24311	40.6	5.7	8.0	36.4	9.2
	U	5433	40.6	8.9	5.4	31.0	14.1

Contd.

Contd.

1		2	3	4	5	6	7	8
Faridabad		T	37484	46.1	5.3	6.0	32.5	10.1
		R	18642	43.5	5.2	7.2	36.1	8.1
		U	18842	48.6	5.4	4.8	29.1	12.1
DELHI		T	235886	51.2	6.6	3.7	27.5	11.0
		R	13432	36.7	7.7	5.3	38.9	11.5
		U	222454	52.0	6.5	3.6	26.8	11.0
North West	*	T	45872	45.1	6.9	3.9	31.7	12.4
		R	4180	37.8	8.4	4.8	37.5	11.5
		U	41692	45.8	6.8	3.8	31.1	12.5
North	*	T	16460	57.7	5.7	2.9	23.5	10.2
		R	751	50.2	4.5	4.1	30.1	11.1
		U	15709	58.1	5.7	2.8	23.2	10.2
North East	*	T	31137	45.9	6.7	3.9	33.2	10.3
		R	2260	36.9	7.4	5.5	38.3	11.9
		U	28877	46.6	6.7	3.8	32.8	10.2
East	*	T	22235	50.2	7.1	4.0	26.2	12.5
		R	177	24.3	6.8	7.9	49.2	11.9
		U	22058	50.4	7.1	4.0	26.1	12.5
New Delhi		T	3735	65.6	4.4	2.5	19.3	8.1
		R	0	0.0	0.0	0.0	0.0	0.0
		U	3735	65.6	4.4	2.5	19.3	8.1
Central	*	T	13807	61.6	5.6	2.9	19.1	10.8
		R	0	0.0	0.0	0.0	0.0	0.0
		U	13807	61.6	5.6	2.9	19.1	10.8
West	*	T	37578	50.7	6.7	4.0	26.9	11.7
		R	1418	40.4	6.4	5.0	37.7	10.4
		U	36160	51.1	6.7	4.0	26.5	11.7
South West	*	T	26617	48.5	7.0	3.8	30.0	10.7
		R	2984	33.0	7.8	5.9	41.9	11.4
		U	23633	50.5	6.9	3.5	28.5	10.6
South	*	T	38445	57.7	6.2	3.5	23.0	9.5
		R	1662	32.1	8.7	5.6	41.5	12.1
		U	36783	58.8	6.1	3.4	22.2	9.4

Contd.

Contd.

1	2	3	4	5	6	7	8
RAJASTHAN	T	1411979	53.4	5.2	5.3	28.4	7.7
	R	1109383	53.3	5.0	5.8	28.7	7.2
	U	302596	53.7	5.8	3.8	27.1	9.6
Ganganagar	T	39414	40.8	7.5	5.8	34.9	11.1
	R	29766	39.3	6.7	6.5	36.3	11.1
	U	9648	45.2	9.8	3.7	30.4	10.9
Hanumangarh *	T	28276	34.5	7.0	6.9	39.9	11.6
	R	23293	35.0	7.0	7.2	39.7	11.1
	U	4983	32.6	7.3	5.5	41.0	13.6
Bikaner	T	27308	45.2	7.0	7.0	30.6	10.2
	R	17141	44.3	7.0	8.2	31.2	9.3
	U	10167	46.7	7.1	5.1	29.7	11.5
Churu	T	37116	40.8	7.1	7.8	34.2	10.2
	R	26042	39.9	6.8	8.7	34.5	10.0
	U	11074	42.8	7.6	5.7	33.5	10.5
Jhunjhunun	T	33293	41.1	7.0	6.6	34.4	10.9
	R	27140	41.3	6.8	7.0	34.3	10.7
	U	6153	40.5	7.9	5.2	34.7	11.6
Alwar	T	72223	52.7	5.3	4.5	30.3	7.2
	R	59625	51.3	5.2	4.8	31.7	7.0
	U	12598	59.6	5.4	3.1	24.1	7.9
Bharatpur	T	55789	58.7	4.4	4.5	26.7	5.7
	R	44238	58.3	4.3	4.8	27.1	5.5
	U	11551	60.3	4.7	3.3	24.9	6.7
Dhaulpur	T	28338	62.5	4.1	3.4	24.8	5.3
	R	23763	63.5	3.9	3.4	24.3	4.9
	U	4575	57.1	5.0	3.6	27.4	7.0
Karauli *	T	25481	42.4	5.8	6.2	38.0	7.5
	R	21969	43.1	5.7	6.6	37.7	7.0
	U	3512	38.5	6.7	4.3	39.9	10.6
Sawai Madhopur	T	27832	50.0	5.3	6.0	31.0	7.7
	R	21883	49.3	5.3	6.6	31.5	7.3
	U	5949	52.7	5.3	3.9	28.9	9.3

Contd.

Contd.

1	2	3	4	5	6	7	8
Dausa *	T	32637	57.6	4.8	4.5	27.1	6.0
	R	29624	57.7	4.8	4.6	27.0	5.9
	U	3013	56.1	5.1	4.0	27.9	7.0
Jaipur	T	136829	57.6	5.2	3.8	25.7	7.8
	R	72732	57.6	4.8	4.0	27.2	6.4
	U	64097	57.6	5.6	3.4	24.0	9.4
Sikar	T	62433	61.9	4.5	4.3	22.7	6.5
	R	50047	61.4	4.5	4.6	23.2	6.3
	U	12386	64.0	4.6	3.3	20.9	7.2
Nagaur	T	57746	45.3	5.9	6.7	33.5	8.6
	R	49193	44.9	5.7	7.2	33.8	8.4
	U	8553	47.9	6.8	4.0	31.5	9.9
Jodhpur	T	77925	57.6	5.3	5.3	23.6	8.1
	R	51949	55.5	5.4	6.5	24.9	7.7
	U	25976	61.8	5.1	3.1	21.0	9.0
Jaisalmer	T	12144	54.7	5.9	6.7	25.7	7.1
	R	10320	55.1	5.7	6.9	25.3	6.9
	U	1824	52.0	7.0	5.2	28.1	7.7
Jarmer	T	53488	58.9	5.0	6.3	22.5	7.3
	R	48154	57.4	5.1	6.7	23.3	7.4
	U	5334	72.3	4.1	2.4	15.3	5.9
Jalor	T	56769	67.8	3.8	5.0	18.2	5.1
	R	53477	68.2	3.7	5.1	18.0	5.0
	U	3292	61.7	5.9	3.4	21.2	7.9
Sirohi	T	21780	53.5	5.8	5.9	27.4	7.4
	R	18845	54.7	5.6	6.2	26.6	7.0
	U	2935	45.9	7.3	3.9	32.5	10.4
Pali	T	77719	67.5	3.6	4.1	19.9	5.0
	R	64551	68.0	3.6	4.2	19.4	4.7
	U	13168	64.8	3.9	3.1	22.1	6.1
Ajmer	T	45889	45.6	5.3	5.3	34.5	9.3
	R	29528	45.3	4.8	5.7	36.2	8.0
	U	16361	46.2	6.1	4.7	31.4	11.6

Contd.

Contd.

1	2	3	4	5	6	7	8
Tonk	T	29059	41.1	5.7	7.0	37.9	8.4
	R	23873	41.5	5.5	7.5	37.7	7.8
	U	5186	39.0	6.4	4.5	38.6	11.5
Bundi	T	23974	47.7	5.7	5.8	32.3	8.4
	R	19088	46.9	5.7	6.2	32.8	8.3
	U	4886	51.1	5.5	4.5	30.2	8.7
Bhilwara	T	44884	45.2	5.7	5.3	35.5	8.4
	R	36470	45.5	5.4	5.5	35.8	7.8
	U	8414	43.6	6.6	4.6	34.3	10.9
Rajsamand *	T	27420	55.0	4.2	4.6	28.5	7.7
	R	23508	53.1	4.2	4.9	30.1	7.7
	U	3912	66.5	4.3	2.8	19.0	7.4
Udaipur	T	63377	52.9	4.7	5.3	28.7	8.3
	R	54749	53.6	4.5	5.5	28.9	7.6
	U	8628	49.0	6.4	3.9	27.9	12.8
Dungarpur	T	41078	62.5	4.2	5.2	22.5	5.6
	R	37905	61.7	4.2	5.5	23.0	5.6
	U	3173	71.8	3.8	2.0	15.9	6.5
Banswara	T	46773	61.7	4.0	4.6	24.0	5.7
	R	43922	61.6	3.9	4.8	24.2	5.5
	U	2851	63.7	4.5	2.4	20.9	8.5
Chittaurgarh	T	44200	48.5	4.6	6.4	32.7	7.9
	R	38439	49.1	4.5	6.6	32.5	7.3
	U	5761	44.6	5.8	4.4	33.6	11.5
Kota	T	32862	44.4	5.7	5.1	33.5	11.3
	R	16754	42.8	5.7	6.9	34.9	9.7
	U	16108	46.1	5.7	3.3	32.1	12.9
Baran *	T	21795	43.2	6.1	8.4	33.4	8.8
	R	18417	43.3	6.1	9.0	33.1	8.5
	U	3378	42.8	6.5	5.3	34.6	10.9
Jhalawar	T	26128	47.9	5.1	6.2	32.3	8.5
	R	22978	48.0	5.1	6.5	32.2	8.2
	U	3150	47.0	5.2	4.5	32.7	10.6

Contd.

Contd.

1	2	3	4	5	6	7	8
UTTAR	T	3453369	53.6	7.4	3.7	26.9	8.3
PRADESH	R	2705784	53.4	7.4	3.9	27.5	7.8
	U	747585	54.4	7.5	3.1	25.0	10.0
Saharanpur	T	56378	48.7	9.2	4.2	27.5	10.4
	R	45090	50.5	9.2	4.2	26.9	9.2
	U	11288	41.7	9.0	4.0	30.1	15.2
Muzaffarnagar	T	66869	42.3	7.7	4.8	35.3	9.9
	R	50884	42.0	7.6	4.9	36.5	9.1
	U	15985	43.4	8.1	4.5	31.6	12.4
Bijnor	T	47135	32.9	11.0	5.2	40.4	10.4
	R	36917	32.8	11.0	5.3	41.5	9.4
	U	10218	33.6	11.0	4.9	36.5	14.0
Moradabad	T	50301	34.1	12.8	4.9	37.7	10.6
	R	36680	35.1	12.3	4.9	38.5	9.1
	U	13621	31.3	14.3	4.7	35.2	14.5
Rampur	T	58730	67.6	5.2	2.5	18.4	6.3
	R	42651	66.4	5.3	2.5	19.9	5.9
	U	16079	70.9	4.8	2.4	14.6	7.3
Jyotiba Phule	T	24288	48.5	8.0	3.8	32.0	7.7
Nagar *	R	17875	44.8	8.9	4.2	35.1	7.0
	U	6413	58.9	5.7	2.7	23.2	9.5
Meerut	T	44092	36.5	7.3	4.7	40.4	11.0
	R	24385	34.1	7.7	5.0	44.1	9.2
	U	19707	39.6	6.9	4.3	35.9	13.2
Baghpat *	T	19964	30.3	6.9	5.7	47.2	9.8
	R	16241	29.7	7.0	5.9	48.0	9.5
	U	3723	33.4	6.3	5.2	43.9	11.1
Ghaziabad	T	50696	40.0	9.0	4.4	36.4	10.2
	R	24879	36.6	9.4	5.3	39.7	9.1
	U	25817	43.3	8.6	3.6	33.2	11.2
Gautam Buddha	T	24632	50.1	8.1	3.8	28.8	9.2
Nagar *	R	16512	45.9	8.2	4.5	32.8	8.7
	U	8120	58.7	7.8	2.5	20.7	10.3

Contd.

Contd.

1	2	3	4	5	6	7	8
Bulandshahr	T	64011	49.7	6.7	4.6	31.0	8.0
	R	46904	44.0	6.7	5.1	35.9	8.4
	U	17107	65.3	6.5	3.3	17.8	7.1
Aligarh	T	71674	51.7	7.9	3.6	28.8	8.0
	R	48982	47.4	7.8	4.1	32.7	7.9
	U	22692	61.0	7.9	2.7	20.2	8.1
Hathras *	T	43298	62.5	7.2	2.5	22.0	5.9
	R	34591	60.7	7.3	2.7	23.4	5.9
	U	8707	69.6	6.6	1.6	16.3	5.9
Mathura	T	49682	56.8	5.0	3.4	28.0	6.8
	R	35411	55.0	5.0	3.5	30.3	6.2
	U	14271	61.5	4.9	3.0	22.3	8.3
Agra	T	93959	62.9	6.8	3.3	20.2	6.8
	R	54170	60.0	5.8	3.5	24.8	5.8
	U	39789	66.7	8.2	3.0	13.9	8.2
Firozabad	T	53723	55.5	5.8	2.9	28.4	7.3
	R	37089	55.7	5.8	3.2	28.5	6.8
	U	16634	55.2	5.9	2.4	28.1	8.5
Etah	T	74961	59.7	5.4	2.6	24.8	7.4
	R	61576	60.0	5.3	2.6	24.9	7.1
	U	13385	58.5	5.7	2.6	24.4	8.8
Mainpuri	T	27165	42.1	6.7	4.6	37.7	8.9
	R	22917	42.0	6.7	4.9	37.7	8.7
	U	4248	42.5	6.8	2.9	37.7	10.0
Budaun	T	50771	39.0	7.5	4.7	39.7	9.1
	R	40675	38.4	7.8	4.7	40.4	8.7
	U	10096	41.2	6.6	4.3	36.9	11.0
Bareilly	T	54814	29.4	8.1	5.3	44.3	12.9
	R	37126	29.5	8.0	5.5	46.1	11.0
	U	17688	29.0	8.5	5.0	40.7	16.8
Pilibhit	T	36548	50.2	7.1	4.2	30.2	8.3
	R	29795	49.7	7.2	4.3	31.0	7.9
	U	6753	52.6	6.6	3.5	27.1	10.2

Contd.

Contd.

1	2	3	4	5	6	7	8
Shahjahanpur	T	46278	50.0	6.4	3.5	32.0	8.1
	R	37885	52.9	5.6	3.5	30.8	7.2
	U	8393	36.6	10.1	3.8	37.1	12.3
Kheri	T	70530	56.5	7.6	3.6	24.9	7.4
	R	63551	56.7	7.7	3.7	24.8	7.1
	U	6979	54.3	6.9	2.8	25.9	10.0
Sitapur	T	63249	45.9	7.2	5.1	33.6	8.2
	R	56072	46.1	7.2	5.2	33.8	7.7
	U	7177	43.8	7.4	4.6	32.2	12.0
Hardoi	T	68884	52.2	6.4	4.4	29.2	7.8
	R	60514	53.0	6.4	4.4	29.0	7.3
	U	8370	46.7	6.7	4.3	30.6	11.7
Unnao	T	55306	43.7	8.4	4.3	34.8	8.8
	R	46367	43.5	8.5	4.5	35.0	8.5
	U	8939	44.6	8.0	3.4	33.9	10.1
Lucknow	T	68182	48.7	8.3	3.8	27.4	11.8
	R	22255	38.6	9.2	5.0	35.9	11.3
	U	45927	53.6	7.9	3.2	23.3	12.0
Rae Bareli	T	54228	46.5	8.9	4.6	30.1	9.8
	R	48509	46.7	8.5	4.8	30.3	9.7
	U	5719	45.1	12.1	3.6	28.4	10.9
Farrukhabad	T	48362	64.9	4.9	2.4	22.4	5.3
	R	37066	65.3	5.1	2.4	22.1	5.0
	U	11296	63.8	4.0	2.4	23.4	6.3
Kannauj *	T	25416	40.1	6.8	4.3	40.8	8.1
	R	21439	40.9	6.7	4.4	40.2	7.7
	U	3977	35.4	7.4	3.5	43.8	10.0
Etawah	T	24548	40.4	6.3	4.9	39.5	8.8
	R	19164	41.7	6.2	5.2	38.8	8.1
	U	5384	35.6	6.9	3.8	42.2	11.5
Auraiya *	T	24876	40.9	8.0	4.7	38.1	8.4
	R	21405	41.4	7.6	4.8	38.1	8.2
	U	3471	38.2	10.0	4.0	38.4	9.4

Contd.

Contd.

1	2	3	4	5	6	7	8
Kanpur Dehat	T	57022	62.6	5.1	3.5	22.7	6.0
	R	52835	62.4	5.0	3.6	22.8	6.2
	U	4187	64.9	6.0	3.0	21.7	4.4
Kanpur Nagar	T	148444	66.0	5.0	2.4	18.8	7.8
	R	47075	66.1	4.3	3.6	20.7	5.4
	U	101369	65.9	5.3	1.9	17.9	9.0
Jalaun	T	39312	57.9	7.4	4.3	24.1	6.3
	R	29141	57.0	7.6	4.9	24.4	6.1
	U	10171	60.8	6.6	2.4	23.2	7.0
Jhansi	T	44386	56.9	6.0	3.5	25.9	7.7
	R	25638	58.6	5.8	4.0	25.8	5.8
	U	18748	54.5	6.2	2.9	26.2	10.2
Lalitpur	T	26782	62.5	4.8	2.9	24.6	5.2
	R	22389	63.0	4.9	3.0	24.2	4.8
	U	4393	59.8	4.3	2.7	26.3	6.9
Hamirpur	T	17646	41.1	8.0	7.6	34.7	8.6
	R	14555	40.7	7.7	8.4	34.6	8.5
	U	3091	43.0	9.0	4.0	35.0	9.0
Mahoba *	T	13674	45.0	7.1	5.6	34.8	7.4
	R	10592	45.2	7.3	5.9	34.7	6.9
	U	3082	44.4	6.6	4.7	34.9	9.4
Banda	T	31530	44.7	7.5	5.7	34.1	8.1
	R	24521	42.5	7.9	6.4	34.9	8.2
	U	7009	52.2	6.1	3.1	30.9	7.6
Chitrakoot *	T	16065	50.9	9.1	4.2	28.6	7.2
	R	14173	51.1	9.1	4.4	28.5	7.0
	U	1892	49.5	9.4	3.3	29.5	8.2
Fatehpur	T	40711	44.7	6.7	5.4	33.3	9.9
	R	37007	45.7	6.6	5.5	32.5	9.7
	U	3704	34.7	7.3	4.2	41.2	12.7
Pratapgarh	T	54062	53.3	9.7	3.2	25.7	8.1
	R	51165	53.6	9.7	3.3	25.5	8.0
	U	2897	48.9	9.1	2.3	30.1	9.5

Contd.

Contd.

1	2	3	4	5	6	7	8
Kaushambi *	T	23409	52.9	6.6	2.9	30.4	7.1
	R	21395	52.7	6.6	2.9	30.8	6.9
	U	2014	55.2	7.0	2.5	26.6	8.8
Allahabad	T	122262	60.0	8.0	2.8	21.4	7.8
	R	93590	61.6	7.2	2.8	21.4	6.9
	U	28672	54.6	10.6	2.7	21.4	10.7
Barabanki	T	79104	65.8	6.7	2.9	18.6	5.9
	R	70786	65.2	6.9	3.0	19.1	5.8
	U	8318	71.5	5.3	2.0	14.2	7.0
Faizabad	T	28137	33.4	8.2	5.7	40.1	12.7
	R	24453	34.1	7.9	5.7	39.9	12.4
	U	3684	28.7	9.8	5.2	41.7	14.7
Ambedkar	T	44530	59.8	6.5	3.0	21.4	9.2
Nagar *	R	40777	60.2	6.4	3.0	21.2	9.1
	U	3753	56.1	7.1	2.7	23.5	10.5
Sultanpur	T	72316	58.3	6.3	3.5	22.5	9.5
	R	69194	58.4	6.3	3.5	22.5	9.4
	U	3122	55.7	6.4	3.0	22.8	12.0
Bahraich	T	45292	56.5	8.9	4.0	22.6	8.0
	R	40740	57.9	8.7	4.0	21.7	7.6
	U	4552	44.1	10.8	3.4	30.0	11.8
Shrawasti *	T	14169	38.0	13.7	5.8	32.8	9.8
	R	13759	38.1	13.7	5.7	32.7	9.8
	U	410	35.1	12.2	7.3	35.6	9.8
Balrampur *	T	35846	64.9	8.4	3.0	17.1	6.7
	R	32109	64.8	8.4	3.0	17.1	6.6
	U	3737	65.2	8.1	2.4	16.9	7.5
Gonda	T	49977	58.4	7.7	3.4	23.1	7.5
	R	45277	57.6	7.8	3.5	23.5	7.6
	U	4700	66.3	6.1	2.0	19.1	6.6
Siddharthnagar	T	43811	68.6	6.0	2.9	16.0	6.5
	R	41490	68.7	6.0	2.9	15.9	6.5
	U	2321	66.7	6.3	2.3	17.5	7.1

Contd.

Contd.

1	2	3	4	5	6	7	8
Basti	T	43888	56.5	9.5	3.4	20.7	9.9
	R	40979	56.2	9.7	3.5	20.7	9.9
	U	2909	60.5	6.1	2.6	20.6	10.2
Sant Kabir	T	25482	58.2	7.6	3.92	2.0	8.4
Nagar *	R	23662	58.4	7.6	3.9	21.8	8.3
	U	1820	56.0	7.1	3.5	24.0	9.5
Maharajganj	T	63909	72.8	5.6	2.7	13.4	5.5
	R	61208	73.1	5.5	2.7	13.2	5.4
	U	2701	65.2	7.2	2.3	17.3	8.0
Gorakhpur	T	56631	43.3	11.0	4.7	31.5	9.5
	R	45017	44.3	10.6	4.8	31.3	9.0
	U	11614	39.6	12.4	4.2	32.1	11.6
Kushinagar *	T	39099	45.4	10.9	5.3	30.9	7.4
	R	37062	45.9	10.8	5.3	30.6	7.4
	U	2037	36.4	12.6	5.5	36.9	8.5
Deoria	T	65497	60.5	8.6	3.5	20.8	6.6
	R	59370	61.6	8.3	3.4	20.4	6.4
	U	6127	50.5	11.4	4.9	24.3	8.9
Azamgarh	T	106710	69.3	5.9	2.4	14.9	7.5
	R	97770	69.0	6.0	2.5	15.0	7.6
	U	8940	72.2	5.5	1.7	13.5	7.1
Mau	T	24817	42.2	8.6	4.6	32.7	11.8
	R	19542	42.1	8.7	4.8	33.0	11.4
	U	5275	42.7	8.4	3.9	31.6	13.4
Ballia	T	52629	50.3	8.3	3.9	28.5	9.0
	R	47908	50.6	8.3	3.9	28.3	8.9
	U	4721	46.7	8.4	3.8	30.9	10.3
Jaunpur	T	75673	59.8	6.7	3.1	21.6	8.8
	R	69805	59.9	6.6	3.2	21.7	8.7
	U	5868	58.8	7.4	2.0	20.9	10.9
Ghazipur	T	49766	49.8	9.2	3.3	28.0	9.7
	R	45034	49.1	9.3	3.3	28.5	9.7
	U	4732	56.1	8.5	3.1	23.1	9.1

Contd.

Contd.

1	2	3	4	5	6	7	8
Chandauli *	T	30388	49.3	8.4	3.5	29.8	9.1
	R	26106	48.4	8.5	3.7	30.5	8.9
	U	4282	54.5	8.0	2.4	25.1	10.0
Varanasi	T	80071	63.4	6.6	2.6	19.3	8.1
	R	47795	64.1	6.0	2.7	19.8	7.4
	U	32276	62.4	7.4	2.4	18.5	9.2
Sant Ravidas	T	24818	53.9	7.8	2.6	26.8	8.9
Nagar Bhadohi*	R	22642	54.8	7.5	2.5	26.4	8.7
	U	2176	44.4	10.1	2.8	31.2	11.4
Mirzapur	T	33476	45.2	8.9	3.8	33.4	8.7
	R	28670	45.5	9.1	3.8	33.3	8.3
	U	4806	43.3	7.9	3.7	34.3	10.9
Sonbhadra	T	18478	42.3	10.4	5.2	32.8	9.3
	R	14976	42.4	10.1	5.6	33.0	8.9
	U	3502	41.8	11.6	3.7	32.1	10.8
BIHAR	T	1887611	53.3	6.9	3.9	27.1	8.8
	R	1692454	53.4	6.9	4.0	27.1	8.6
	U	195157	52.6	6.6	3.3	27.3	10.3
Pashchim	T	49803	49.6	8.4	5.5	29.7	6.9
Champaran	R	43279	48.4	8.6	5.7	30.5	6.8
	U	6524	57.2	6.7	4.5	24.5	7.1
Purba	T	122856	68.4	5.8	2.5	16.8	6.5
Champaran	R	115947	68.8	5.8	2.5	16.5	6.4
	U	6909	62.0	5.6	2.7	21.6	8.1
Sheohar *	T	13346	61.1	6.1	3.6	21.6	7.6
	R	12965	61.4	6.0	3.6	21.3	7.6
	U	381	50.1	10.0	3.7	28.9	7.3
Sitamarhi	T	49273	45.9	9.4	5.3	29.7	9.7
	R	46908	46.3	9.3	5.3	29.6	9.5
	U	2365	38.1	10.5	5.0	33.4	13.0
Madhubani	T	72405	48.7	7.6	4.3	29.1	10.3
	R	70452	48.9	7.6	4.4	28.9	10.2
	U	1953	38.4	8.0	3.3	37.1	13.2

Contd.

Contd.

1	2	3	4	5	6	7	8
Supaul *	T	45655	62.9	5.7	4.4	20.9	6.2
	R	43931	63.3	5.6	4.4	20.6	6.1
	U	1724	52.8	6.9	3.8	28.0	8.5
Araria	T	63414	57.3	8.4	5.0	21.0	8.3
	R	59307	56.9	8.5	5.1	21.4	8.2
	U	4107	63.9	7.6	3.2	15.6	9.8
Kishanganj	T	27083	53.2	9.3	5.5	21.1	10.9
	R	23953	53.4	9.3	5.7	20.9	10.8
	U	3130	51.9	9.3	4.0	22.5	12.3
Purnia	T	74871	58.5	9.3	3.9	20.6	7.7
	R	69847	59.2	9.3	3.8	20.2	7.5
	U	5024	49.0	9.2	4.8	26.2	10.8
Katihar	T	73260	64.0	7.4	3.8	17.4	7.4
	R	64379	62.9	7.7	4.0	18.0	7.4
	U	8881	72.1	5.4	2.1	13.2	7.1
Madhepura	T	29404	52.1	8.2	3.9	27.6	8.1
	R	27523	51.3	8.3	4.0	28.2	8.2
	U	1881	64.9	6.6	2.6	19.4	6.6
Saharsa	T	27952	49.4	7.4	4.2	32.9	6.2
	R	25347	50.8	7.2	4.2	31.9	6.0
	U	2605	35.3	9.3	4.2	42.8	8.4
Darbhanga	T	75771	53.6	6.8	3.4	27.1	9.1
	R	70035	54.1	6.7	3.4	26.9	8.9
	U	5736	47.2	8.5	3.6	29.4	11.3
Muzaffarpur	T	81743	54.0	7.4	4.4	26.6	7.5
	R	74120	54.1	7.4	4.5	26.7	7.3
	U	7623	53.7	6.4	4.0	26.5	9.3
Gopalganj	T	42612	52.3	8.3	4.3	26.6	8.4
	R	39809	52.2	8.4	4.3	26.8	8.4
	U	2803	53.7	7.5	4.2	25.0	9.5
Siwan	T	45419	41.9	7.9	5.4	32.2	12.7
	R	42792	41.3	8.0	5.5	32.6	12.7
	U	2627	51.4	6.9	3.0	25.9	12.8

Contd.

Contd.

1	2	3	4	5	6	7	8
Saran	T	57589	42.6	6.9	4.8	32.3	13.4
	R	52051	42.4	6.9	4.8	32.4	13.4
	U	5538	44.3	6.9	4.6	30.9	13.2
Vaishali	T	59135	55.5	6.2	3.5	27.2	7.6
	R	54859	55.4	6.3	3.5	27.3	7.5
	U	4276	56.6	5.8	3.0	26.3	8.3
Samastipur	T	97347	58.4	6.3	3.4	25.0	7.0
	R	95290	58.8	6.3	3.3	24.7	6.9
	U	2057	41.5	7.8	4.4	35.2	11.0
Begusarai	T	61031	51.8	6.7	3.1	29.0	9.4
	R	58369	51.7	6.7	3.2	29.1	9.4
	U	2662	53.6	6.7	2.1	26.8	10.8
Khagaria	T	31759	54.3	6.8	3.7	27.5	7.7
	R	29999	54.7	6.8	3.7	27.2	7.6
	U	1760	48.0	6.1	3.7	33.4	8.8
Bhagalpur	T	58765	52.5	5.6	3.2	29.3	9.4
	R	48921	52.9	5.6	3.2	29.1	9.2
	U	9844	50.5	5.7	2.9	30.4	10.6
Banka *	T	28937	49.5	7.3	5.1	30.4	7.8
	R	27881	49.6	7.3	5.1	30.3	7.8
	U	1056	46.6	6.9	5.0	34.4	7.1
Munger	T	38252	61.6	5.3	2.4	23.3	7.4
	R	25540	60.0	5.4	2.5	24.8	7.3
	U	12712	64.9	5.1	2.3	20.2	7.5
Lakhisarai *	T	20714	53.4	5.9	4.0	28.6	8.1
	R	17470	52.7	6.0	4.0	29.3	8.1
	U	3244	57.2	5.8	3.7	25.2	8.2
Sheikhpura *	T	11171	50.1	6.6	3.8	30.7	8.7
	R	9531	50.6	6.5	3.9	30.8	8.3
	U	1640	47.1	7.6	3.5	30.4	11.4
Nalanda	T	63028	49.9	5.7	3.4	32.4	8.6
	R	54536	50.1	5.6	3.5	32.6	8.2
	U	8492	48.6	6.4	2.8	31.3	10.9

Contd.

Contd.

1	2	3	4	5	6	7	8
Patna	T	98862	48.3	6.0	3.4	32.2	10.1
	R	60957	48.1	5.7	3.6	33.5	9.1
	U	37905	48.6	6.5	3.1	29.9	11.8
Bhojpur	T	44648	51.5	6.0	3.6	28.3	10.6
	R	39622	52.5	6.0	3.7	27.8	10.1
	U	5026	43.5	6.5	3.4	32.1	14.5
Buxar *	T	23308	46.2	6.6	4.3	31.3	11.6
	R	20532	45.2	6.7	4.5	32.2	11.5
	U	2776	53.6	5.6	3.4	25.1	12.3
Kaimur	T	26978	58.8	5.9	3.1	24.1	8.0
(Bhabua) *	R	25797	58.3	6.0	3.2	24.4	8.1
	U	1181	69.1	4.9	1.6	17.0	7.4
Rohtas	T	60094	56.9	5.4	3.4	27.1	7.3
	R	50911	55.6	5.4	3.6	28.2	7.3
	U	9183	64.2	4.9	2.7	20.8	7.3
Jehanabad	T	34590	42.5	7.4	4.0	34.8	11.2
	R	31792	42.6	7.4	4.0	34.9	11.1
	U	2798	42.2	7.8	3.7	34.0	12.3
Aurangabad	T	41352	44.7	6.8	4.5	34.0	10.0
	R	37896	44.7	6.9	4.6	34.0	9.8
	U	3456	44.1	6.5	4.2	33.9	11.4
Gaya	T	73769	46.4	6.5	4.0	33.4	9.7
	R	63257	46.2	6.5	4.2	33.8	9.3
	U	10512	47.8	7.0	2.5	30.9	11.8
Nawada	T	34240	41.3	7.0	4.5	35.5	11.6
	R	31446	41.1	7.0	4.7	35.8	11.5
	U	2794	44.1	6.7	2.9	32.7	13.7
Jamui *	T	27175	45.8	7.7	4.9	30.3	11.3
	R	25203	46.6	7.7	4.9	29.6	11.2
	U	1972	35.5	7.6	5.3	39.2	12.4
SIKKIM	T	20367	53.0	15.6	16.9	10.7	3.9
	R	18571	50.9	16.4	17.9	11.0	3.9
	U	1796	74.4	7.2	6.1	7.6	4.7

Contd.

Contd.

1	2	3	4	5	6	7	8
North	T	1501	59.7	12.1	13.1	11.9	3.2
	R	1474	59.7	12.1	13.4	11.7	3.2
	U	27	59.3	14.8	0.0	22.2	3.7
West	T	4618	52.7	15.9	16.8	11.0	3.6
	R	4518	52.1	16.0	17.1	11.2	3.6
	U	100	83.0	10.0	2.0	3.0	2.0
South	T	5828	47.8	18.0	20.0	9.9	4.3
	R	5690	47.3	18.2	20.2	10.0	4.2
	U	138	65.2	10.9	11.6	5.1	7.2
East	T	8420	55.5	14.3	15.4	10.8	4.0
	R	6889	51.2	16.1	17.5	11.4	3.8
	U	1531	74.9	6.6	5.9	7.9	4.6
ARUNACHAL	T	33315	69.3	7.3	9.2	10.4	3.8
PRADESH	R	27456	66.8	7.9	10.5	10.9	3.9
	U	5859	81.1	4.3	3.3	8.0	3.3
Tawang	T	1327	60.2	9.0	16.0	12.2	2.6
	R	1128	54.8	10.3	18.2	14.1	2.7
	U	199	91.0	2.0	3.5	1.5	2.0
West Kameng	T	2661	72.3	7.6	9.8	8.3	2.0
	R	2460	71.0	7.8	10.2	8.8	2.1
	U	201	87.6	5.0	5.0	1.5	1.0
East Kameng	T	2683	75.0	5.6	8.1	9.4	2.0
	R	2184	74.0	5.6	9.0	9.3	2.1
	U	499	79.2	5.6	4.2	9.6	1.4
Papum Pare *	T	4128	81.3	4.7	3.9	7.8	2.3
	R	2384	79.6	5.3	5.2	7.8	2.1
	U	1744	83.5	3.8	2.2	7.8	2.6
Lower Subansiri	T	3376	74.8	5.2	8.0	9.5	2.5
	R	3017	72.9	5.6	8.7	10.1	2.7
	U	359	90.8	1.7	1.7	4.5	1.4
Upper Subansiri	T	2076	76.3	5.5	6.9	8.1	3.2
	R	1550	73.1	6.4	8.3	9.2	3.1
	U	526	85.6	3.0	3.0	4.9	3.4

Contd.

Contd.

1	2	3	4	5	6	7	8
West Siang	T	3556	72.6	7.6	7.9	8.5	3.5
	R	2769	68.7	8.7	9.6	9.3	3.7
	U	787	86.0	3.6	1.9	5.8	2.7
East Siang	T	2708	66.1	6.7	10.5	11.0	5.6
	R	2212	62.8	7.5	12.0	11.8	5.9
	U	496	80.6	3.4	4.0	7.5	4.4
Upper Siang *	T	1339	67.9	6.6	13.3	10.1	2.2
	R	1339	67.9	6.6	13.3	10.1	2.2
	U	0	0.0	0.0	0.0	0.0	0.0
Dibang Valley	T	1844	65.7	8.6	9.7	11.5	4.5
	R	1562	64.1	9.2	10.4	11.9	4.5
	U	282	74.8	5.7	5.7	9.2	4.6
Lohit	T	3069	63.1	9.4	8.6	13.0	5.9
	R	2724	64.1	9.1	9.0	12.3	5.6
	U	345	55.9	11.6	5.8	18.8	7.8
Changlang	T	2635	50.8	12.4	15.9	14.0	6.9
	R	2423	49.3	13.0	16.7	13.8	7.1
	U	212	67.5	5.2	6.1	16.5	4.7
Tirap	T	1913	58.3	8.4	10.6	16.4	6.4
	R	1704	57.2	8.7	11.4	16.6	6.1
	U	209	67.5	5.3	3.8	14.4	9.1
NAGALAND	T	26499	37.6	16.6	19.8	16.1	9.9
	R	23520	34.9	17.3	21.5	16.4	9.9
	U	2979	59.0	11.1	6.5	13.2	10.1
Mon	T	3741	33.3	16.8	22.8	15.9	11.3
	R	3587	32.6	17.0	23.1	16.1	11.2
	U	154	49.4	12.3	14.9	11.0	12.3
Tuensang	T	7477	31.2	20.1	27.0	13.7	8.0
	R	7297	30.9	20.2	27.2	13.6	8.1
	U	180	44.4	15.0	18.3	17.8	4.4
Mokokchung	T	2596	37.6	15.3	17.8	17.2	12.1
	R	2399	36.2	15.4	19.0	17.5	11.8
	U	197	54.3	13.7	3.6	13.2	15.2

Contd.

Contd.

1	2	3	4	5	6	7	8
Zunheboto	T	2675	39.1	16.4	18.1	15.9	10.4
	R	2368	35.6	17.7	19.4	16.5	10.8
	U	307	66.1	7.2	8.5	11.1	7.2
Wokha	T	1847	39.6	16.9	14.3	20.2	8.9
	R	1523	35.2	16.8	15.9	23.3	8.8
	U	324	60.2	17.3	7.1	5.9	9.6
Dimapur *	T	3205	49.8	11.9	11.8	17.0	9.6
	R	2120	45.5	13.1	15.5	17.3	8.6
	U	1085	58.2	9.4	4.7	16.3	11.4
Kohima	T	3394	39.4	14.7	18.0	17.6	10.3
	R	2830	35.1	15.4	20.7	18.5	10.2
	U	564	60.6	11.2	4.3	13.1	10.8
Phek	T	1564	45.1	15.2	11.1	16.2	12.4
	R	1396	41.6	16.0	11.8	17.0	13.5
	U	168	74.4	8.9	4.8	8.9	3.0
MANIPUR	T	28376	41.3	9.8	10.6	21.8	16.6
	R	20955	41.7	9.5	11.7	21.9	15.2
	U	7421	40.2	10.6	7.4	21.3	20.7
Senapati	T	1800	45.2	9.5	15.6	20.2	9.6
	R	1800	45.2	9.5	15.6	20.2	9.6
	U	0	0.0	0.0	0.0	0.0	0.0
Tamenglong	T	1405	39.4	11.1	16.9	20.9	11.7
	R	1405	39.4	11.1	16.9	20.9	11.7
	U	0	0.0	0.0	0.0	0.0	0.0
Churachandpur	T	2638	49.7	9.5	18.1	11.4	11.2
	R	2638	49.7	9.5	18.1	11.4	11.2
	U	0	0.0	0.0	0.0	0.0	0.0
Bishnupur	T	3506	41.4	7.9	10.6	22.3	17.9
	R	2196	44.6	7.8	9.8	21.9	15.8
	U	1310	36.1	7.9	11.8	22.8	21.3
Thoubal	T	5285	34.8	10.5	8.0	27.3	19.3
	R	3509	32.8	10.2	8.6	29.4	19.0
	U	1776	38.9	11.1	6.9	23.3	19.9

Contd.

Contd.

1	2	3	4	5	6	7	8
Imphal West	T	5385	43.7	10.0	7.1	19.6	19.6
	R	2511	46.5	9.1	8.7	19.2	16.4
	U	2874	41.3	10.8	5.7	19.9	22.3
Imphal East *	T	5164	40.8	9.7	8.4	21.9	19.1
	R	3936	40.7	8.9	8.9	22.6	18.9
	U	1228	41.2	12.4	6.8	19.9	19.7
Ukhrul	T	1677	41.4	9.5	9.7	25.6	13.7
	R	1677	41.4	9.5	9.7	25.6	13.7
	U	0	0.0	0.0	0.0	0.0	0.0
Chandel	T	1516	38.7	10.4	14.8	24.7	11.5
	R	1283	35.9	10.7	15.8	25.4	12.2
	U	233	53.6	8.6	9.0	21.0	7.7
MIZORAM	T	16011	39.1	12.5	15.1	15.5	17.8
	R	9691	38.9	12.6	15.8	15.7	17.1
	U	6320	39.4	12.5	14.1	15.2	18.9
Mamit *	T	1080	26.0	11.1	17.2	26.0	19.6
	R	870	24.9	11.8	17.4	25.3	20.6
	U	210	30.5	8.1	16.7	29.0	15.7
Kolasib *	T	1268	43.8	10.5	14.7	14.8	16.2
	R	584	37.8	12.5	18.3	15.1	16.3
	U	684	48.8	8.8	11.7	14.6	16.1
Aizawl	T	5120	39.2	12.6	13.6	14.8	19.7
	R	1879	39.6	13.6	13.6	15.0	18.3
	U	3241	39.0	12.1	13.6	14.7	20.6
Champhai *	T	2327	31.8	17.4	17.8	16.2	16.8
	R	1619	29.8	18.0	18.6	16.9	16.7
	U	708	36.4	16.2	16.0	14.5	16.8
Serchhip *	T	1168	35.6	13.4	16.0	15.5	19.5
	R	725	34.5	11.9	17.5	15.3	20.8
	U	443	37.5	15.8	13.5	15.8	17.4
Lunglei	T	2533	40.5	12.3	15.0	14.6	17.6
	R	1735	42.2	12.3	14.7	14.3	16.5
	U	798	36.7	12.4	15.5	15.2	20.2

Contd.

Contd.

1	2	3	4	5	6	7	8
Lawngtlai	T	1530	60.5	7.0	8.6	11.0	12.9
	R	1530	60.5	7.0	8.6	11.0	12.9
	U	0	0.0	0.0	0.0	0.0	0.0
Saiha *	T	985	31.0	12.7	24.6	15.4	16.3
	R	749	26.3	11.9	27.2	17.0	17.6
	U	236	45.8	15.3	16.1	10.6	12.3
TRIPURA	T	58940	46.7	8.7	9.7	23.7	11.3
	R	48800	46.2	8.7	10.1	23.7	11.2
	U	10140	48.8	8.2	7.7	23.5	11.7
West Tripura	T	26938	45.9	9.0	9.7	24.3	11.1
	R	19669	45.2	9.1	10.4	24.6	10.7
	U	7269	48.0	8.9	7.8	23.2	12.0
South Tripura	T	14335	43.3	8.8	10.6	25.9	11.5
	R	13272	43.4	8.8	10.9	25.6	11.4
	U	1063	42.1	8.4	7.3	29.4	12.8
Dhalai *	T	5325	50.2	7.9	8.2	22.3	11.4
	R	4868	50.6	8.2	7.8	21.8	11.6
	U	457	45.3	5.3	12.9	27.4	9.2
North Tripura	T	12342	50.7	8.0	9.1	20.6	11.6
	R	10991	49.6	8.3	9.5	20.8	11.8
	U	1351	59.6	5.5	5.8	18.9	10.2
MEGHALAYA	T	28803	46.5	11.9	12.7	17.8	11.1
	R	22740	42.4	12.9	14.4	18.8	11.5
	U	6063	61.7	8.2	6.4	13.9	9.8
West Garo Hills	T	6970	39.4	17.4	13.0	17.1	13.1
	R	6197	38.1	18.6	13.8	16.6	13.0
	U	773	49.9	8.2	6.5	21.5	14.0
East Garo Hills	T	2528	45.5	13.4	12.7	17.7	10.6
	R	2215	44.8	13.6	13.2	17.9	10.5
	U	313	50.8	11.8	9.3	16.3	11.8
South Garo Hills *	T	1426	45.3	10.2	15.8	18.0	10.7
	R	1313	44.8	10.7	16.1	17.7	10.7
	U	113	51.3	4.4	11.5	21.2	11.5

Contd.

Contd.

1	2	3	4	5	6	7	8
West Khasi Hills	T	4077	35.5	10.2	18.4	24.9	10.9
	R	3805	34.8	10.5	19.2	24.5	11.0
	U	272	44.5	7.0	8.5	29.8	10.3
Ri Bhoi *	T	2180	41.8	11.7	14.4	17.6	14.4
	R	1949	43.3	11.7	15.0	17.1	12.9
	U	231	29.9	11.3	9.1	22.1	27.7
East Khasi Hills	T	9084	57.1	8.2	9.7	16.3	8.7
	R	4917	48.1	8.6	12.9	20.8	9.5
	U	4167	67.6	7.7	6.0	11.0	7.7
Jaintia Hills	T	2538	51.1	12.4	10.4	13.8	12.3
	R	2344	49.8	12.2	11.2	14.3	12.5
	U	194	66.5	13.9	1.5	7.7	10.3
ASSAM	T	530300	53.2	10.7	9.8	17.3	9.0
	R	468113	52.1	11.0	10.3	17.7	8.8
	U	62187	61.0	8.7	5.7	14.6	9.9
Kokrajhar	T	15764	44.7	14.7	10.4	17.3	12.9
	R	14727	44.4	15.0	10.6	17.0	13.0
	U	1037	49.1	9.5	7.4	21.7	12.2
Dhubri	T	31589	55.7	8.8	8.4	17.9	9.3
	R	27550	55.2	8.9	8.7	18.1	9.1
	U	4039	59.1	7.5	6.2	16.3	10.8
Goalpara	T	16792	49.7	8.8	13.0	18.6	9.8
	R	15563	49.4	8.7	13.5	18.9	9.6
	U	1229	53.9	10.3	7.4	15.6	12.7
Bongaigaon	T	20243	56.4	9.6	9.8	15.1	9.1
	R	17840	55.5	9.7	10.4	15.2	9.1
	U	2403	63.1	9.0	5.2	14.1	8.7
Barpeta	T	24400	39.7	12.6	12.1	23.9	11.6
	R	22452	39.2	12.7	12.5	24.0	11.6
	U	1948	45.6	11.7	7.8	22.8	12.1
Kamrup	T	43883	54.4	10.7	8.7	16.9	9.3
	R	29473	49.3	11.5	10.7	19.0	9.5
	U	14410	64.9	9.0	4.7	12.5	8.9

Contd.

Contd.

1	2	3	4	5	6	7	8
Nalbari	T	21922	50.8	13.6	10.5	16.7	8.3
	R	21466	50.3	13.7	10.7	16.8	8.4
	U	456	73.9	7.2	1.5	11.6	5.7
Darrang	T	40029	53.6	14.2	10.4	14.1	7.7
	R	38489	53.7	14.3	10.6	13.9	7.6
	U	1540	52.5	10.7	6.6	19.4	10.8
Marigaon	T	11547	36.7	14.8	12.8	24.4	11.3
	R	11141	36.3	14.8	13.0	24.6	11.3
	U	406	47.5	14.8	7.9	17.5	12.3
Nagaon	T	44624	45.9	11.5	10.9	21.2	10.4
	R	39462	45.4	11.7	11.2	21.4	10.2
	U	5162	49.6	10.2	8.6	19.8	11.9
Sonitpur	T	31861	40.8	15.0	14.3	18.8	11.0
	R	29043	40.2	15.6	15.1	19.2	10.0
	U	2818	46.7	9.6	6.1	15.3	22.3
Lakhimpur	T	15298	40.0	14.8	14.1	21.6	9.5
	R	14390	39.4	14.9	14.5	21.7	9.5
	U	908	49.0	12.1	7.5	21.3	10.1
Dhemaji	T	10323	48.9	13.2	12.7	17.1	8.0
	R	9634	48.4	13.4	13.0	17.1	8.0
	U	689	55.3	10.7	9.4	17.1	7.4
Tinsukia	T	17235	42.4	13.7	13.2	20.4	10.3
	R	14150	40.6	14.1	14.6	20.8	9.8
	U	3085	50.5	11.5	6.9	18.7	12.4
Dibrugarh	T	17325	48.2	11.9	9.9	20.4	9.6
	R	14374	46.1	12.3	10.8	21.2	9.5
	U	2951	58.0	9.6	5.8	16.5	10.1
Sibsagar	T	23500	63.5	8.8	7.2	13.2	7.4
	R	21596	63.0	8.8	7.5	13.3	7.4
	U	1904	69.6	8.3	4.1	11.1	6.9
Jorhat	T	20739	60.4	9.1	8.1	14.7	7.6
	R	17260	58.4	9.5	8.8	15.6	7.7
	U	3479	70.7	7.2	4.9	10.3	6.9

Contd.

Contd.

1	2	3	4	5	6	7	8
Golaghat	T	13241	39.9	13.1	12.6	23.9	10.4
	R	12161	39.7	13.1	13.0	24.0	10.2
	U	1080	42.8	13.1	8.7	22.5	12.9
Karbi Anglong	T	14905	53.7	9.8	11.5	16.7	8.3
	R	13527	54.0	9.7	11.9	16.4	8.0
	U	1378	51.2	10.4	7.1	20.3	11.0
North Cachar	T	2657	46.6	15.4	13.1	16.8	8.1
Hills	R	1836	45.5	15.7	13.5	16.9	8.4
	U	821	49.2	14.5	12.2	16.6	7.6
Cachar	T	53438	74.0	4.3	4.4	11.8	5.6
	R	45696	73.0	4.4	4.7	12.5	5.5
	U	7742	79.4	3.8	3.2	7.6	6.0
Karimganj	T	30327	69.0	5.4	5.3	13.8	6.5
	R	28240	68.7	5.5	5.4	13.9	6.5
	U	2087	73.4	4.6	3.8	11.6	6.6
Hailakandi	T	8658	52.1	10.0	7.3	20.0	10.6
	R	8043	52.5	10.1	7.3	19.7	10.5
	U	615	46.7	9.8	7.2	23.7	12.7
WEST BENGAL	T	1847174	46.7	9.2	7.1	22.3	14.7
	R	1354253	45.1	9.8	8.1	23.6	13.4
	U	492921	51.1	7.5	4.5	18.9	18.0
Darjiling	T	56982	60.0	11.5	9.1	10.7	8.8
	R	43881	59.7	12.4	9.8	10.1	8.1
	U	13101	61.1	8.3	6.7	12.7	11.1
Jalpaiguri	T	84236	52.2	12.6	7.7	15.3	12.3
	R	71230	52.2	13.1	8.0	15.0	11.7
	U	13006	52.1	9.6	5.6	17.1	15.6
Koch Bihar	T	65954	52.7	10.2	8.2	17.9	11.0
	R	58131	51.0	10.7	8.8	18.4	11.0
	U	7823	65.0	6.4	3.8	14.2	10.7
Uttar Dinajpur	T	40900	43.5	11.6	8.9	25.4	10.5
	R	36750	43.1	11.9	9.0	25.7	10.3
	U	4150	46.5	9.6	8.1	23.2	12.7

Contd.

Contd.

1	2	3	4	5	6	7	8
Dakshin	T	30450	47.8	9.0	5.8	21.8	15.6
Dinajpur *	R	26221	46.2	9.6	6.0	23.1	15.1
	U	4229	57.8	5.8	4.3	13.2	18.9
Maldah	T	61379	40.9	10.7	7.6	25.0	15.7
	R	56822	40.3	10.8	7.9	25.5	15.4
	U	4557	48.2	10.0	3.5	18.7	19.5
Murshidabad	T	156305	54.4	8.0	5.2	20.5	11.8
	R	136706	54.1	8.0	5.3	20.9	11.6
	U	19599	56.5	7.9	4.4	17.8	13.4
Birbhum	T	59855	32.9	10.8	8.8	32.8	14.7
	R	55059	32.4	10.9	9.1	33.1	14.6
	U	4796	39.0	9.6	6.1	29.2	16.0
Barddhaman	T	147597	48.4	8.5	5.3	22.9	14.9
	R	98087	48.0	8.9	5.8	23.0	14.3
	U	49510	49.2	7.6	4.5	22.6	16.2
Nadia	T	108631	46.6	8.5	7.2	24.0	13.6
	R	84803	46.0	8.6	7.7	24.4	13.3
	U	23828	48.8	8.3	5.6	22.5	14.8
North Twenty	T	201594	48.6	8.0	6.2	19.8	7.5
Four Parganas	R	96390	46.3	8.6	7.8	21.9	15.3
	U	105204	50.7	7.4	4.6	17.8	19.5
Hugli	T	110540	46.6	9.0	5.6	22.7	16.1
	R	73847	44.0	9.6	6.2	24.8	15.4
	U	36693	51.9	7.7	4.4	18.6	17.5
Bankura	T	68737	35.7	10.8	10.3	29.1	14.1
	R	64588	35.5	10.8	10.6	29.2	13.9
	U	4149	38.5	10.1	7.0	26.7	17.8
Puruliya	T	58721	43.9	9.9	11.3	23.2	11.7
	R	53292	43.8	10.0	11.6	23.3	11.3
	U	5429	44.0	8.8	8.0	23.0	16.2
Medinipur	T	229357	38.5	10.2	9.6	27.1	14.6
	R	209335	38.3	10.3	9.9	27.3	14.2
	U	20022	40.2	9.6	6.1	25.3	18.7

Contd.

Contd.

1	2	3	4	5	6	7	8
Haora	T	96402	**46.6**	8.8	5.1	22.8	16.7
	R	49661	**43.8**	9.9	6.4	25.0	14.8
	U	46741	**49.5**	7.7	3.7	20.5	18.6
Kolkata	T	107818	**53.6**	6.1	3.5	16.2	20.6
	R	0	**0.0**	0.0	0.0	0.0	0.0
	U	107818	**53.6**	6.1	3.5	16.2	20.6
South Twenty Four Parganas	T	161716	**45.9**	8.4	7.6	23.3	4.8
	R	139450	**45.2**	8.4	8.2	24.0	14.2
	U	22266	**50.0**	8.0	4.0	19.0	18.9
JHARKHAND	T	448377	**41.5**	8.9	6.3	30.8	12.5
	R	348928	**40.7**	9.0	6.7	31.6	11.9
	U	99449	**44.4**	8.2	4.7	28.2	14.6
Garhwa *	T	21611	**46.6**	7.2	4.3	30.8	11.2
	R	20786	**46.6**	7.2	4.4	30.7	11.1
	U	825	**45.0**	7.3	2.5	32.2	13.0
Palamu	T	54799	**49.5**	6.3	4.3	28.7	11.2
	R	51698	**49.7**	6.2	4.3	28.5	11.2
	U	3101	**45.4**	7.5	4.2	30.8	12.0
Chatra *	T	13747	**41.0**	8.0	5.5	31.4	14.1
	R	12985	**41.3**	8.0	5.5	31.4	13.7
	U	762	**36.6**	8.3	4.3	31.5	19.3
Hazaribag	T	29674	**34.6**	9.5	7.9	35.6	12.4
	R	23678	**33.7**	9.5	8.5	36.2	12.0
	U	5996	**38.0**	9.5	5.4	33.2	14.0
Kodarma *	T	7502	**33.2**	9.4	5.3	37.4	14.8
	R	6148	**31.8**	9.7	5.8	38.5	14.2
	U	1354	**39.4**	8.1	3.0	32.4	17.1
Giridih	T	26340	**33.2**	10.9	7.0	34.7	14.2
	R	24466	**33.3**	11.0	7.0	34.7	14.0
	U	1874	**32.9**	9.4	6.7	34.3	16.7
Deoghar	T	15412	**31.7**	13.1	7.3	35.8	12.1
	R	13319	**32.0**	13.6	7.5	35.4	11.5
	U	2093	**29.5**	10.0	5.8	38.6	16.2

Contd.

Contd.

1	2	3	4	5	6	7	8
Godda	T	16995	37.5	8.7	5.1	37.3	11.3
	R	16439	37.5	8.7	5.2	37.3	11.3
	U	556	38.8	8.3	2.9	38.7	11.3
Sahibganj	T	13756	31.1	9.4	7.8	40.1	11.6
	R	11954	31.6	9.2	7.9	40.1	11.2
	U	1802	28.0	10.7	6.8	40.5	14.2
Pakaur *	T	10592	47.0	8.6	6.2	27.2	11.0
	R	9817	46.1	8.7	6.4	27.7	11.0
	U	775	58.6	6.6	2.8	20.5	11.5
Dumka	T	25555	33.9	11.8	7.6	34.3	12.5
	R	23551	33.4	11.9	7.8	34.6	12.4
	U	2004	40.0	10.4	5.0	30.5	14.0
Dhanbad	T	43013	47.5	8.7	5.2	26.8	11.8
	R	22192	46.7	9.0	6.3	27.1	10.9
	U	20821	48.4	8.2	4.0	26.6	12.8
Bokaro *	T	24963	33.1	10.6	7.0	34.5	14.9
	R	14425	33.7	11.5	8.0	32.7	14.1
	U	10538	32.2	9.3	5.5	37.1	15.9
Ranchi	T	49341	45.4	8.0	6.4	26.3	13.9
	R	30818	44.1	8.4	7.6	27.5	12.3
	U	18523	47.6	7.2	4.2	24.4	16.6
Lohardaga	T	5026	23.7	9.1	8.2	44.3	14.6
	R	4376	24.3	9.2	8.5	44.0	14.0
	U	650	19.5	8.8	6.3	46.6	18.8
Gumla	T	22757	40.9	8.3	7.3	32.4	11.2
	R	21452	40.7	8.3	7.4	32.4	11.1
	U	1305	44.1	7.3	4.8	31.2	12.6
Pashchimi	T	28552	39.4	9.5	8.1	30.6	12.3
Singhbhum	R	22453	38.4	9.6	8.8	31.7	11.5
	U	6099	43.1	9.4	5.6	26.8	15.0
Purbi Singhbhum	T	38742	51.2	8.0	6.4	22.3	12.1
	R	18371	51.4	9.0	8.0	21.4	10.3
	U	20371	51.0	7.2	4.9	23.1	13.8

Contd.

Contd.

1	2	3	4	5	6	7	8
ORISSA	T	1021335	50.3	6.7	8.2	24.6	10.1
	R	877709	49.6	6.8	8.7	24.9	9.9
	U	143626	54.8	6.3	5.4	22.2	11.3
Bargarh *	T	42135	51.7	6.7	8.5	24.1	8.9
	R	38832	50.6	6.7	8.9	24.9	8.9
	U	3303	64.6	7.4	3.5	14.8	9.6
Jharsuguda *	T	15300	50.9	6.3	8.8	24.3	9.7
	R	10824	49.6	6.5	9.9	24.8	9.2
	U	4476	54.1	5.7	6.0	23.0	11.1
Sambalpur	T	28283	50.9	6.8	8.1	25.0	9.2
	R	21340	47.7	6.6	9.4	27.2	9.0
	U	6943	60.9	7.3	4.0	18.1	9.7
Debagarh *	T	9892	55.7	5.7	8.1	23.0	7.5
	R	9297	56.8	5.8	7.7	22.3	7.3
	U	595	38.2	5.2	13.1	33.1	10.4
Sundargarh	T	41465	45.3	6.9	10.0	27.6	10.2
	R	28391	41.2	7.3	12.3	29.0	10.3
	U	13074	54.3	5.9	5.0	24.6	10.1
Kendujhar	T	34728	44.5	8.3	10.2	26.4	10.6
	R	29924	42.9	8.3	10.8	27.2	10.8
	U	4804	55.0	8.2	6.3	21.4	9.1
Mayurbhanj	T	54661	46.1	7.9	10.9	25.5	9.7
	R	51067	46.4	7.8	11.0	25.3	9.5
	U	3594	42.5	9.1	9.0	27.5	11.9
Baleshwar	T	53752	40.0	8.2	11.8	28.5	11.4
	R	48455	39.5	8.4	12.2	28.6	11.4
	U	5297	45.4	7.0	8.4	27.5	11.6
Bhadrak *	T	44271	55.6	6.1	7.7	20.9	9.7
	R	40146	55.8	6.1	7.8	21.0	9.3
	U	4125	53.7	6.8	6.2	19.2	14.0
Kendrapara *	T	37408	45.7	6.1	8.1	28.0	12.1
	R	35332	45.6	6.1	8.2	28.1	12.0
	U	2076	47.9	6.4	5.9	25.9	13.9

Contd.

Contd.

1	2	3	4	5	6	7	8
Jagatsinghapur *	T	27161	39.4	6.7	8.9	31.0	14.0
	R	24629	37.5	6.9	9.2	32.1	14.3
	U	2532	58.2	5.0	6.1	19.7	11.0
Cuttack	T	65567	43.9	6.3	7.8	27.8	14.2
	R	49033	43.6	6.4	8.6	27.6	13.8
	U	16534	44.8	5.9	5.4	28.6	15.4
Jajapur *	T	51730	47.9	6.4	8.9	25.5	11.2
	R	49418	47.6	6.4	9.0	25.6	11.3
	U	2312	54.8	5.7	6.2	23.8	9.6
Dhenkanal	T	29188	46.5	6.7	8.9	26.4	11.5
	R	26615	47.5	6.4	9.0	26.2	10.9
	U	2573	36.6	10.2	8.7	27.7	16.8
Anugul *	T	29559	54.5	6.6	6.5	23.6	8.9
	R	25787	53.5	6.8	6.7	24.4	8.7
	U	3772	61.6	5.2	4.7	17.9	10.7
Nayagarh *	T	23799	51.9	5.9	6.9	24.2	11.1
	R	22800	52.1	5.8	7.1	24.3	10.7
	U	999	46.6	6.7	4.4	22.9	19.3
Khordha *	T	62526	56.9	5.2	6.3	20.0	11.7
	R	37650	55.9	5.1	7.3	20.4	11.4
	U	24876	58.3	5.5	4.8	19.4	12.0
Puri	T	57083	55.9	4.9	7.1	21.2	10.9
	R	51075	55.5	4.8	7.5	21.3	10.9
	U	6008	59.4	5.4	3.9	20.6	10.8
Ganjam	T	93197	58.7	6.7	4.7	22.3	7.6
	R	78504	58.2	6.8	4.9	22.7	7.4
	U	14693	61.4	5.8	4.0	20.1	8.7
Gajapati *	T	13489	46.3	8.5	9.4	29.0	6.8
	R	12495	46.5	8.6	9.7	28.8	6.4
	U	994	43.9	7.5	5.5	31.7	11.4
Kandhamal	T	18030	50.4	6.0	10.5	25.5	7.6
	R	16511	48.9	6.3	11.0	26.2	7.6
	U	1519	66.4	3.4	5.0	17.8	7.4

Contd.

Contd.

1	2	3	4	5	6	7	8
Baudh *	T	10086	52.4	8.1	8.3	23.9	7.2
	R	9669	52.8	8.0	8.5	23.7	7.0
	U	417	44.1	10.6	4.8	28.5	12.0
Sonapur *	T	13431	41.4	8.7	9.8	30.2	9.9
	R	12551	41.8	8.7	10.0	29.8	9.7
	U	880	35.0	9.8	6.6	36.5	12.2
Balangir	T	32006	40.2	8.8	10.0	31.5	9.5
	R	28563	40.0	8.8	10.4	31.7	9.2
	U	3443	41.9	9.0	6.4	30.4	12.3
Nuapada *	T	13696	45.3	9.5	8.6	27.2	9.3
	R	12866	44.7	9.6	8.8	27.5	9.4
	U	830	55.5	8.1	4.7	22.7	9.0
Kalahandi	T	32421	50.4	8.2	8.6	23.5	9.3
	R	30025	50.3	8.3	8.6	23.6	9.2
	U	2396	52.0	6.9	8.1	22.4	10.7
Rayagada *	T	20605	62.8	5.5	6.5	17.4	7.8
	R	17769	62.5	5.5	6.7	17.7	7.6
	U	2836	64.6	5.7	5.1	15.8	8.8
Nabarangapur *	T	28104	60.9	6.0	7.3	17.8	8.0
	R	26050	60.6	6.0	7.5	18.0	7.9
	U	2054	64.8	6.7	4.5	15.5	8.5
Koraput	T	26625	59.3	6.2	7.8	18.9	7.8
	R	21757	58.3	6.5	8.1	19.5	7.6
	U	4868	63.9	4.8	6.5	16.1	8.8
Malkangiri *	T	11137	53.4	5.7	9.3	21.8	9.7
	R	10334	53.0	5.8	9.6	22.0	9.7
	U	803	59.4	4.7	6.2	20.2	9.5
CHHATTISGARH	T	419887	38.1	7.2	8.1	36.1	10.4
	R	344993	37.5	7.3	8.8	36.4	9.9
	U	74894	41.0	6.9	4.9	34.7	12.4
Koriya *	T	10317	42.9	7.7	6.3	32.1	11.0
	R	7648	43.5	7.8	6.9	31.3	10.5
	U	2669	41.2	7.5	4.4	34.2	12.6

Contd.

Contd.

1	2	3	4	5	6	7	8
Surguja	T	36299	43.7	8.4	6.9	31.0	10.1
	R	33699	43.0	8.6	7.1	31.2	10.1
	U	2600	52.1	6.0	3.9	28.0	9.9
Jashpur *	T	11347	35.4	9.4	8.8	35.2	11.2
	R	10754	35.3	9.5	8.9	35.2	11.1
	U	593	38.8	6.7	6.9	35.2	12.3
Raigarh	T	23472	25.1	8.3	10.0	44.3	12.3
	R	20596	25.4	8.4	10.5	43.6	12.1
	U	2876	22.8	7.6	6.6	49.4	13.6
Korba *	T	17089	38.8	8.2	7.2	34.8	10.8
	R	11510	35.0	8.9	8.9	36.8	10.4
	U	5579	46.7	6.9	3.9	30.7	11.8
Janjgir - Champa*	T	24585	28.3	6.9	8.0	46.7	10.1
	R	21972	28.5	7.0	8.2	46.2	10.2
	U	2613	26.6	6.8	6.2	50.9	9.4
Bilaspur	T	41374	33.9	7.6	7.2	41.1	10.3
	R	32828	32.5	7.7	7.6	42.6	9.5
	U	8546	38.9	7.3	5.3	35.5	13.0
Kawardha *	T	12572	32.1	6.6	7.8	44.8	8.7
	R	11830	32.4	6.5	8.0	44.6	8.4
	U	742	27.2	7.4	4.3	48.1	12.9
Rajnandgaon	T	28021	37.3	6.3	9.2	36.6	10.5
	R	23440	37.3	6.3	9.8	36.4	10.2
	U	4581	37.4	6.7	5.9	37.7	12.3
Durg	T	63976	38.9	6.3	7.5	36.8	10.5
	R	42494	35.8	6.3	9.1	39.0	9.8
	U	21482	45.0	6.3	4.3	32.3	12.0
Raipur	T	71510	43.9	6.3	8.0	32.1	9.6
	R	56052	45.0	6.0	8.8	31.5	8.6
	U	15458	39.8	7.3	5.2	34.4	13.3
Mahasamund *	T	15351	34.1	8.3	9.0	36.6	12.0
	R	13906	34.6	8.2	9.3	36.4	11.5
	U	1445	29.4	8.4	6.4	39.4	16.5

Contd.

Contd.

1	2	3	4	5	6	7	8
Dhamtari *	T	15748	39.6	6.6	8.4	34.9	10.6
	R	13990	40.3	6.4	8.7	34.6	10.0
	U	1758	34.0	7.4	5.7	37.8	15.2
Kanker *	T	14859	41.0	6.7	10.3	30.3	11.7
	R	14180	40.5	6.8	10.5	30.4	11.8
	U	679	50.8	4.3	5.9	29.2	9.9
Bastar	T	21810	39.5	8.4	9.7	32.0	10.4
	R	19821	39.2	8.5	10.1	32.1	10.1
	U	1989	42.1	8.0	5.7	30.8	13.4
Dantewada*	T	11557	46.8	9.1	8.6	27.9	7.6
	R	10273	44.8	9.5	9.4	28.7	7.5
	U	1284	62.3	5.4	2.4	21.2	8.7
MADHYA	T	1408528	45.2	5.4	6.135.28.2		
PRADESH	R	1060433	45.1	5.3	6.7	35.6	7.4
	U	348095	45.4	5.6	4.2	34.1	10.6
Sheopur *	T	13552	57.8	4.4	5.2	26.2	6.4
	R	11164	57.6	4.5	5.8	25.7	6.3
	U	2388	58.3	3.9	2.5	28.2	7.1
Morena	T	35821	54.5	5.0	3.1	30.7	6.7
	R	29188	57.5	4.8	3.0	28.5	6.2
	U	6633	41.4	5.9	3.6	40.2	8.9
Bhind	T	30588	50.1	5.8	4.3	33.0	6.8
	R	22637	50.2	6.2	4.7	32.5	6.5
	U	7951	49.8	4.7	3.3	34.5	7.7
Gwalior	T	39059	45.9	4.7	3.5	37.7	8.2
	R	15446	47.2	4.2	4.1	38.6	5.8
	U	23613	45.0	5.1	3.1	37.1	9.7
Datia	T	13990	45.7	5.4	5.1	37.4	6.5
	R	10998	48.3	5.3	5.1	35.3	6.1
	U	2992	36.1	5.5	5.0	45.4	8.0
Shivpuri	T	32560	54.5	4.8	5.0	30.0	5.7
	R	27777	56.2	4.5	5.1	28.8	5.3
	U	4783	44.4	6.4	4.4	36.9	7.9

Contd.

Contd.

1	2	3	4	5	6	7	8
Guna	T	32975	38.9	5.8	7.4	40.5	7.5
	R	27167	41.2	5.5	7.7	38.9	6.7
	U	5808	28.3	6.9	5.9	47.7	11.3
Tikamgarh	T	27389	42.2	5.3	5.4	40.9	6.2
	R	22192	42.9	5.3	5.5	40.4	5.9
	U	5197	39.1	5.3	5.0	43.0	7.7
Chhatarpur	T	30311	43.5	6.6	5.7	36.5	7.7
	R	24726	45.4	6.5	6.0	35.0	7.0
	U	5585	35.0	7.1	4.2	42.7	11.0
Panna	T	19189	50.1	5.1	5.0	32.0	7.7
	R	16644	50.6	5.0	5.3	31.6	7.4
	U	2545	46.6	5.6	3.2	35.0	9.5
Sagar	T	57272	44.7	5.4	6.2	36.6	7.1
	R	41075	42.4	5.8	6.9	38.3	6.6
	U	16197	50.6	4.5	4.2	32.2	8.5
Damoh	T	26801	43.3	5.5	5.8	37.7	7.6
	R	21721	42.9	5.7	6.3	38.0	7.1
	U	5080	45.0	5.0	3.9	36.3	9.8
Satna	T	42803	39.0	6.2	5.4	39.6	9.8
	R	35556	40.3	6.0	5.6	39.1	9.1
	U	7247	33.0	7.3	4.2	42.1	13.6
Rewa	T	50093	48.3	6.2	4.4	33.2	7.8
	R	39342	44.5	6.7	4.8	36.0	8.0
	U	10751	62.1	4.5	3.3	23.0	7.0
Umaria *	T	12319	50.6	5.2	5.8	30.8	7.6
	R	10330	48.9	5.1	6.2	31.9	7.9
	U	1989	59.1	5.4	3.8	25.3	6.4
Shahdol	T	28161	36.1	7.8	7.8	38.0	10.2
	R	22519	36.6	7.6	8.4	37.8	9.5
	U	5642	34.1	8.6	5.3	38.8	13.1
Sidhi	T	29961	36.3	8.3	6.5	39.6	9.2
	R	26443	36.5	8.1	6.7	39.8	9.0
	U	3518	35.3	10.0	5.0	38.6	11.0

Contd.

Contd.

1	2	3	4	5	6	7	8
Neemuch *	T	21885	52.4	3.8	4.6	31.8	7.4
	R	17374	55.5	3.5	4.4	29.8	6.8
	U	4511	40.1	4.9	5.5	39.7	9.8
Mandsaur	T	31993	46.8	4.2	6.0	35.3	7.8
	R	27267	47.1	4.1	6.2	35.3	7.3
	U	4726	44.8	5.0	4.5	35.0	10.7
Ratlam	T	28218	45.2	4.1	6.8	35.6	8.3
	R	20376	44.8	3.7	7.7	36.7	7.1
	U	7842	46.3	5.2	4.5	32.7	11.3
Ujjain	T	38146	50.1	4.5	5.7	30.6	9.0
	R	26770	53.5	3.8	6.1	29.6	6.9
	U	11376	42.1	6.2	4.7	33.0	14.0
Shajapur	T	37638	52.0	3.3	6.6	31.5	6.6
	R	31781	52.1	3.1	6.9	31.6	6.2
	U	5857	51.3	4.2	5.0	30.9	8.6
Dewas	T	36304	52.1	4.4	5.2	31.4	6.9
	R	27218	51.7	4.4	5.7	32.0	6.2
	U	9086	53.4	4.5	3.6	29.8	8.8
Jhabua	T	21171	33.1	5.2	7.6	46.6	7.5
	R	19375	34.5	5.2	7.7	45.8	6.8
	U	1796	18.3	5.8	5.8	54.8	15.2
Dhar	T	31076	41.3	5.1	7.2	38.5	7.9
	R	26944	42.5	4.9	7.4	37.8	7.3
	U	4132	33.7	6.1	5.5	43.1	11.6
Indore	T	48978	48.8	6.2	4.4	29.9	10.7
	R	15591	43.3	5.2	6.0	37.1	8.5
	U	33387	51.4	6.6	3.7	26.6	11.7
West Nimar	T	29070	41.1	5.2	6.5	39.2	7.9
	R	25499	42.4	5.0	6.7	38.6	7.3
	U	3571	31.8	7.0	5.3	43.5	12.4
Barwani *	T	19874	49.1	6.2	6.0	30.8	7.9
	R	16634	48.8	6.3	6.1	31.3	7.5
	U	3240	50.6	5.3	5.5	28.4	10.2

Contd.

Contd.

1	2	3	4	5	6	7	8
East Nimar	T	36661	48.8	5.6	6.4	31.2	7.9
	R	26169	48.7	5.6	7.1	31.4	7.2
	U	10492	49.2	5.8	4.6	30.8	9.6
Rajgarh	T	36799	47.7	3.9	7.5	34.5	6.4
	R	31433	47.1	3.8	8.0	35.0	6.1
	U	5366	51.0	4.4	4.8	31.5	8.4
Vidisha	T	31897	42.4	5.0	7.2	38.3	7.1
	R	26011	42.3	5.0	7.8	38.1	6.7
	U	5886	42.9	4.8	4.7	39.0	8.5
Bhopal	T	52570	53.6	4.5	4.1	28.3	9.6
	R	10514	46.3	4.3	6.7	35.0	7.6
	U	42056	55.4	4.6	3.4	26.6	10.1
Sehore	T	34241	48.0	4.2	7.2	33.1	7.5
	R	29313	48.8	4.1	7.5	32.4	7.2
	U	4928	43.3	4.4	5.1	37.7	9.6
Raisen	T	31655	47.6	5.2	7.3	32.7	7.2
	R	27252	48.5	5.1	7.5	32.1	6.8
	U	4403	41.8	5.8	6.0	36.3	10.1
Betul	T	31998	40.2	6.1	7.8	36.3	9.6
	R	25972	40.5	6.0	8.3	35.8	9.4
	U	6026	38.9	6.4	5.8	38.5	10.3
Harda *	T	12679	52.9	5.0	7.0	28.2	7.0
	R	9977	53.5	4.9	7.7	27.5	6.4
	U	2702	50.6	5.4	4.3	30.7	9.0
Hoshangabad	T	31253	47.2	5.6	6.1	33.1	8.0
	R	22678	47.6	5.6	6.8	32.5	7.4
	U	8575	46.1	5.4	4.2	34.7	9.7
Katni *	T	28062	42.1	5.0	6.9	37.7	8.4
	R	24118	44.3	4.7	7.2	36.9	6.9
	U	3944	28.3	7.0	4.9	42.2	17.5
Jabalpur	T	46992	34.7	6.2	5.8	41.5	11.8
	R	23252	36.2	5.9	7.2	41.9	8.7
	U	23740	33.2	6.4	4.4	41.2	14.8

Contd.

Contd.

1	2	3	4	5	6	7	8
Narsimhapur	T	26655	45.5	6.0	6.2	33.6	8.7
	R	22812	45.3	6.0	6.6	33.7	8.4
	U	3843	46.4	5.6	4.3	33.0	10.7
Dindori *	T	11699	36.6	6.7	8.5	40.6	7.7
	R	11123	36.7	6.7	8.5	40.7	7.4
	U	576	33.9	6.9	6.9	38.5	13.7
Mandla	T	20262	39.6	6.1	7.8	38.1	8.4
	R	18464	39.7	6.0	8.1	38.3	8.0
	U	1798	38.7	7.5	4.9	36.8	12.2
Chhindwara	T	44591	39.5	6.1	6.9	38.4	9.1
	R	34735	39.4	6.2	7.4	38.6	8.3
	U	9856	40.0	5.8	4.9	37.5	11.8
Seoni	T	27913	36.2	5.6	7.8	41.3	9.0
	R	25373	35.4	5.6	8.2	42.1	8.7
	U	2540	44.3	5.6	4.3	33.1	12.8
Balaghat	T	35404	37.8	5.9	9.0	36.5	10.8
	R	31483	38.1	5.7	9.4	36.5	10.4
	U	3921	36.1	6.9	6.4	36.6	14.0
GUJARAT	T	1045465	47.3	6.4	6.7	29.7	9.9
	R	719367	46.9	6.4	7.3	30.3	9.1
	U	326098	48.3	6.3	5.5	28.4	11.6
Kachchh	T	35139	46.2	6.2	8.3	28.7	10.5
	R	27143	45.4	6.2	8.8	29.5	10.1
	U	7996	48.7	6.5	6.7	26.2	11.9
Banas Kantha	T	57288	46.1	6.8	7.7	31.2	8.3
	R	52441	46.7	6.7	7.9	30.8	7.9
	U	4847	39.7	7.6	5.1	35.5	12.1
Patan *	T	35236	51.7	5.4	7.1	28.1	7.7
	R	29364	52.6	5.4	7.4	27.5	7.1
	U	5872	47.2	5.8	5.5	31.1	10.4
Mahesana	T	40182	38.9	6.7	5.9	38.7	9.9
	R	32966	38.7	6.6	6.3	38.8	9.6
	U	7216	39.7	6.9	4.1	38.0	11.3

Contd.

Contd.

1	2	3	4	5	6	7	8
Sabar Kantha	T	44630	42.2	7.2	5.4	35.6	9.5
	R	40309	42.1	7.0	5.4	36.1	9.4
	U	4321	43.4	9.3	5.0	31.3	11.0
Gandhinagar	T	32874	50.0	5.5	4.5	31.4	8.6
	R	22261	49.2	5.3	4.8	32.2	8.5
	U	10613	51.8	5.9	3.6	29.9	8.8
Ahmadabad	T	125840	52.8	5.3	4.6	27.7	9.6
	R	35816	53.8	5.2	6.2	27.5	7.4
	U	90024	52.4	5.3	4.0	27.8	10.5
Surendranagar	T	41743	44.5	6.0	8.6	31.9	9.0
	R	31859	44.2	5.9	9.1	32.1	8.5
	U	9884	45.3	6.1	6.7	31.1	10.8
Rajkot	T	64734	41.8	6.5	7.8	31.8	12.1
	R	36221	42.4	6.2	8.7	31.5	11.1
	U	28513	41.1	6.7	6.6	32.2	13.4
Jamnagar	T	40168	41.5	6.7	8.2	30.9	12.8
	R	24348	37.1	7.0	9.8	33.5	12.6
	U	15820	48.3	6.1	5.7	26.9	13.0
Porbandar *	T	12895	47.3	5.6	6.9	27.7	12.6
	R	7591	46.7	5.4	7.5	28.2	12.3
	U	5304	48.1	5.8	6.0	27.2	13.0
Junagadh	T	47021	36.9	7.3	8.4	34.0	13.3
	R	33964	36.3	7.5	8.5	34.6	13.1
	U	13057	38.6	6.9	7.9	32.6	14.0
Amreli	T	39287	52.4	5.0	7.7	26.2	8.7
	R	30996	51.3	5.2	8.3	26.5	8.7
	U	8291	56.7	4.3	5.7	24.8	8.5
Bhavnagar	T	51527	39.8	6.7	7.9	35.3	10.3
	R	36266	40.6	6.4	8.1	35.6	9.2
	U	15261	37.7	7.5	7.4	34.7	12.8
Anand *	T	38678	43.2	7.2	6.8	32.1	10.7
	R	29639	41.9	7.4	7.2	33.0	10.4
	U	9039	47.2	6.2	5.7	29.2	11.7

Contd.

Contd.

1	2	3	4	5	6	7	8
Kheda	T	47718	48.0	6.5	5.8	30.2	9.5
	R	39602	47.9	6.6	5.5	30.9	9.0
	U	8116	48.7	5.9	7.3	26.5	11.7
Panch Mahals	T	40017	48.3	6.8	6.1	30.1	8.7
	R	35535	48.4	6.8	6.2	30.5	8.2
	U	4482	47.6	6.8	5.2	27.0	13.3
Dohad *	T	41138	60.4	4.1	5.8	24.7	5.0
	R	38177	60.6	4.0	5.9	24.9	4.6
	U	2961	56.6	6.0	4.4	22.8	10.2
Vadodara	T	51481	39.1	7.5	7.7	32.4	13.3
	R	30535	38.2	7.4	8.5	34.5	11.5
	U	20946	40.3	7.6	6.6	29.4	16.1
Narmada *	T	10537	49.2	7.1	8.8	26.4	8.4
	R	9561	49.1	7.2	9.0	26.4	8.3
	U	976	50.4	6.7	7.0	26.1	9.8
Bharuch	T	30057	59.0	5.8	6.3	20.3	8.6
	R	23562	57.8	5.8	6.5	21.5	8.4
	U	6495	63.2	5.7	5.6	16.1	9.4
Surat	T	63790	49.7	7.3	6.6	26.2	10.2
	R	29877	48.4	7.8	7.4	26.8	9.5
	U	33913	50.9	6.8	5.9	25.7	10.7
The Dangs	T	4066	51.4	5.4	11.8	24.3	7.1
	R	4066	51.4	5.4	11.8	24.3	7.1
	U	0	0.0	0.0	0.0	0.0	0.0
Navsari *	T	23434	56.3	8.8	5.5	20.0	9.4
	R	16658	54.4	9.3	5.6	21.2	9.4
	U	6776	60.8	7.6	5.1	17.1	9.4
Valsad	T	25985	60.7	6.6	5.9	18.8	7.9
	R	20610	61.2	6.7	6.3	18.6	7.2
	U	5375	58.8	6.2	4.3	19.7	11.0
DAMAN & DIU	T	3171	59.9	6.0	3.8	21.8	8.6
	R	1880	61.8	6.0	2.9	22.0	7.3
	U	1291	57.1	5.9	5.0	21.5	10.5

Contd.

Contd.

1	2	3	4	5	6	7	8
Diu	T	1400	60.1	4.9	3.9	22.4	8.7
	R	742	57.7	5.7	2.8	26.7	7.1
	U	658	62.9	4.0	5.0	17.6	10.5
Daman	T	1771	59.6	6.8	3.7	21.2	8.6
	R	1138	64.4	6.2	3.0	18.9	7.5
	U	633	51.0	7.9	5.1	25.4	10.6
Dadra & Nagar Haveli	T	4048	58.0	7.3	8.3	19.6	6.8
	R	3269	56.9	7.0	9.5	19.9	6.8
	U	779	62.4	8.5	3.6	18.7	6.8
MAHARASHTRA	T	1569582	37.0	7.2	5.9	36.3	13.6
	R	1020371	36.8	6.9	6.8	37.2	12.2
	U	549211	37.3	7.7	4.2	34.6	16.1
Nandurbar *	T	23588	55.9	5.1	3.9	26.9	8.3
	R	20576	57.7	4.8	4.0	26.0	7.6
	U	3012	43.5	7.5	2.7	33.2	13.1
Dhule	T	28329	34.7	6.9	5.7	41.4	11.3
	R	21422	36.1	6.7	6.2	40.7	10.3
	U	6907	30.5	7.6	4.2	43.4	14.3
Jalgaon	T	57264	27.8	7.3	6.4	46.3	12.1
	R	43503	28.4	6.8	7.1	46.2	11.5
	U	13761	26.2	8.7	4.5	46.4	14.2
Buldana	T	41774	27.8	6.5	9.6	43.5	12.7
	R	34521	28.6	6.5	9.6	43.0	12.3
	U	7253	23.8	6.4	9.2	46.0	14.6
Akola	T	29142	32.1	6.8	8.4	39.9	12.7
	R	19823	35.3	6.8	8.8	37.7	11.4
	U	9319	25.2	7.0	7.7	44.6	15.6
Washim *	T	18211	29.0	7.1	9.4	43.5	11.1
	R	15539	29.6	6.8	10.1	42.8	10.7
	U	2672	25.3	8.9	5.3	47.3	13.2
Amravati	T	61461	45.4	6.3	6.2	30.6	11.5
	R	42024	45.4	5.7	7.4	30.3	11.1
	U	19437	45.5	7.5	3.6	31.2	12.3

Contd.

Contd.

1	2	3	4	5	6	7	8
Wardha	T	22192	34.6	6.3	8.6	35.9	14.7
	R	16844	35.5	5.8	9.4	34.9	14.3
	U	5348	31.6	7.8	6.0	39.0	15.7
Nagpur	T	62473	30.8	6.8	5.5	38.9	17.9
	R	23718	33.4	6.9	7.5	37.3	14.9
	U	38755	29.2	6.8	4.4	39.9	19.7
Bhandara	T	19811	31.6	5.7	7.5	41.8	13.3
	R	17187	32.4	5.6	7.6	41.6	12.8
	U	2624	26.2	6.7	7.3	42.9	16.9
Gondiya *	T	26730	44.3	4.3	6.8	34.1	10.6
	R	24097	45.4	4.3	6.9	33.4	10.0
	U	2633	33.8	4.4	5.3	41.0	15.4
Gadchiroli	T	14200	29.8	8.7	10.9	38.0	12.7
	R	13296	30.1	8.9	11.2	37.4	12.5
	U	904	25.7	5.6	6.4	46.3	15.9
Chandrapur	T	39514	42.7	6.5	7.2	32.3	11.3
	R	29440	44.5	6.2	8.1	31.0	10.2
	U	10074	37.6	7.2	4.5	36.0	14.6
Yavatmal	T	41977	35.3	7.6	7.3	37.3	12.5
	R	35766	36.6	7.1	7.6	36.7	12.0
	U	6211	28.2	10.2	5.4	40.6	15.6
Nanded	T	77329	53.0	6.1	4.9	27.1	8.9
	R	64766	56.9	5.6	4.9	24.5	8.1
	U	12563	32.7	8.9	5.0	40.3	13.1
Hingoli *	T	21541	36.9	6.3	8.3	38.3	10.2
	R	18845	38.2	6.0	8.7	37.4	9.7
	U	2696	27.9	8.1	5.5	44.8	13.7
Parbhani	T	33267	33.6	7.0	7.6	41.6	10.3
	R	23595	33.9	6.2	8.7	41.1	10.1
	U	9672	32.9	8.8	4.9	42.8	10.6
Jalna	T	38796	43.1	5.9	6.2	34.6	10.2
	R	32413	43.2	5.8	6.6	34.4	10.0
	U	6383	42.4	6.3	4.4	35.7	11.2

Contd.

Contd.

1	2	3	4	5	6	7	8
Aurangabad	T	58580	39.6	6.3	5.7	37.1	11.3
	R	41436	39.5	5.9	6.5	37.5	10.6
	U	17144	39.9	7.3	3.9	36.0	13.0
Nashik	T	70120	33.3	6.8	6.3	40.7	13.0
	R	45071	34.5	6.9	6.8	40.0	11.8
	U	25049	31.0	6.7	5.4	41.9	15.1
Thane	T	70407	26.1	9.0	5.6	39.9	19.4
	R	24229	25.3	9.8	7.1	42.9	14.9
	U	46178	26.5	8.6	4.7	38.4	21.8
Mumbai	T	115810	50.7	7.0	3.1	24.5	14.7
(Suburban) *	R	0	0.0	0.0	0.0	0.0	0.0
	U	115810	50.7	7.0	3.1	24.5	14.7
Mumbai	T	53967	53.6	6.9	3.1	22.3	14.1
	R	0	0.0	0.0	0.0	0.0	0.0
	U	53967	53.6	6.9	3.1	22.3	14.1
Raigarh	T	27795	32.0	8.8	6.7	38.8	13.8
	R	22831	31.6	8.6	7.2	39.4	13.2
	U	4964	33.8	9.7	4.0	36.1	16.5
Pune	T	91282	29.4	7.8	5.4	39.5	17.8
	R	43867	31.2	7.7	6.1	40.8	14.3
	U	47415	27.8	8.0	4.7	38.4	21.1
Ahmadnagar	T	83560	42.5	6.6	5.5	33.3	12.0
	R	71459	43.9	6.5	5.4	32.7	11.5
	U	12101	34.5	7.6	6.1	36.7	15.1
Bid	T	40242	30.4	7.0	6.0	44.5	12.1
	R	33493	31.0	6.5	6.4	44.2	11.9
	U	6749	27.4	9.4	3.9	46.2	13.2
Latur	T	44818	32.7	7.2	6.5	41.6	12.0
	R	34875	32.2	6.8	7.1	42.2	11.7
	U	9943	34.3	8.5	4.6	39.5	13.1
Osmanabad	T	35057	36.8	6.5	5.9	38.9	11.8
	R	30489	36.8	6.3	6.2	39.0	11.8
	U	4568	37.2	7.7	4.2	38.7	12.1

Contd.

Contd.

1	2	3	4	5	6	7	8
Solapur	T	66084	32.4	8.7	4.9	39.7	14.3
	R	47266	32.9	8.4	5.4	39.1	14.2
	U	18818	31.2	9.5	3.6	41.3	14.5
Satara	T	37457	25.1	8.8	6.0	42.4	17.7
	R	33507	25.3	8.8	6.3	42.5	17.1
	U	3950	22.8	9.1	4.0	41.2	22.9
Ratnagiri	T	27228	35.1	8.0	9.1	32.3	15.5
	R	24844	35.5	7.9	9.4	32.4	14.8
	U	2384	30.7	8.3	6.0	31.5	23.4
Sindhudurg	T	12808	30.7	10.4	6.1	32.0	20.8
	R	11841	30.7	10.3	6.2	32.0	20.8
	U	967	31.0	10.7	5.8	30.9	21.6
Kolhapur	T	43826	30.8	9.5	3.6	39.0	17.0
	R	32010	32.1	9.3	3.7	38.5	16.3
	U	11816	27.3	10.2	3.4	40.3	18.8
Sangli	T	32942	26.5	10.3	4.4	40.1	18.7
	R	25778	26.7	10.3	4.6	40.2	18.2
	U	7164	25.8	10.1	3.8	39.6	20.6
ANDHRA PRADESH	T	1364981	42.6	10.2	5.430.511.4		
	R	1050400	41.4	10.2	5.8	31.4	11.1
	U	314581	46.5	10.0	3.9	27.4	12.2
Adilabad	T	33722	40.5	11.3	4.5	31.5	12.2
	R	26550	40.8	11.2	4.8	31.6	11.6
	U	7172	39.0	11.7	3.5	31.2	14.6
Nizamabad	T	39939	45.6	8.9	4.1	30.4	11.0
	R	33874	45.2	8.9	4.3	31.0	10.6
	U	6065	47.9	8.7	3.2	26.8	13.4
Karimnagar	T	60650	48.8	9.7	4.8	25.2	11.6
	R	48876	46.6	9.9	5.0	26.7	11.8
	U	11774	57.8	9.1	3.8	18.7	10.6
Medak	T	47272	45.9	9.4	4.5	30.1	10.0
	R	42078	45.5	9.3	4.6	30.7	9.8
	U	5194	48.7	10.5	3.4	25.5	11.8

Contd.

Contd.

1	2	3	4	5	6	7	8
Hyderabad	T	52590	50.1	9.0	3.3	23.3	14.3
	R	0	0.0	0.0	0.0	0.0	0.0
	U	52590	50.1	9.0	3.3	23.3	14.3
Rangareddi	T	59075	48.7	8.7	3.9	27.9	10.8
	R	30641	46.8	8.5	4.6	30.9	9.2
	U	28434	50.7	8.9	3.2	24.7	12.5
Mahbubnagar	T	66015	44.9	8.6	5.2	32.0	9.3
	R	60318	44.7	8.6	5.3	32.2	9.1
	U	5697	46.7	8.8	3.0	29.9	11.5
Nalgonda	T	73616	46.7	8.2	4.6	30.2	10.3
	R	65774	46.3	8.3	4.8	30.5	10.2
	U	7842	50.3	7.9	2.8	27.4	11.6
Warangal	T	67121	48.1	9.7	4.3	28.3	9.5
	R	56430	46.7	9.8	4.7	29.4	9.4
	U	10691	55.7	9.0	2.4	22.7	10.3
Khammam	T	63695	49.9	8.9	4.3	26.7	10.3
	R	52641	49.6	8.7	4.4	26.9	10.4
	U	11054	51.1	9.8	3.5	25.8	9.8
Srikakulam	T	51608	43.6	10.2	6.1	29.5	10.6
	R	47248	44.2	10.1	6.2	29.2	10.4
	U	4360	36.5	11.3	5.7	33.4	13.1
Vizianagaram	T	49406	46.7	9.7	6.2	28.6	8.8
	R	41383	46.6	9.6	6.4	28.7	8.7
	U	8023	46.8	10.3	5.0	28.2	9.7
Visakhapatnam	T	67263	48.5	10.4	4.8	25.9	10.3
	R	40026	43.1	11.1	6.3	29.4	10.0
	U	27237	56.4	9.2	2.7	20.9	10.8
East Godavari	T	92680	48.7	9.9	4.1	27.5	9.8
	R	71364	47.6	10.1	4.3	28.1	10.0
	U	21316	52.4	9.6	3.4	25.5	9.1
West Godavari	T	61135	29.7	12.3	6.2	38.6	13.3
	R	49797	29.4	12.3	6.3	38.6	13.4
	U	11338	31.0	12.3	5.4	38.5	12.7

Contd.

Contd.

1	2	3	4	5	6	7	8
Krishna	T	71156	35.8	11.5	5.7	33.8	13.2
	R	53656	35.0	11.5	6.0	34.1	13.4
	U	17500	37.9	11.4	4.9	32.9	12.8
Guntur	T	76735	39.2	11.3	4.9	31.5	13.1
	R	54778	37.3	11.9	5.2	31.8	13.8
	U	21957	43.9	9.7	4.0	30.8	11.6
Prakasam	T	48931	34.3	12.3	5.5	35.3	12.6
	R	42510	34.2	12.0	5.6	35.6	12.6
	U	6421	35.0	14.0	4.5	33.5	12.9
Nellore	T	49653	36.0	11.4	7.8	32.4	12.4
	R	41697	35.7	11.4	8.1	32.4	12.3
	U	7956	37.3	10.9	6.3	32.4	13.1
Cuddapah	T	46029	36.0	11.3	8.2	31.8	12.7
	R	38103	36.0	11.2	8.5	31.9	12.4
	U	7926	35.8	11.9	6.7	31.4	14.2
Kurnool	T	65261	40.2	9.3	6.9	32.6	11.0
	R	53091	40.0	9.2	7.4	32.7	10.8
	U	12170	41.2	9.7	4.8	32.5	11.8
Anantapur	T	63895	33.6	10.6	8.0	35.2	12.6
	R	52750	33.6	10.6	8.6	35.1	12.2
	U	11145	33.9	10.7	5.4	35.7	14.3
Chittoor	T	57534	33.5	12.5	6.9	34.0	13.1
	R	46815	33.1	11.9	7.3	34.3	13.4
	U	10719	35.5	14.8	5.2	32.8	11.7
KARNATAKA	T	940643	46.9	9.6	5.3	28.3	9.8
	R	661139	46.1	9.9	5.7	29.0	9.4
	U	279504	48.7	9.1	4.5	26.9	10.8
Belgaum	T	58900	30.5	11.0	6.1	40.2	12.3
	R	46070	29.1	11.1	6.7	41.2	11.9
	U	12830	35.3	10.5	4.1	36.4	13.7
Bagalkot *	T	28042	45.7	9.2	5.0	31.8	8.4
	R	21173	45.7	8.7	5.5	32.1	8.1
	U	6869	45.4	10.6	3.5	31.0	9.6

Contd.

Contd.

1	2	3	4	5	6	7	8
Bijapur	T	37315	51.0	8.5	4.2	27.1	9.2
	R	31041	52.5	8.6	4.3	25.9	8.6
	U	6274	43.1	8.2	3.8	32.7	12.1
Gulbarga	T	60657	46.5	8.8	5.1	31.9	7.6
	R	42354	42.0	9.4	6.0	34.8	7.7
	U	18303	57.0	7.3	2.9	25.2	7.6
Bidar	T	30224	44.0	8.5	4.9	34.1	8.5
	R	24814	44.5	8.4	5.3	33.6	8.3
	U	5410	41.6	9.1	3.3	36.5	9.6
Raichur	T	23349	47.1	9.0	5.0	30.7	8.2
	R	16243	41.0	9.8	6.0	34.4	8.8
	U	7106	61.0	7.3	2.7	22.2	6.7
Koppal *	T	21041	37.9	10.3	5.3	36.4	10.1
	R	17912	37.6	10.3	5.6	36.8	9.8
	U	3129	39.7	10.3	3.5	34.6	11.9
Gadag *	T	18355	39.9	8.7	6.5	35.4	9.5
	R	12867	44.8	8.8	5.7	32.7	8.1
	U	5488	28.6	8.7	8.3	41.7	12.7
Dharwad	T	23031	30.3	10.8	6.3	39.3	13.4
	R	11989	33.1	10.2	6.4	38.6	11.7
	U	11042	27.2	11.4	6.2	40.0	15.3
Uttara Kannada	T	28313	46.9	8.8	5.8	27.6	10.8
	R	21698	47.7	8.4	5.9	27.6	10.4
	U	6615	44.4	9.8	5.6	27.9	12.4
Haveri *	T	26635	42.1	10.3	5.2	31.4	11.0
	R	21252	42.6	10.7	4.8	31.2	10.7
	U	5383	40.4	8.6	6.5	32.1	12.4
Bellary	T	37270	48.6	9.1	4.3	29.4	8.6
	R	24396	45.3	9.2	4.8	32.8	8.0
	U	12874	55.0	9.1	3.4	22.9	9.6
Chitradurga	T	31971	48.7	10.1	5.3	27.9	8.1
	R	26307	47.6	10.5	5.7	27.8	8.3
	U	5664	53.8	8.0	3.1	27.9	7.1

Contd.

Contd.

1	2	3	4	5	6	7	8
Davanagere*	T	33904	45.8	10.3	4.5	29.5	9.9
	R	24689	48.2	9.8	4.7	28.1	9.2
	U	9215	39.4	11.8	3.9	33.3	11.7
Shimoga	T	26612	39.9	10.3	6.3	32.1	11.4
	R	19068	41.5	10.2	6.1	31.3	10.9
	U	7544	35.8	10.7	6.5	34.3	12.7
Udupi *	T	17050	39.5	12.9	4.7	24.8	17.9
	R	14777	40.6	13.2	4.7	24.4	17.0
	U	2273	32.6	11.3	4.8	27.5	23.9
Chikmagalur	T	25263	57.7	8.0	5.0	21.6	7.6
	R	20886	56.7	8.1	5.4	22.0	7.8
	U	4377	62.4	7.6	3.4	19.6	7.0
Tumkur	T	49391	46.1	11.4	5.8	27.7	9.0
	R	41178	45.4	11.5	6.2	27.9	9.0
	U	8213	49.6	11.1	3.9	26.2	9.1
Kolar	T	44426	45.5	10.6	5.6	28.0	10.4
	R	35540	45.3	10.6	5.7	28.3	10.2
	U	8886	46.2	10.8	5.2	26.6	11.2
Bangalore	T	94228	50.7	8.2	5.0	25.1	11.0
	R	13108	44.4	9.5	5.9	28.9	11.2
	U	81120	51.7	8.0	4.9	24.5	11.0
Bangalore Rural	T	39616	48.0	9.6	5.6	27.2	9.6
	R	32735	48.1	9.7	6.0	26.7	9.5
	U	6881	47.2	9.1	3.7	29.9	10.0
Mandya	T	41842	59.8	9.7	4.3	19.1	7.1
	R	35693	59.3	9.7	4.5	19.4	7.1
	U	6149	62.4	9.6	3.3	17.7	7.1
Hassan	T	29481	42.3	10.5	8.1	30.0	9.1
	R	25392	43.1	10.2	8.6	29.2	9.0
	U	4089	37.2	12.9	5.2	34.9	9.9
Dakshina Kannada	T	37999	52.2	8.6	4.3	20.6	14.2
	R	21978	46.4	9.6	5.1	23.6	15.2
	U	16021	60.2	7.2	3.3	16.4	12.9

Contd.

Contd.

1	2	3	4	5	6	7	8
Kodagu	T	7666	44.4	9.7	8.8	26.1	11.0
	R	6798	44.4	9.8	9.2	25.9	10.7
	U	868	44.2	8.9	5.8	28.1	13.0
Mysore	T	44094	54.6	11.0	5.8	20.1	8.5
	R	29972	55.5	10.7	5.8	20.3	7.8
	U	14122	52.8	11.7	5.8	19.8	9.9
Chamarajanagar*	T	23968	67.3	8.3	3.6	14.6	6.2
	R	21209	67.7	8.2	3.6	14.6	5.9
	U	2759	64.5	8.8	3.1	15.2	8.4
GOA	T	15749	27.9	11.9	6.3	31.2	22.7
	R	8559	26.3	12.0	7.1	31.5	23.0
	U	7190	29.8	11.7	5.4	30.8	22.3
North Goa	T	9004	27.8	11.6	6.0	29.5	25.1
	R	5289	26.9	11.8	6.5	30.1	24.6
	U	3715	29.0	11.3	5.2	28.6	25.8
South Goa	T	6745	28.0	12.2	6.8	33.4	19.5
	R	3270	25.3	12.4	8.1	33.7	20.5
	U	3475	30.6	12.1	5.6	33.1	18.6
Lakshadweep	T	1678	35.9	12.3	8.8	30.1	12.9
	R	989	37.3	10.6	9.9	29.4	12.7
	U	689	34.0	14.8	7.1	31.1	13.1
KERALA	T	860794	38.9	7.8	9.3	27.6	16.5
	R	647782	38.8	7.9	9.4	27.6	16.3
	U	213012	39.1	7.5	8.8	27.8	16.8
Kasaragod	T	28422	37.6	9.2	10.3	28.5	14.5
	R	23119	38.1	9.3	10.6	27.5	14.5
	U	5303	35.4	8.5	8.9	32.6	14.5
Kannur	T	57931	36.3	8.5	11.1	27.3	16.8
	R	29399	35.6	9.0	11.6	27.2	16.6
	U	28532	37.1	8.1	10.6	27.3	16.9
Wayanad	T	18401	37.7	8.6	10.7	28.0	15.0
	R	17656	37.7	8.7	10.6	27.8	15.1
	U	745	38.1	5.8	13.0	30.7	12.3

Contd.

Contd.

1	2	3	4	5	6	7	8
Kozhikode	T	81853	38.2	7.0	10.3	27.1	17.4
	R	51970	38.9	7.1	10.8	26.1	17.0
	U	29883	37.0	6.8	9.5	28.7	18.1
Malappuram	T	88430	38.4	7.6	9.5	25.2	19.3
	R	79479	38.1	7.7	9.6	25.1	19.5
	U	8951	40.3	7.4	8.9	25.5	17.9
Palakkad	T	65329	41.7	8.1	9.7	26.4	14.0
	R	56809	41.3	8.2	9.8	26.7	14.1
	U	8520	44.8	7.2	9.2	25.0	13.8
Thrissur	T	74615	40.8	8.5	8.2	25.9	16.5
	R	54389	40.9	8.7	8.2	26.3	15.9
	U	20226	40.7	8.2	8.1	24.9	18.1
Ernakulam	T	79234	37.5	8.2	8.9	28.1	17.2
	R	44981	37.4	8.2	9.7	27.9	16.8
	U	34253	37.7	8.2	7.9	28.2	17.9
Idukki	T	36143	44.5	7.0	8.6	25.1	14.8
	R	34479	44.9	6.9	8.6	24.8	14.8
	U	1664	35.3	8.9	9.4	31.6	14.8
Kottayam	T	55732	36.0	7.9	10.6	27.5	18.1
	R	46762	35.0	8.1	10.8	27.8	18.4
	U	8970	41.1	6.4	9.5	26.1	16.9
Alappuzha	T	63539	40.2	7.5	8.7	29.1	14.5
	R	45186	39.9	7.8	8.7	29.5	14.1
	U	18353	40.8	6.9	8.8	28.2	15.3
Pathanamthitta	T	35280	34.9	9.3	9.6	30.3	15.8
	R	32200	35.4	8.6	9.7	30.3	16.0
	U	3080	29.9	16.9	8.2	30.7	14.2
Kollam	T	82922	40.0	6.8	8.8	29.0	15.3
	R	67168	39.3	6.9	8.9	29.4	15.5
	U	15754	42.9	6.7	8.4	27.5	14.5
Thiruvanantha-puram	T	92963	38.9	7.1	7.3	29.8	6.9
	R	64185	38.4	7.3	7.4	30.1	16.8
	U	28778	40.0	6.6	7.3	29.0	17.1

Contd.

Contd.

1	2	3	4	5	6	7	8
TAMIL NADU	T	1642497	58.7	7.6	4.4	21.5	7.8
	R	945019	58.6	8.0	4.7	21.7	7.1
	U	697478	58.9	7.1	4.1	21.4	8.6
Thiruvallur	T	69045	50.7	8.9	6.1	26.4	7.9
	R	34037	50.7	8.6	7.0	26.6	7.1
	U	35008	50.7	9.1	5.3	26.1	8.7
Chennai	T	96440	53.3	7.0	4.5	22.6	12.5
	R	0	0.0	0.0	0.0	0.0	0.0
	U	96440	53.3	7.0	4.5	22.6	12.5
Kancheepuram	T	71231	49.4	9.0	6.9	26.6	8.0
	R	35630	48.8	9.3	7.7	26.9	7.2
	U	35601	50.1	8.6	6.2	26.2	8.9
Vellore	T	84576	51.1	8.7	5.1	26.0	9.0
	R	50977	46.8	9.5	5.9	28.5	9.3
	U	33599	57.7	7.4	4.0	22.3	8.7
Dharmapuri	T	81448	67.6	6.6	3.0	17.7	5.0
	R	69794	68.2	6.6	3.1	17.3	4.8
	U	11654	63.8	6.9	2.7	20.2	6.4
Tiruvannamalai	T	49036	44.3	10.1	7.8	28.6	9.1
	R	42059	46.0	10.2	7.8	27.4	8.6
	U	6977	34.1	9.7	8.0	36.0	12.2
Viluppuram	T	66071	49.5	9.1	5.9	28.1	7.5
	R	58030	50.5	9.2	5.9	27.3	7.1
	U	8041	42.1	8.4	5.8	33.6	10.1
Salem	T	49560	45.4	9.8	4.8	30.3	9.6
	R	25397	42.9	10.7	5.3	31.6	9.5
	U	24163	48.0	8.8	4.4	29.0	9.8
Namakkal	T	29696	52.5	8.5	5.2	25.3	8.5
	R	18438	51.7	8.9	5.8	24.8	8.8
	U	11258	53.8	7.8	4.4	26.0	8.0
Erode	T	66695	64.4	6.6	4.0	18.1	6.9
	R	35422	63.1	7.1	4.4	18.0	7.4
	U	31273	65.8	6.1	3.5	18.2	6.5

Contd.

Contd.

1	2	3	4	5	6	7	8
The Nilgiris	T	21456	61.5	5.7	4.9	20.9	7.0
	R	8939	59.5	6.2	4.7	22.3	7.2
	U	12517	62.8	5.4	5.1	19.8	6.8
Coimbatore	T	115738	67.1	6.1	3.4	15.7	7.6
	R	42019	65.6	6.3	3.9	16.7	7.5
	U	73719	67.9	6.0	3.1	15.2	7.7
Dindigul	T	63535	69.4	6.0	3.0	15.1	6.5
	R	43423	71.6	5.9	2.8	13.8	5.9
	U	20112	64.8	6.3	3.2	18.0	7.8
Karur *	T	15342	39.3	11.5	6.9	32.3	10.1
	R	10537	40.2	11.9	6.7	31.8	9.4
	U	4805	37.2	10.5	7.2	33.5	11.7
Tiruchirappalli	T	76445	63.5	8.3	4.0	18.1	6.2
	R	40650	64.3	8.2	4.0	17.9	5.6
	U	35795	62.5	8.3	4.0	18.4	6.8
Perambalur *	T	12820	59.9	9.7	4.2	20.2	5.9
	R	10510	57.7	10.8	4.3	21.0	6.1
	U	2310	69.8	4.7	3.8	16.6	5.1
Ariyalur *	T	21352	59.8	9.0	4.7	21.4	5.2
	R	19245	60.2	9.0	4.7	20.9	5.1
	U	2107	56.7	8.3	3.8	25.4	5.8
Cuddalore	T	64426	61.3	6.9	5.1	20.5	6.2
	R	44519	60.4	7.4	5.5	20.6	6.0
	U	19907	63.3	5.8	4.1	20.2	6.6
Nagapattinam *	T	50958	66.4	6.0	3.5	17.0	7.0
	R	37345	64.8	6.7	3.6	17.6	7.3
	U	13613	70.8	4.2	3.4	15.4	6.2
Thiruvarur	T	37371	64.3	7.2	4.1	18.4	6.1
	R	29682	63.8	7.2	4.1	18.8	6.2
	U	7689	66.2	7.3	4.1	16.8	5.6
Thanjavur	T	59468	54.3	9.2	5.2	23.4	7.9
	R	40867	55.5	9.2	5.1	23.2	7.0
	U	18601	51.8	9.0	5.3	24.0	9.9

Contd.

Contd.

1	2	3	4	5	6	7	8
Pudukkottai	T	40289	61.6	8.2	4.5	19.1	6.6
	R	33339	62.3	8.1	4.3	18.9	6.4
	U	6950	57.8	8.6	5.5	20.2	7.8
Sivaganga	T	39119	66.2	6.0	3.8	16.8	7.2
	R	29010	66.5	6.0	4.0	16.5	7.0
	U	10109	65.0	6.0	3.2	17.9	7.9
Madurai	T	70256	62.8	6.3	3.4	18.7	8.8
	R	32988	63.9	6.6	3.8	18.1	7.6
	U	37268	61.7	6.0	3.0	19.3	9.9
Theni *	T	30752	63.6	7.1	2.9	18.8	7.6
	R	15304	65.4	6.9	2.9	18.1	6.7
	U	15448	61.8	7.2	2.9	19.5	8.6
Virudhunagar	T	43277	58.5	7.7	3.6	21.9	8.4
	R	23952	57.1	8.6	3.6	21.9	8.8
	U	19325	60.2	6.7	3.5	21.8	7.8
Ramanathapuram	T	35524	59.3	8.3	3.5	20.2	8.7
	R	27022	58.0	8.9	3.8	20.4	9.0
	U	8502	63.6	6.4	2.6	19.7	7.7
Thoothukkudi	T	45845	58.7	6.6	3.9	22.2	8.6
	R	26248	56.8	7.1	4.1	23.0	8.9
	U	19597	61.3	5.9	3.5	21.2	8.1
Tirunelveli	T	74087	57.9	7.8	4.0	23.2	7.1
	R	39268	58.4	7.8	3.5	23.2	7.0
	U	34819	57.3	7.8	4.5	23.2	7.2
Kanniyakumari	T	60639	63.5	5.5	2.7	21.4	6.9
	R	20368	62.0	5.0	2.7	23.4	6.9
	U	40271	64.3	5.7	2.7	20.4	6.9
PONDICHERRY	T	25857	41.2	7.0	8.8	34.1	8.8
	R	9541	40.9	7.5	9.2	34.7	7.7
	U	16316	41.4	6.7	8.6	33.8	9.5
Yanam	T	632	52.2	9.7	5.4	26.6	6.2
	R	0	0.0	0.0	0.0	0.0	0.0
	U	632	52.2	9.7	5.4	26.6	6.2

Contd.

Contd.

1	2	3	4	5	6	7	8
Pondicherry	T	19151	39.2	6.9	9.2	35.7	8.9
	R	6687	39.6	7.4	9.5	36.0	7.6
	U	12464	39.1	6.6	9.1	35.6	9.7
Mahe	T	685	32.4	12.6	8.5	27.6	19.0
	R	0	0.0	0.0	0.0	0.0	0.0
	U	685	32.4	12.6	8.5	27.6	19.0
Karaikal	T	5389	47.9	6.6	7.8	30.2	7.5
	R	2854	43.9	7.8	8.7	31.6	8.0
	U	2535	52.3	5.3	6.7	28.7	6.9
ANDAMAN &	T	7057	47.1	9.27.726.5		9.5	
NICOBAR	R	5082	44.9	8.9	9.1	27.3	9.8
ISLANDS	U	1975	52.6	10.2	4.2	24.4	8.7
Andamans	T	5979	45.7	9.9	7.9	26.5	10.1
	R	4004	42.3	9.7	9.7	27.5	10.7
	U	1975	52.6	10.2	4.2	24.4	8.7
Nicobars	T	1078	54.7	5.8	6.9	26.4	6.2
	R	1078	54.7	5.8	6.9	26.4	6.2
	U	0	0.0	0.0	0.0	0.0	0.0

Bibliography

Broeck, Jacobus, *Public Welfare and the Blind,* University of California Press, 1959.

Ethical Issues in Disability and Rehabilitation: World Institute on Disability, 1989.

Jacyshyn, Maria, *Australian Disability Review,* Vol. 1, No. 3, 1988.

Keller, Helen, *The Story of My Life,* Garden City, 1954.; *The World I Live In,* Century Co., 1908.

Lane, Harlan, *When the Mind Hears: A History of the Deaf,* Random House, 1984.

Legislative History of Public Law 101-336 *The Americans With Disabilities Act,* vol. 1-3, U.S. Government Printing Office, 1990.

Liachowitz, Claire, *Disability as a Social Construct,* University of Pennsylvania Press, 1988.

Pelka, Fred, *The ABC-CLIO Companion to the Disability Rights Movement,* ABC-CLIO Inc., 1997.

Percy, Stephen, *Disability, Civil Rights, and Public Policy,* University of Alabama Press, 1989.

Shapiro, Joe, *No Pity: People With Disabilities Forging A New Civil Rights Movement,* Times Books, 1993.

The Last Civil Rights Movement : Disabled Peoples' International, St. Martin's Press, 1989.

West, Jane, *The Americans With Disabilities Act,* Milbank Memorial Fund, 1991.

Williams, Paul and Bonnie Schoultz, *We Can Speak For Ourselves: Self Advocacy by Mentally Handicapped People*, Indiana University Press, 1982.

Zola, Irving, "Any Distinguishing Features — The Portrayal of Disability in the Crime Mystery Genre - I," Vol. 10, No. 4, Fall 1990, Disability Studies Quarterly. *The Changing World of Impaired and Disabled People in Society*, ed. Stephen C. Hey, Gary Kiger, and Daryle Evans, Salem, Oregon: Society for Disability Studies and Willamette University.

Index